Critical Neurophilosophy and Indigenous Wisdom

Critical Neurophilosophy and Indigenous Wisdom

Four Arrows
Fielding Graduate University, Santa Barbara, USA

Greg Cajete
University of New Mexico, USA

Jongmin Lee
Kyungpook National University Hospital, South Korea

SENSE PUBLISHERS
ROTTERDAM/BOSTON/TAIPEI

A C.I.P. record for this book is available from the Library of Congress.

ISBN: 978-94-6091-108-8 (paperback)
ISBN: 978-94-6091-109-5 (hardback)
ISBN: 978-94-6091-110-1 (e-book)

Published by: Sense Publishers,
P.O. Box 21858,
3001 AW Rotterdam
The Netherlands
http://www.sensepublishers.com

Printed on acid-free paper

Cover image: The hoop dancer, juggling the great Lakota virtues, was painted by Richard Red Owl, a member of the Oglgla Sioux Tribe. He was born on the Pine Ridge Indian Reservation in 1940. The painting was commissioned by Four Arrows.

CONTENTS

WHY A BOOK SUCH AS THIS?

BRAIN, n. An apparatus with which we think that we think.
MIND, n. A mysterious form of matter secreted by the brain. Its chief activity consists in the endeavor to ascertain its own nature, the futility of the attempt being due to the fact that it has nothing but itself to know itself with.

(From Ambrose Bierce's The Devil's Dictionary)

THE CREDIBILITY OF NEUROSCIENCE

In a May 12, 2008 interview on C-Span radio, futurist Paul Saffo predicted that the world is on the cusp of a technological revolution as relates to neuroscience (brain research). He joked that one can tell when a new scientific revolution is underway because people start writing books about how the new ideas can bring about such global improvements as world peace. He added, however, that such ambitions are soon replaced with books about financially profitable industrial applications, such as using functional magnetic resonance imaging machines (fMRI) to verify marketing strategies or to replace conventional lie detectors.

Admittedly, this book is in the "world peace" camp as far as neuroscience textbooks go. However, as Bierce's definitions above imply, the authors are cautious about any grand expectations for the new brain research technologies. This book contends, in fact, that we must utilize these technologies in concert with a more organic grounding. Without such a grounding, Western neuroscientists and the philosophers who attempt to make sense of their "objective" findings may lead us further away from, not closer to, the truth about what humans can do to live in harmony on this planet.

There are about 100 billion neurons in the human brain and each is connected to thousands of others. Most behaviours, beliefs and emotions engage multiple parts of the brain and the variety of possible interactions with memory, culture and DNA is unfathomable. To expect relatively new brain imaging technologies and the interpretations of human beings to explain why we behave as we do and how we can do better is to place too much confidence in technology and Western science. The authors of this text are not the first, however, to express this concern. More than twenty years ago the well known Harvard researcher, Howard Gardner, was among the first to be critical of brain research and its conclusions. In his book, *Art, Mind and the Brain*, he says "The packaging of current research on the human brain threatens to tell us more about academic huckstering than about neurological function (2004, p. 278)." Although I am personally familiar with Dr. Gardner's skeptical disposition (See his counter-position against my stand for arts- based dissertations in my book, *The Authentic Dissertation: Alternative ways of knowing, research and representation*), I agree with his early warning about this subject and research supports it as well. A study conducted by neuroethicists at Stanford University in 2005 found that of 132 reports on brain research published in the daily press and in scientific journals, 79 percent were optimistic, 16 percent were balanced and only 5 percent were critical. After reporting on this study in the article, "Of Two Minds" for *Haaretz Magazine*, Illani and Feldman continue:

> Many scientists are taking issue with the rising dominance of brain sciences within the study of the human mind and human behavior. Psychologists, philosophers and even a large number of brain researchers maintain that many of the studies that are attracting public interest are scientifically untenable, rely on as-yet-unproven technologies, or simply show the obvious after appalling financial investments. Others argue that the studies are unethical and subject to commercial manipulation (Ilani & Feldman, 2008).

David McCabe, an assistant professor in the Department of Psychology at Colorado State, and his colleague Alan Castel, an assistant professor at University of California-Los Angeles, found that simply by attaching an image of a brain indicating patterns of activity, they were able to increase the likelihood that research subjects would believe an assertion, regardless of whether the article described a fictitious, implausible finding or realistic research (Colorado State University, 2007). Although this reveals a lack of critical thinking skills perhaps as well as an overconfidence in technology, this kind of response to neuropsychological research provides both a reason for this text as well as a call to consider its message critically.

There are also the technological limitations mentioned earlier. Technologies, such as fMRI and positron emission tomography (PET), that the neurosciences are relying on, are still in their infancy. For example, the best spatial resolution they can achieve is around 1mm, which leaves much of the activity of the brain unexplored. Time-span is also not short enough to "see" all the activity that may be taking place in response to a stimulus. Of course, there is also the possibility that there may be important aspects of consciousness and decision making that cannot be measured because it has nothing to do with physical aspects of the brain. (See, for example, the work relating to "outside agency" in Daniel Wegner's 2002 book, *The Illusion of Conscious Will.*)

Even with these concerns, however, social neurosciences still have a significant contribution to make if only to stimulate reflection on human behaviour in new ways. For example, in their article for *Science Communication*, "Brain Imaging: A Decade of Coverage in the Print Media," the authors conclude that "neuroscience provides an ideal model for exploring science communication and ethics in a multicultural context (Racine, Bar-Ilan, Illes, 2006, p. 122)." Similarly, in a special edition of the journal entitled *Current Directions in Psychological Science*, Peter Hagoort provides evidence of (possible) contributions from fMRI measurements to our understanding of the functional architecture of language processing (2008) and John O'Doherty and Peter Bossaerts provide several examples of how functional neuroimaging data have helped to shape and inform theories of decision making over and above results available from traditional behavioral measures (2008).

In the introduction of their edited text, *Social Neuroscience: Integrating Biological and Psychological Explanations of Social Behavior*, Eddie Harmon-Jones and Piotr Winkielman go so far as to say this kind of research may be indispensable:

> So, to summarize the benefits, good social neuroscience research integrates the theory and methods of neuroscience and social psychology to derive novel psychological hypotheses. It then tests these hypotheses using a multidisciplinary set of methods, including the behavioral measures of social psychology and the "wetter" measures of neuroscience. It goes beyond using new methods to measure existing constructs; it incorporates ideas from other domains to better understand a problem in another domain. In the end, both parent fields are benefited-theoretically, practically and methodologically. Given these benefits, it seems that the potential of social neuroscience for addressing questions about psychological mechanisms will make it indispensable to the field (2007, p. 6–7).

NEUROPHILOSOPHY

In an effort to consider interpretations and possible applications of neuroscientific research conclusions, a number of scholars have emerged as "neurophilosophers." These individuals are posing such questions as:

- Is deception a mainstay evolutionary survival mechanism in human beings?
- What ways can we prevent harmful prejudice in light of research on bias that exists below awareness and does not rely on conscious deliberation (Amodio et al, 2004)?
- What are the implications that relate to the prevention of war or of prejudice (See Plant, 1998)?
- What is the biological and spiritual basis for social trust and how can social experiences be healing and restorative (see Carter, 2007)?
- What can neuropsychological studies tell us about the mind-body-spirit connection (Harmon-Jones, 2007, p. 6)?

Neurophilosophy attempts to make practical sense of the technical research that is changing views about such things as perception, belief-formation, and consciousness (Mandik & Brook, 2005, p. 1). It engages many of the disciplines that describe various approaches to cognitive and social behavior that neuroscience embraces, such as neuropsychology, cognitive neuroscience, affective neuroscience, social psychophysiology and social neuroscience. All of these involve the study of the relationships between brain functions and behaviors, such as arousal, attention, consciousness, decision making, language, learning, memory, sensory perception, bias, deception, planning, problem solving, social interaction and cognition, response to cultural influences, etc. Most of these disciplines depend upon advanced technologies, such as functional magnetic resonance imaging and positron emission tomography.

In this book we refer to neurophilosophy as an umbrella term that covers other related disciplines that try to help guide human behaviours for the best. One of these is "neuroeconomics." This is a relatively new transdisciplinary field of research that emerged from bioeconomics which uses evolutionary biology to build models that predict human behavior (Zak 2002). It uses neuroscientific measurement techniques to identify neural substrates associated with economic choices, economics being defined by any evaluation of alternatives whereby individuals make choices according to some sense of reward or punishment. One of the most important researchers in this field is Paul J. Zak from the Center for Neuroeconomics Studies at Claremont Graduate University. Our first chapter on generosity relies heavily on research from this arena.

There is also a concentration in neuroeconomics that the late Margaret Gruter of the Gruter Institue for Law and Behavioral research calls, "neurojurisprudence." It looks at the usefulness of laws and punishments to determine the impact of legal punishment on the perpetration of crime. This field's focus on empathy and trust tend, as will be seen, to be supportive of Indigenous wisdom while at the same time are vulnerable to the kind of criticisms mentioned above. For example, Western researchers in this field make assumptions when describing their experiments that presume that humans have a strong sense of ownership (Camerer 2003). As will be seen, this may be a feature of Western cultures but not of Indigenous ones. Another arena under this category is "neuroethics." It studies what parts of the brain are activated as relates to behaviors that are universally considered to be wrong or right.

Neuroanthropology," which has a collaborative blog headquartered in the departments of Anthropology at Macquarie University (Sydney, Australia) and the University of Notre Dame (South Bend, USA) has this to say about its goals:

> We hope to bring together scholars from around the world interested in the implications of new findings in the brain sciences for social, cultural, and psychological theory in anthropology… With links to social, cultural, and psychological anthropology, neuroanthropology also brings a critical perspective on how biological ideas are often used to essentialize and naturalize what are largely sociocultural processes (http://anthropology.net, accessed July 22, 2008)

"Neuroreligion" also has its own blogs. Those who study in this arena are looking at what happens to our brains when we conceive in one way or the other about the concept of God. Monastersky (2006) writes in the *Chronicle of Higher Education*:

> Wander down the halls of some neurobiology departments these days and you may catch a few decidedly nonscientific terms floating by in conversations there. Researchers reared in the hard materialism of Western science may well be chatting about Franciscan nuns, the Dalai Lama, the soul, or enduring happiness. These scholars are part of a small but growing group of metaphysically minded investigators exploring the connections between the

> brain and spirituality. Some of them are treating religion as just another object to put under the microscope – or inside a brain scanner. But others are breaking the bounds of accepted scientific tradition, raising taboo topics such as whether the mind exists beyond the body or whether basic scientific knowledge must be linked to human values (p. A 14).

All of these expanding fields of study surrounding neuroscience relate to the early history of neuropsychology which began during the 1950s when social norms against overt racial prejudice emerged. "Being wary that participants' concerns over these norms might threaten the veracity of their self-reported racial attitudes, researchers turned to biological measures that might be resistant to overt control efforts" (Harmon-Jones, 2007, p. 4). This wariness included challenges to psychology and philosophy, whereby the new scientists refuted the idea that one could know anything true by merely self-reflecting. (According to Indigenous wisdom, self-reflection is, under certain conditions, the best source for understanding reality, as will be seen.)

In 1956, Wilfred Sellars replaced an emphasis on introspection with the theory that people develop a common sense "theory of mind" by observing dispositions and behaviors until a sense of consistency leads to predictability, or perceived predictability of others. This became known as "folk psychology" and the idea that it is a theory has become known as "theory-theory" (Morton 1980). Folk psychology, however, will not always coincide with neuroscientific explanations and therefore a number of scholars like Churchland (1981) have completely dismissed folk psychology, claiming neuroscience as "the proper scientific approach to the mind and arguing that folk psychology will not fit with mature neuroscience; as a result, the folk ontology should be rejected in favor of a neuroscientific ontology (Nichols 2002). This outright dismissal of folk psychology or common sense as a valid theory of mind is referred to as "eliminative materialism."

We mention these debates about how we might understand human nature, beliefs, behaviors, etc. and make predictions based upon some theory of mind to introduce the concept of "Indigenous Wisdom" and bring it into the discussion. Lehrer reminds us that "Neuroscience is a reductionist science (2008). If it is, then Indigenous wisdom stands at the other end of the scale. Therefore, it may be vital to have a collaboration between neuroscience and a holistic, inductive way of seeing the world if we are to successfully transform human social systems so they can be sustainable in the future. Indigenous worldviews offer this opportunity and the remainder of this Introduction attempts to be sufficiently convincing in the centuries-old effort to bring forth this ancient wisdom that still lives, however, ignored, throughout the world.

INDIGENOUS WISDOM

Indigenous Wisdom is not folk psychology, although intuition, self-reflection (especially as relates to experience with both the visible and invisible worlds), meta-cognition, self-reflection and observation of human nature have certainly contributed to it. It is the product of careful and methodologically sound observations of the natural world (which includes humans). It has been tested and re-tested for thousands of years in the most rigorous real-life laboratories for survival and well-being. Indigenous Peoples, meaning those cultures who themselves or the ancestors have, by inhabiting a location for thousands of years and retaining ancient ways of understanding it, produced a "theory of mind" that is every bit as scientific as modern ideas, especially as relate to predicting outcomes, perhaps more so. This is not only true as relates to the many inventions and contributions that relate to food development, storage and preparation; herbal-based medicines; forms of clothing and transportation; astronomy; sustainable practices, etc., but also relates to contributions to democratic government concepts; child discipline; and inter-personal relationship psychology. Indigenous wisdom about world history may also be as scientifically based as any modern theories. In her article, "A Scientific Spiritual Philosophy," renowned theosophist, Blair A. Moffett, wrote:

> Indigenous wisdom is neither utilized nor thoroughly appreciated (1975). The ancient American perspective of our past is manifestly grander and more logically appealing than any we ourselves have so far conceived. It is also thoroughly evolutionary, hence scientific. The Indian at the same time likewise had a strong conviction of the absolute necessity for right living and right action as the key to successful human progress in harmony with surrounding nature. His profoundly spiritual conceptions of life, the universe, and his relations to them are demonstrated again and again in his philosophy and culture. Only in certain few expressions such as the Aztec culture, which had degenerated into a bloody perversion of the earlier, pure emphasis on a life of self-sacrifice for the good of the race and the world, is this spiritual outlook lacking. We have good reason to believe that the primeval American wise men knew that these serial humanities represented no more than facets in time and space – phases – of an immensely rich and complex evolution of the consciousnesses composing the solar universe. We, trying to comprehend their vision solely with our minds or intellects, all too often see but its shell and remain baffled by the terse, elliptical symbolism they used to record their cosmic insights. The Indian accounts can in fact be studied successfully only by means of our intuitions and awakened spiritual vision. It is not too much to say that until these faculties are brought by us into more active use generally, the theosophy formulated and lived by these remarkable peoples through long epochs can be neither fully.

Many scholars and philosophers have noted the tragedy of dismissing Indigenous wisdom and Indigenous science as it relates to contemporary affairs. For example, Niaz Ahmed Khan, a professor at Dhaka University in Bangladesh and an honorary research fellow at the Centre for Development Studies at the University of Wales, UK recently compiled and collated academic studies on indigenous knowledge and was able to identify and record only seventy seven peer-reviewed articles/book chapters. In an editorial he refers to this figure and laments that such wisdom remains a generally ignored subject (2008). Edgar Mitchel, Apollo astronaut and found of the Institute of Noetic Sciences has said that "only a handful of visionaries have recognized that indigenous wisdom can aid the transition to a sustainable world." (amazon.com reviews at http://www.amazon.com/ Shapeshifting-Techniques - Global-Personal-Transformation/dp/0892816635).

As for the topic of "world peace," Indigenous wisdom has also been suppressed, even misrepresented. In Four Arrows' text, *Unlearning the Language of Conquest: Scholars Expose Anti-Indianism in America (2006)*, contributing author, James DeMeo, wrote the chapter, "Peaceful Versus Warlike Societies in Pre-Columbian America: What do Archeology and Anthropology Tell Us?" It challenges the conclusions of such popular books as *Constant Battles: The Myth of the Peaceful Nobel Savage,* written by Professors Steven LaBlank and Kathyrn Register or *Wild in the Woods: The Myth of the Peaceful Eco-Savage* by Robert Whelan, with its chapter titles like "Dances with Garbage." All one needs to do is study Yale's Human Resource Area Files, an internationally recognized organization in the field of cultural anthropology founded in 1949 to facilitate worldwide comparative studies of human behaviour, to see that most human societies prior to the rise of monarchies in the West were relatively peaceful and did not practice war as we understand it today. The remarkable research of Johan M.G. van der Dennen, published in her doctoral thesis and subsequent book, *The Origin of War: The Evolution of a Male-Coalitional Reproductive Strategy* (1995) also supports the idea that Indigenous Wisdom can help re-member ways of living in harmony that can lead to peaceful co-existence.

> Peaceable preindustrial (preliterate, primitive, etc.) societies constitute a nuisance to most theories of warfare and they are, with few exceptions, either denied or 'explained away.' In this contribution I shall argue that the claim of universal human belligerence is grossly exaggerated; and that those students who have been developing theories of **war**, proceeding from the premise that peace is the 'normal' situation, have not been starry-eyed utopians…(p. 2).

She goes on to offer evidence the shows all war is a deliberate and seemingly rational political strategy, based on perceived cost/benefit considerations and ethical judgments by those in power. She describes the complexities that may have led Indigenous people to develop social mores that actually limit rather than promote violence. For example, she refers to Plains Indians' emphasis on individual feats of bravery such as a counting coup or stealing horses were far more important objectives than killing an enemy. She offers a comprehensive literature review of both biological and cultural theories of war, including many references that establish that primitive societies placed a great emphasis on healthy reciprocity as opposed to competition. For example, Leavitt's research found war absent or rare in 73% of hunting and gathering societies and it nearly half of those employing agriculture of some form (1977).

Although we have been talking about reclaiming our Indigenous Science and remaining critical of an over-reliance on Western Science, keep in mind that this book partners the two approaches in a complementary dialogue that intends to better understand how humans can regain our ability to live in harmony on Mother Earth.

This partnership is discussed by Dr. Elisabet Sahtouris, an evolution biologist, futurist, author, consultant and speaker who did her post-doctoral work at the American Museum of Natural History in New York, taught at the University of Massachusetts and M.I.T., was a science writer for the HORIZON/ NOVA TV series, and co-founded the Worldwide Indigenous Science Network because she was "convinced that the knowledge indigenous people have about living in balance with other living systems is critical to our own species' survival" (http://www.ratical.org/LifeWeb/Articles/survival.txt).

In her presentations about a sort of partnership between Western and Indigenous understandings, she often refers to an ancient Hopi Indian prophecy:

> Red and White Brothers, sons of the Earth Mother and the Great Spirit who gave them different missions. The Red Brother was to stay at home and keep the land in sacred trust while the White Brother went abroad to record things and make inventions. One day the White Brother was to return and share his inventions in a spirit of respect for the wisdom his Red Brother had gained. It was told that his inventions would include cobwebs through which people could speak to each other from house to house across mountains, even with all doors and windows closed; there would be carriages crossing the sky on invisible roads, and eventually a gourd of ashes that when dropped would scorch the earth and even the fishes in the sea. If the White Brother's ego grew so large in making these inventions that he would not listen to the wisdom of the Red Brother, he would bring this world to an end in the Great Purification of nature. Only a few would survive to bring forth the next world in which there would again be abundance and harmony.

She also tells about the Colombian Kogi's creation story that has a similar motif:

> Aluna, the Great Mother, the primeval waters, is the source of all creation… put humans, including Elder and Younger Brothers, into the world. From the beginning, Younger Brother caused so much trouble that eventually he was given knowledge of technology and sent far, far away across the waters. Five hundred years ago, the Kogi say, he found his way back across the waters and he has been causing trouble ever since. If he does not listen to the Kogi, to Elder Brother, who is telling him to stop destroying the Mother, to stop digging out her heart in his mining and cutting up her liver in his deforestation, he will bring this world to an end.

She refers to other Indigenous prophesies that warn that although technology is an important aspect of humanity, "it must be brought into harmony with the sacred natural world through the deep Earth wisdom of indigenous peoples." She asks how indigenous peoples knew what technology would bring without this balance and she answers:

> The answer to this question lies in a fundamental difference between the worldviews of indigenous and industrial peoples. The failure of Euro-American scientists to predict the consequences of the technology they spawned is

> directly related to the fact that their mechanical worldview is diametrically opposed to the organic worldview of indigenous peoples…Native science, which by Euro-American scientific categorization includes biology, geology, astronomy, navigation, meteorology, botany, medicine/ pharmacology, psychology, agricultural engineering, plant genetics, ecology, social and political sciences is based on thousands of years of observations…Pre-Inca and Inca agriculture developed hundreds of varieties of potatoes, high protein grain and beans, corn and many other carefully bred crops, feeding millions of people on the same lands without destroying them. Over half the food eaten in the world today traces its roots to the Andes. Their mountain agriculture included automatic irrigation systems and climate-control to prevent freezing. .. Much indigenous science is extremely sophisticated in what we call "interdisciplinary sciences," such as geology and meteorology. The Hopi, for example discovered that in the Southwest underground copper deposits draw down lightning, bringing life-giving rains to the desert. They know that mining can change weather patterns as surely as the Kogi know that deforestation and mining are drying the climate around them so their mountains no longer have adequate snow to feed the rivers on which their crops and lives depend.
>
> When the White Brother's inventive genius comes together with the Red Brother's deep wisdom, we will develop an appropriate technology that does not violate the Earth, but restores it and permits all creatures to live in health (IBID).

Perhaps such a dialogue with its radically different views from Western science, may help engage a neurophilosophy that will more likely lead toward a more healthy balance in human affairs.

AN IMPORTANT CONCERN

The reader may have noted that the above references to those who offer support for the application of Indigenous wisdom into matters of human behaviour have been non-Indian. I have done this almost defensively to help assure that the many non-Indian readers will be motivated to acknowledge the credibility of Indigenous worldviews without the bias of self-promotion, something Indian people shy away from anyway. For more than 500 years American Indians and their ways were treated with disgust and dismissal. Many still hold on to negative stereotypes and it does not help that academics continue to write through the conqueror's lens as James Clifton does in his 1990 book, *The Invented Indian*, where he says "acknowledging anything positive in the native pas is an entirely wrongheaded proposition because no genuine Indian accomplishments have ever really been substantiated (p. 36)." There are many more contemporary versions of this kind of work that still embrace the opinion of British historian Hugh Trevor-Roper who wrote, "How unrewarding is any serious study of the gyrations of barbarous tribes in picturesque but irrelevant corners of the globe, whose chief function in history, in my opinion, is to show to the present an image of the past from which, by history, it has escaped (1965, p. 9)."

However, there is a risk in quoting non-Indian authors who promote Indigenous wisdom. The risk is to promote, if indirectly, a more indirect continuation of anti-Indianism by honouring the conqueror's voice to speak for us. New-agers, non-Indian Native Studies scholars who make their living teaching about Indigenous ways of knowing, and entrepreneurs who appropriate Indigenous spiritual ceremonies and charge money for participation, all in their own ways continue to cast a shadow over the authentic voices of Indian Peoples.

BOOK STRUCTURE AND CHAPTER TOPICS

There are eight chapters in this text. Each focuses on a different concept that has significant implications for healthful, harmonious, human civilizations. Each has been the target of neuroscientific studies and each is of major importance to Indigenous Peoples. The concepts, in order of their presentation, are generosity/altruism, truthfulness/deception, courage/fear, humour, art/music, Nature, spirituality and, finally, the concept of balance.

Chapters open with a relevant quote that offers an Indigenous perspective chosen to initiate critical thinking about Part I which follows. Part I presents a synopsis of state-of-the-art neuroscientific studies on the chapter topic. These study reviews were conducted and written by Ph.D. candidates who are completing the doctoral degree in neuropsychology at Fielding Graduate University. They are straightforward literature reviews that begin with an overview of the material then proceed to summaries and descriptions of a number of specific research studies. The reason the opening quote may inspire critical thinking when reading the research summaries is that it offers a hint at how the Indigenous perspective might either not be in synch with the scientific interpretations, might support them, or might offer a complementary view of human nature. The reader can either study the details of the experiments; simply scan the scientific studies and jump quickly to the conclusion; or begin with Part II and refer back to Part I as needed.

Part II changes gears. Here, two Indigenous scholars, Greg Cajete and Four Arrows, join with a South Korean neuroscientist, who also happens to be a student of Buddhism, to engage in a conversation about the chapter topics and the neurophilosophical conclusions offered by the researchers. Our goal is to begin a dialogue we hope that you, the reader, and your associates will continue. We augment and, as it turns out, often challenge, the neurophilosophical possibilities that stem from the Western scientific interpretations.

Part III, "Continuing the Dialogue," presents the reader with some questions to help stimulate a continuation of the dialogue and increase an understanding of the material, especially as relates to the similarities, differences and complementary perspectives gleaned from considering both the Western neuroscience and the Indigenous wisdom. We end this chapter with such an exercise.

CONTINUING THE DIALOGUE

1. Considering the history and various traditional academic disciplines that interact with social neuroscience, what would you say is the ultimate goal of social neuroscience?
2. Do you believe that the social sciences will offer viable solutions for the problems facing humanity today? Why or why not?
3. In your own history of learning, what has been the general regard for "Indigenous wisdom?"
4. How would you characterize the differences and similarities between Western neuroscience and Indigenous science at this point?

REFERENCES

Amodio, D. M., Harmon-Jones, E., Devine, P. G., Curtin, J. J., Hartley, S., & Covert, A. (2004). Neural signals for the detection of unintentional race bias. *Psychological Science, 15*, 88–93.

Brothers, L. (1997). *Friday's footprint: How society shapes the human mind*. New York: Oxford University Press.

Camerer, D. F. (2003). Strategizing in the brain. *Science, 300*, 1673–1675.

Carter, S. C. (2007). Neuropeptides and the protective effects of social bonds. In Harmon-Jones & P. Winkielman (Eds.), *Social neuroscience*.

Clifton, J. A. (1990). *The invented idian: Cultural fictions and government policies*. New Bruswick, NJ: Transactions Books.

Colorado State University. (2007, October 8). Brain images make cognitive research more believable. *Science Daily*. Retrieved May 12, 2008, from http://www.sciencedaily.com/releases/2007/10/071002151837.htm

Four Arrows. (2008, November). *Don Trent. The authentic dissertation: Alternative ways of knowing, research and representation*. London: Routledge.

Four Arrows. (Ed.). (2006). *Unlearning the language of conquest: Scholars challenge anti-Indianism in America*. Austin, TX: University of Texas Press.

Gardner, H. (1984). *Art, mind and brain: A cognitive approach to creativity*. Oshkosh, WI: Basic Books.

Hagoort, P. (2008, April). Should psychology ignore the language of the brain? In "Special Issue: The Interface Between Neuroscience and Psychological Science". *Current Directions in Psychological Science, 17*(2), 61–176.

Harmon-Jones, E., & Winkielman, P. (2007). *Social neuroscience: Integrating biological and psychological explanations of social behavior*. New York: The Guilford Press. Retrieved from http://chronicle.com/free/v52/i38/38a01401.htm

Ilani, O., & Feldman, Y. (2008, March 20). Of two minds. *Haaretz Daily News*. Retrieved from http://www.haaretz.com/hasen/spages/964062.html

Jacobs, D. (1997). *Primal awareness: A true story of survival, transformation and awakening with the raramuri shamans of mexico*. Rochester, VT: Inner Traditions International.

Jacobs, D., & Jacobs-Spencer, J. (2001). *Teaching virtues: Building character across the curriculum*. Landham, MD: Scarecrow Education Press, a division of Roman and Littlefield.

Klein, S. B., & Kihlstron, J. F. (1998). On bridging the gap between social personality psychology and neuropsychology. *Personality and Social Psychology Review, 2*, 228–242.

Leavitt, G. C. (1977). The frequency of warfare: An evolutionary perspective. *Sociology Inquiry, 47*, 49–58.

Lehrer, J. (2008, January–February). Out of the Blue. In Seed No 14. New York: Seed Media Group.

Mandik, P., & Brook, A. (2005). In A. Brook & S. Akins (Eds.), *Cognition and the brain: The philosophy and neuroscience movement*. Cambridge: Cambridge University Press.

Monastersky, R. (2006, May 26). Religion on the brain in chronicle of higher education.

O'Doherty, & Bossaerts, P. (2008, April). Toward a mechanistic understanding of human decision making: Contributions of functional neuroimaging. In "Special Issue: The Interface Between Neuroscience and Psychological Science". *Current Directions in Psychological Science, 17*(2), 61–176.

Parabola article (Sun and Moon), by Howard *Teich*, 1994 (*Twins*), *XIX*(2), 56 & 58.

Plant, E. A., & Devine, P. G. (1998). Internal and external motivation to respond without prejudice. *Journal of Personality and Social Psychology*, *75*, 811–832.

Racine, E., Bar-Ilan, O., & Illes, J. (2006, September). Brain imaging: A decade of coverage in the print media. In *Science communication* (Vol. 28, Issue 1, p. 122). Thousand Oaks, CA: Sage.

Trevor-Roper, H. (1965). *The rise of Christian Europe*. London: Thames and Hudson.

Van der Dennen, J. M. G. (1995). *Origin of war: The evolution of a male-coalitional reproductive strategy*. Groningen: Origin Press. Dissertation can be accessed at University of Groningen. Retrieved from http://dissertations.ub.rug.nl/faculties/jur/1995/j.m.g.van.der.dennen/? FullItemRecord = ON

Zak, P. J. (2002). Genetics, family structure, and economic growth. *Journal of Evolutionary Economics*, *12*, 343–365.

BEGINNING WITH WHO WE ARE

In the Indian Way

"One of the most fundamental principles of Aboriginal research methodology is the necessity for the research to locate him or herself... We resist colonial models of writing by talking about ourselves first and then relating pieces of our stories and ideas to the research topic."

(Kathy Absolon & Cam Willet in Research as Resistance, edited by Leslie Brown and Susan Strega, 2005, p. 99).

FOUR ARROWS, *aka Don Trent Jacobs*

Equally proud of both my Cherokee and Scots-Irish blood, I nonetheless go by my Lakota name, Wahinkpe Topa (Four Arrows), given to me in a naming ceremony subsequent to a vision I had in preparation for my third Sun Dance. The story is too long and complex for here. Suffice it to say that by going by "Four Arrows" as I have been guided to do, I hope at least acknowledge the importance of Indigenous perspectives. In saying this, I must admit that I, not being raised among traditional Indian people, am far from being qualified to be a spokesperson. Nonetheless, I bring to this work a variety of relevant experiences. I have worked as a fire fighter and medic, a school teacher, a health psychologist and hypnotherapist, a director of a school for troubled youth, a night-club piano player, a horse trainer, and a professor. I have written eighteen books, a number of invited book chapters, and nearly a hundred articles. I possess doctorates in Health Psychology, specializing in psychoneuroimmunology, and in Curriculum and Instruction, specializing in Indigenous Worldviews. I lived with a number of First Nations over the past twenty years and, when serving as Dean of Education at Oglala Lakota College, I fulfilled my Sundance vows. Before coming to my current position as faculty in the College of Educational Leadership and Change at Fielding Graduate University, I was an Associate Professor at Northern Arizona University where I had the fortune to work with Navajo and Hopi students and elders. I currently live in a remote fishing village in Mexico during the winters and in an equally remote village on the west coast of Vancouver Island, British Columbia during the summer. My wife Bea is a polo photographer and website designer; my daughter Jessica is the mother of two boys, a math teacher, and an agent for her actor son. As for my grandsons, I hope they will inherit a more balanced world than now exists and that in some small way this book will help. In the meantime, I continue to see the beauty of life while living in a remote fishing village in Mexico with people who, like me, are essentially "mixed bloods" in the winter and on the west coast of Vancouver Island in the summer.

As we begin this journey together, I offer this "prayer" into the universe: May our work, our reflections and our learning be motivated by a deep concern for all sentient life, for now and for future generations.
Mitakuye Oyasin (We are all related)

GREG CAJETE

I am an educator of Native American people. What I have been doing and where provides context for understanding what is meant by indigenous science, and the role I play as a Native American educator. I am a Tewa Indian from Santa Clara Pueblo which is one of six Tewa speaking villages north of Santa Fe, New Mexico. Each of these Pueblos is autonomous but is related to others through custom and language. I grew up in this pueblo in New Mexico and was raised partly by my grandmother because my mother worked in Los Alamos, New Mexico where she had to spend long periods of time. As a result, I grew up with my grandmother in a distinctly traditional way. Of course, at the time I didn't know that this was education, as it involved an old style of teaching and old ways of learning, ways children had learned essentials important to my people for thousands of years. The public school was close by so I didn't have to be enrolled in boarding school, as my mother and grandmother had. I was able to grow up in my own community, which allowed me to gain sensitivity to the differences between the way we understood ourselves and the way the Pueblo community was different from mainstream society.

When you grow up in a community with other people of your culture who are related or are living the same way, you don't realize your difference. You don't really understand until you face mainstream society process and culture, and I wasn't affected until I began to interact with other cultural groups. Then I realized how different Indian people were, and how we viewed life and education in some very distinct ways. When I was ready to go to college, I had to fight to stay in New Mexico. At that time there was a full scale attempt to recruit native people from reservations and take them off to Ivy League schools. I was courted by schools like Harvard, Dartmouth and Stanford. Many of my friends did go to those places, but I stayed home. I went to a college that was not far from my home, and that allowed me to maintain constant contact with my community.

After I graduated, I was given the opportunity to teach at a school which had opened in 1962, the Institute of American Indian Arts (IAIA) in Santa Fe. The purpose of the IAIA was to evolve a context in which the artistic potentials of young Native American people from all over the United States could be cultivated and expressed. The IAIA was an experiment in cultural education, an experiment using the arts as a primary vehicle, but also aimed at helping native young people learn about themselves, their culture and their identity. After its opening in 1962, the Institute became famous as a model school as it was recognized by UNESCO as being one of four culturally based schools of note in the world.

For five to eight years it was indeed a shining light in the world of Indian education. But, as is the case when an entity is connected with the US government, and especially with the Bureau of Indian Affairs, it was vulnerable to the winds of political change. In the Seventies the Institute fell on difficult times and was moved from its original campus to The College of Santa Fe, where it became a "tenant" of that college.

In 1988, Congress enacted new legislation entitled the American Indian Arts and Development Act, which chartered the IAIA as a public/private entity with its own direct congressional funding. It remains a kind of experiment because even this new legislation is designed to see whether this arrangement will work and maintain both its ideals and the congressional mandate.

I began to teach high school science at the Institute of American Indian Arts in 1974. At that time the school had a junior and senior high program as a feeder program for the two year Associate of Fine Arts degree program in the college. During my first year of teaching, I realized that many of the ways of teaching and approaching science, or so called text book science, were just not appropriate for my students. These Native American students came from all over the United States, from urban environments, rural environments. Some were very traditional in terms of their upbringing, others were not. All had a common thread and that was an interest and a willingness to explore the arts. They also possessed a common alienation from science educational approaches they had experienced in reservation and community schools. Charged with making a program work for these students, I put aside all the textbook methods I had brought with me from the Teacher Education College and created new curricula based on my own experiences as a native person. It was a grand experience in that I was allowed to do things that would not have been allowed in another school, certainly not in any public school. I explored and created with the students a process that allowed them to learn in ways they felt good about.

A curriculum evolved over the years. It began with the introduction of native uses of plants in a health science class I was teaching, and it grew into a full culturally based science program. Its story is a story of creation, of the process of interaction in science, art and culture and the integration of those aspects into the expression of a curriculum–a learning, teaching process that actually works well for Native students who wish to understand and learn about their lost heritage as it relates to science. The curriculum evolved around the idea that every indigenous culture has an orientation to learning, and that orientation is metaphorically represented in its art forms, its way of community, its language, and its way of understanding itself in relationship to the natural environment that contexts or cradles it.

I am currently Director of Native American Studies at the University of New Mexico and an Associate Professor in the College of Education. The perspective on cognitive brain research, which I address in this book, reflects an extension of the cumulative influences of Indigenous philosophy that also informs my professional work, Native science, cultural education and the creative process. The insights gained from research in these areas and their implications for the way science is communicated to Native American students form the orienting basis for my contribution to this work.

JONGMIN LEE

During the period of active restoration of Korean economy after post-war chaos, I was born in Daegu, Korea. I was named as Jongmin by my father under the family name of Lee. Since we Korean have similar background with the other Far East Asian cultures, we still use Chinese characters in special situation such as naming newborn kid. My first name Jongmin comprises of two components, Jong and Min. The name Jong is registered name in the pedigree of our family. This registered name has been already selected long time ago based on five rotating elements of ancient Oriental philosophy, Taoism and Confucianism. These five elements are metal, wood, water, fire, and earth. The name Jong contains the radical of metal. My father's registered name contains the radical of earth. My son's is water. The rotation of the five elements have common root with Buddhist speculation of circulating life. The name Min was the only name which my father could choose. The meaning of Min is jade gem. Although I don't know the exact intention of my father to choose this character for me, I guess he wanted for me to become a precious person within the society. The exact family name of mine is "Lee from Gwangju". Almost family names in Korea have its origin, the name of home town. When I trace back the pedigree, I could reach up to the 9th century in Silla dynasty. Subsequent Korea dynasty, Chosun dynasty, Japanese colony, and Republic of Korea were stained on our pedigree. These facts imply that the traditional philosophy, including Taoism, Confucianism, and Buddhism, maybe resolved into my mentality or encoded into my gene.

Within the strong obligation of these philosophies, my grand grandmother became Christian during the persecution era in Chosun dynasty. My mother has the family name of "Chang from Indong" and her parents were also Christian during the Japanese colony era. Therefore my parents were very strong in-born Christians and subsequently I had been baptized in Catholic Church as soon as my birth regardless of my own opinion. In addition, my father had studied western law in Tokyo Japan and Leuven Belgium. My mother had studied western music in Tokyo Japan and she became a soprano singer. My father was always reasonable and logical to me (probably for the education of his kid). In contrast, my mother was rich in affection and made me confused whenever I decide something. My brothers and sister were also in reasonable side rather than emotional side, since they studied western science with inherited logical way of thinking.

I grew up in this unusual environment comprising several philosophies from Taosim to western modern science, although my thinking is heavily influenced, I'm sure by my western medical training. Since I had great interest in engineering, I became a radiologist and I am affiliated with both radiology and biomedical engineering departments in a medical college.

A perspective I bring to this book is the idea that homeostasis is a very important concept in neuroscience. There are many reciprocal interactions in medicine such as sympathetic-parasympathetic nervous systems, insulin-glucagon enzymatic system, osteoblast-osteoclast cellular system, and so on. The disruption of the homeostasis will result in pathological situation. The status of homeostasis should be the most efficient way of energy consumption to keep normal physiological function. Therefore the homeostasis can be expressed as the balance of physiological functions. In Confucianism, the doctrine of the middle path is regarded as the supreme virtue in human behaviour. The doctrine gives caution to be in extreme edge where the conflict occurs with high energy consumption. To keep the middle path, human should lay down their avarice which is the source of all conflict within human mentality. The homeostasis and the doctrine of the middle path seem to be a single concept described differently by Oriental or indigenous philosophy and western science.

When Four Arrows invited me to be a co-author of this book, I felt strong ambivalence since I had no academic knowledge beyond the territory of western science. However, I could understand and had agreement with his speculation about indigenous wisdom, I decided to jump on this adventure boat. During the writing our dialogues, I could revisit and reform my ideas about western science and oriental philosophy. This job has been a very exciting journey for me like putting my hand beyond the star gate. I hope our dialogue and my contribution to it will help inspire further conversation that will guide "neurophilosophy" in a useful direction.

CHAPTER 1

GENEROSITY

They are so naive and so free with their possessions that no one who has not witnessed them would believe it. When you ask for something they have, they never say no. To the contrary, they offer to share with anyone.

– Christopher Columbus (quoted in Zinn, 2005, p. 3).

I. NEUROSCIENCE STUDIES OVERVIEW

Jennifer Mitchell and Shahzad Chaudhry

Historically, psychologists believed that altruism is a selfless means to a selfish end; in other words, altruism carried an expectation that the generosity would somehow be returned (Gintis, Bowles, Boyd, & Fehr, 2003). Technological developments have allowed researches to investigate the underlying biological mechanisms involved in generosity, and the results have created a theoretical shift. The following seven studies reflect the current trend to explain human generosity in terms of neuroeconomics. Neuroeconomics combines the study of the brain with economic theory in an attempt to elucidate the decision-making process. Each of the studies summarized below depict critical components of the neuroeconomic theory of generosity. The first study lays a foundation by indicating the crucial role that emotions play in the decision-making process, and illustrates that humans experience emotional reactions to fair and unfair offers. The second study depicts a clear preference for helpful versus unhelpful individuals as early as infancy. The third study introduces the current theory that acting in generous, cooperative and/or altruistic ways activates reward processing centers of the brain. The fourth and fifth studies provide additional support for the idea that being generous is processed as a reward in the brain. The sixth study lends further support to a reward-based theory of generosity by investigating the neural mechanisms involved in altruistic punishment. The final study examines the role that empathy plays in anonymous generosity. All of the studies provide glimpses into the underlying neural explanation behind generosity; the brain processes acts of generosity as a reward, which serves to encourage future acts of generosity in order to obtain additional rewards.

Study 1: "The Neural Basis of Economic Decision-Making in the Ultimatum Game"

Summary. Sanfey, Rilling, Aronson, Nystrom, and Cohen (2003) looked at the role that both cognition and emotions play in the decision-making process. The authors used functional magnetic resonance imaging (fMRI) to highlight the areas of the brain activated during an economic game called the Ultimatum Game. During the game, participants were scanned as they were offered what were considered fair and unfair offers. Unfair offers stimulated brain activity in the anterior insula (region of the brain implicated in emotions) and the dorsolateral prefrontal cortex (region of the brain implicated in cognition). An additional discovery was that when a participant rejected what was deemed an unfair offer, there was increased activation of the anterior insula. These findings suggest that emotions play a central role in the decision-making process. As a key component to virtually all social interactions, understanding decision-making and the emotions behind them can elucidate the motivations behind human interactions.

Description. The authors described a need for research in understanding the role of emotions in the decision-making process. The authors hypothesized that unfair responses would trigger activation in areas of the brain associated with emotion, and that the severity of the emotional reaction would largely determine whether or not offers were accepted or rejected in the Ultimatum Game. In the study, participants were made an offer to split a sum of money, and the trials were evenly split between a human partner making the offer, a computer making the offer, and a control where money was simply doled out. Based on the offer, participants had to determine if the offer was fair and they accepted it, or unfair and they rejected it. All participants received identical offers, but at differing points of the study.

A total of 19 participants in the Ultimatum Game underwent fMRI scans while responding to fair and unfair offers made to them. As expected, all the fair responses were accepted and the unfair responses were rejected increasingly as the amount offered decreased. It is interesting to note that emotional reactions to unfair offers were significantly higher when the partner was a human instead of a computer. The emotional reactions, signified by activation of the bilateral anterior insula, were also higher for offers that were considered less fair. The authors report that this region of the brain has been associated with pain and disgust in previous studies.

Study 2: "Social Evaluation by Preverbal Infants"

Summary. Hamlin, Wynn, and Bloom, (2007) found that humans are capable of evaluating social situations in preverbal stages of infancy. According to the authors, the ability to evaluate social interactions during infancy indicated that the skill is not learned, but inherent in everyone. The infants were not only able to detect differences, but showed a preference for helping others. The presence of this ability at such an early stage confirms its importance, and suggests possible biological underpinnings.

Description. The authors arrived at their findings through experimentation on two groups of healthy infants, 16 10-month-old infants and 12 6-month-old infants. The infants were placed in their mothers' laps for the experiment and the mothers were asked to close their eyes and not interfere in any way.

An initial habituation phase allowed the infants time to become accustomed to the characters made of wooden pieces of various shapes (e.g., square, triangle, etc.) with eyes glued on them. During the actual experimentation phase, one of the characters was either assisted up a hill or hindered by a third character, which physically blocked the climber's way. By allowing the infants to reach for their preferred character, 14 of the 16 10-month-olds and all 12 of the 6-month olds showed a preference for the character that had been helpful towards the climber. Through these outcomes, the authors verified their hypothesis that infants are indeed capable of recognizing social aspects of an event, and determining either like or dislike for people based on their function. The authors also varied the experiments in several ways and verified their findings that social interaction was at the heart of the infants' choice. For example, in one scenario the characters were presented simply as blocks (without eyes), and the infants did not show a preference between the helping and hindering characters.

Based on the findings of this study, the authors argued that the ability to facilitate these evaluations at such an early stage of life suggests evolutionary and developmental components. In past societies, not only would it have been beneficial for people to recognize those who were cooperative but also to distinguish those who would not reciprocate helping behaviour, ultimately damaging group cohesiveness and the ability to complete basic tasks (e.g., food gathering, warfare, hunting, etc.).

This ability to socially evaluate others is also expected to play some role in the moral development of the infant, which could have significant implications for the infant later in life. A specific issue to consider is the relationship between an infant's exposure to others who have been either prosocial or antisocial in their interactions with others and the infant's own helping behaviour later in life.

Study 3: "A Neural Basis for Social Cooperation"

Summary. Rilling, Gutman, Zeh, Pagnoni, Berns, and Kilts, (2002) focused on the concept of reciprocal altruism and how specific areas in the brain (i.e., nucleus accumbens, caudate nucleus, ventromedial frontal/orbitofrontal cortex, and rostral anterior cingulated cortex) may be responsible for the increase in mutual cooperation instead of selfishly accepting favors from others without reciprocating.

Description. the authors note that historically, one behaviour that has helped various groups of humans to survive a variety of harsh situations has been their willingness and ability to share material resources, especially food, for the benefit of each other. Furthermore, while reciprocal altruism has been rare in other animal species, it has been noted in humans with the understanding that two preconditions must have been met for the evolution of this behaviour: first, there must be repetitive social interaction between partners who are to reciprocate altruism, and secondly the individuals must have the capability to distinguish between those who are altruistic and those who are not.

To study reciprocal altruism, the authors used the "Iterated prisoners' dilemma game," where two participants make a choice to cooperate or defect, and their choices impact the amount of money each receives at the end of the experiment. The payoff amounts are setup so that the highest payoff is for a defector when the other is cooperative, while both participants cooperating or defecting earns is in the middle, and the lowest earning is for the cooperative participant when the other is defecting. To earn the maximum amount of money, it is important to defect as much as possible while the other person does not defect at all. The likelihood of one person continuing to cooperate while the other defects, however, is rather low.

For this study, the authors ran two separate experiments where 19 women were paired off with another human and 17 women were paired off with a computer. The participants were informed that the computer did not have a fixed strategy and instead would respond with a choice based on their response on the most recent choice. The authors found a different level of neural activation when the women were paired off with a human versus when they were paired with a computer. They also noted that a previous cooperative or defect response from both participants was more likely to be followed by another cooperative or defect response. During this interaction, there was activation in the participants' brain in the anteroventral striatum, subgenual anterior cingulate cortex, and the ventromedial/orbitofrontal cortex, which are areas of the brain known to be involved in reward processing.

The authors wanted to clarify whether the activation in the brain was resulting from the reinforcement from monetary reward or earning it during social interaction with another participant. The authors studied the brain activations during the human paired portion of the game and when a human and computer were involved. They found that the anteroventral striatum, rostral anterior cingulate cortex, and orbitofrontal cortex were activated more during the reciprocated social cooperation than receiving the monetary reward during the non-social situation. Furthermore, the rostral anterior cingulate cortex and the anteroventral striatum only activated when there was cooperation between two human partners, instead of one human cooperating with a computer. Following a cooperative response, the decision making period on whether to cooperate or not during the next response also showed activity in the left anterior caudate, the right post-central gyrus, rostral anterior cingulate cortex and the anteroventral striatum.

The authors noted that after the experiments the subjects reported mutual cooperation to be the best situation, even though it resulted in a decreased monetary award. This was more desirable than defecting against a cooperative partner, because defecting increased both feelings of guilt and the possibility that the partner would then defect on the next exchange, and could result in a destabilized relationship and decrease in reward. During the cooperative interactions, the activations in the orbitoforntal cortex and ventral striatum support the idea that there is a reward component to mutually cooperative/altruism behavior.

Study 4: "Neural Responses to Taxation and Voluntary Giving Reveal Motives for Charitable Giving"

Summary. Harbaugh, Mayr, and Burghart, (2007) studied the concepts of "pure altruism" and "warm glow," as possible causes for people's feelings of reward and specific neural activity when there is either a mandate to pay taxes or they voluntarily contribute for the benefit of society.

Description. The authors looked at the differences between taxation and voluntary donations to charity in the Unites States and how each of these behaviours impacts a person's neural functioning. They distinguished between two types of possible rewards for helping society. The first occurs when a person feels good or receives satisfaction from simply seeing his/her giving of money as a benefit to society, and is more likely to fall in the category of "true altruism". On the other hand, when a person feels good about having made a decision to donate seeing it as a benefit to another, this is less likely to be true altruism and is termed "warm glow." The authors argued that if a person is in the "true altruism" group then he/she should show neural activity associated with the brain's reward centers whether they donate money on a voluntary or mandatory basis. The authors also argued that those in the "warm glow" group should only show activation in the brain's reward centers when they are voluntarily donating money and not when they are being taxed.

The authors noted that past research showed that the ventral striatum and the insulae are involved in the processing of various types of information. Specifically, they are implicated in reward processing related to rewards of money, food, and drugs, as well as abstract rewards such as contributing to charities, punishing unfair players in sharing games, etc. For this study, the authors used fMRI scanning of 19 females while they played the Dictator Game. The subjects were given $100 at the start of the experiment and were allowed to make decisions on whether or not to donate money to a local food bank, while also having mandatory (tax-like) transfers made to the food bank from their fund. While multiple offers of mandatory and voluntary transfers were made, the participants had to accept the offered transfers with the understanding that the experimenters would remain unaware of their choices. Furthermore, at the end of the experiment, one of their mandatory and one voluntary transfer would be randomly chosen and implemented. The authors also had participants complete satisfaction ratings after the transfers were accepted or refused.

During the study, the authors were able to divide the group into 2, separating out 9 egoists and 10 altruists. The egoists had a higher neural response to their own payoff versus the charity, and the altruists gave money to the charity on an almost 2 to 1 ratio when compared to the egoists. Satisfaction ratings for voluntary giving were almost 10% higher than for the mandatory transfers, and the voluntary transfers also resulted in a higher activation in the caudate, right nucleus accumbens, and the insulae. Based on these findings, the authors conclude that the findings support the "warm-glow" theory of giving, but that both "pure altruism" and "warm glow" are important motives for giving to charities.

Study 5: "Human Fronto-Mesolimbic Networks Guide Decisions about Charitable Donation"

Summary. Moll, Krueger, Zahn, Pardini, Oliveira-Souza, and Grafman (2006) noted that, at times, humans will sacrifice material benefits to endorse or to oppose societal causes based on moral beliefs. At first glance, this seems to go against the evolutionary concept of survival and looking out for one's own needs. The authors set out to study the neural bases for human altruism through their decisions on charitable donations. They found that the mesolimbic reward system is activated by donations in the same way as when monetary rewards are obtained. Additionally, the medial orbitorfrontal-subgenual and lateral orbitofrontal areas mediate decisions to donate or to oppose societal cues and more anterior sectors of the prefrontal cortex are activated when altruistic choices prevail over selfish material interest.

Description. The authors recruited 19 participants to undergo fMRI scans while they either endorsed or opposed societal causes through anonymous donating or refraining from donating. The participants were then given a few seconds to review a specific offer from one of the four following scenarios: (1) the participant would not benefit monetarily but the charity would, (2) the participant would benefit but the charity would not, (3) the participant would lose money and the charity would benefit monetarily, and (4) both the participant and charity would benefit monetarily. To avoid a monetary fine for failing to respond, they had to make a choice within the allotted time. At the end of the experiment, the participants were allowed to keep the balance of money they had remaining.

When participants made the altruistic decisions, whereby the charity received the bulk of the donation, there was an associated activation of the anterior prefrontal cortex, including the frontopolar cortex and the medial frontal gyrus. The authors noted that distinct neural systems are involved in the decision to donate or to oppose societal causes; the mesolimbic reward system provides the general reinforcement mechanism, the subgenual area and the lateral orbitofrontal cortex mediate social attachment and aversion responses, and the anterior prefrontal cortex is crucial for representing more complex reinforcement contingencies related to altruistic decisions. These findings are in line with prior understandings of these brain systems; the mesolimbic system regulates overall reward reinforcement and is activated by a host of stimuli, including food, sex, drugs, and money, and the subgenual area is known to be involved in the social attachment function and release of the neuromodulators oxytocin and vasopressin. The authors further noted that recent studies have indicated that the administration of oxytocin to humans resulted in increased trust and cooperation in economic interactions.

Based on the findings of this study, the authors speculate that humans' ability to feel attachment or aversion to societal causes may have emerged through the same evolutionary mechanisms that resulted in the reciprocity theory. This would allow the primate reward, social attachment, and aversion neural systems to operate beyond the immediate issues of relationships, thereby allowing humans to directly link value to abstract collective causes, principles, and ideologies. While these primitive centers of the brain are linked to altruism, the uniquely developed anterior prefrontal cortex becomes involved when immediate self-interest and moral beliefs are at odds.

Study 6: "The Neural Basis of Altruistic Punishment"

Summary. de Quervain, Fischbacher, Treyer, Schellhammer, Schnyder, Buck, and Fehr (2004) looked at the willingness of people to punish others at a personal cost to promote cooperation. This phenomenon is termed altruistic punishment, and is one aspect of strong reciprocity, which is believed to be the evolutionary root of human cooperation. The term implies that those that cooperate are rewarded, and those that do not cooperate are punished at the punisher's expense. Through neurological imaging, the authors were able to determine that reward processing centers of the brain were activated when non-cooperators were punished. This adds to the current body of literature suggesting that brains are not only hard-wired to reward generous behaviours, but also punishment towards those that are not generous or cooperative.

Description. The authors sought to determine the neurological effects of altruistic punishment. Positron emission tomography (PET) scans were taken while participants took part in an economic game. Although two people took part in each trial, all interactions were anonymous. The first person (A) was given 10 monetary units (MU) and asked whether he wanted to keep the 10 MU or pass it on to the second person (B). If A gave B the 10 MU, B was given an extra 40 MU from the experimenter. If A did not give anything, then the 10 MU was retained and B received nothing. In the second phase, B was asked whether to split the 50 MU with A, or to retain it all. Based on the reaction of B, A was given the option to punish B and allowed a one minute period to decide. The authors posited that if B did not return the generous act, A would consider this unfair and it would create a desire to punish A for violating the cooperation norm. The authors took scans during this 1 minute interval to determine the area of activation when the desire to punish was evoked.

The sample was comprised of 15 males, of which 14 initiated the game by trusting B and passed on all 10 MU. Scans were taken of A whenever B did not respond with trust and kept the 50 MU. Results supported the authors' hypothesis that punishing B increased activation in the caudate nucleus, which has been implicated in reward processing. Activation also increased in the thalamus, which has specifically been tied to the processing of monetary rewards. When B failed to return the generous act and proved untrustworthy, A responded with a desire and willingness to punish, which then activated areas of the brain associated with reward processing. The authors found that the greater the willingness of A to punish B (more costly to A), the greater the activation in the caudate. This suggests that A anticipated the satisfaction or reward that would be experienced if B was punished. The authors argue that punishing norm violators elicits a reward process in the caudate, and that altruistic punishment is a strong motivator in human cooperation.

Study 7: "Oxytocin Increases Generosity in Humans"

Summary. Zak, Stanton, and Ahmadi (2007) pointed out that although there are numerous instances of generous behavior towards strangers, there is as of yet no clear explanation behind one-shot anonymous generosity. A new research interest in the area of neuroeconomics seeks to explain this form of generosity towards strangers in terms of empathy. The authors aimed to elucidate the role of empathy in generous behaviour. Oxytocin was used to stimulate empathy in individuals while they participated in typical neuroeconomics game play. The results indicated that oxytocin increased generosity by 80%, leading researchers to argue that empathy creates an emotional reaction towards another which in turn leads to generosity.

Description. The authors distinguish between altruism and generosity, indicating that both involve the act of giving, but that generosity implies the act of giving more than what is needed or asked for. The authors utilized a double blind placebo experiment to elucidate the underlying mechanisms involved in generous behaviour. The participants were randomly assigned to either the experimental or control groups, with 34 males in each group. The experimental group was given a nasal inhalant containing oxytocin, while the control group received a nasal inhalant comprised of only saline. The design was based on previous research indicating the role empathy plays in generous behaviour. In order to simulate empathy in a controlled environment, the researchers used a neuromodulator called oxytocin. The authors noted previous research which illustrated the ability of oxytocin to promote attachment, trust, and reciprocity.

A total of 68 participants were given the nasal inhalant, with 34 receiving oxytocin and 34 receiving saline. They each filled out demographic information while they waited one hour for the oxytocin to take effect. After the mandatory wait period, the authors tested various money transfer scenarios to determine the effects of oxytocin (empathy) on altruistic and generous behaviours. The authors used two common games from economics theory, the Ultimatum Game and the Dictator Game, to create the test scenarios. Participants within each group were randomly assigned to roles of either the first decision maker (DM1) or the second decision maker (DM2) and took part in both games. For the Ultimatum Game, DM1 was given $10 and asked to present an offer to split the money with DM2, and DM2 was asked to state the lowest offer he would accept. This game aimed to elicit purposive offers from DM1 that reflected a willingness to consider the DM2 participant's perspective. Based on the offer, DM2 could accept and the money would be split, or reject and no one would receive any money. If DM2 rejected the offer, he had the opportunity to punish DM1 for a poor offer, but at a personal cost to DM1. In the Dictator Game, all methods remained the same, except DM2 was forced to accept all offers, which meant that DM1 was not obliged to consider DM2's perspective. The hypothesis stated that taking another's perspective into consideration (showing empathy), would increase generosity. Therefore, the Ultimatum Game offers could be compared with the

Dictator Game offers to determine any difference between altruistic and generous offers. All identities were masked, and no communication was allowed between experimenters or participants.

The authors found that the average offer was 21% higher for the oxytocin group than the average offer for the saline group in the Ultimatum Game. The authors also found that the oxytocin group averaged $1.89 for accepted offers, and the saline group averaged $1.06 for accepted offers. The authors defined a generous offer as one that exceeded the mean acceptable offer given by DM2 prior to beginning the game. For example, if DM1 made an offer at or below the average acceptable offer, then this was classified as altruistic. If, however, the offer was greater than the average acceptable offer, then it was classified as generous because it went above and beyond what was expected or needed. The authors developed a mathematical computation that determined the oxytocin DM1 group showed 80% higher generosity than that of the saline group. Offers made by DM1 in the Dictator Game were then compared to the offer the same DM1 made in the Ultimatum Game. This allowed the researchers to control for altruism, and to partial out only acts of generosity. The findings suggested that even after controlling for altruism present in initial offers of the Dictator Game, the oxytocin (empathy) did result in higher levels of generosity. The authors argued that the act of considering another's perspective (empathy) reflected generous behaviour, and this resulted in 80% higher generosity. Conversely, they argued that not considering another's perspective will decrease the act of generous giving.

The authors briefly review available literature on the effects of oxytocin on neurological functioning. They indicate that it has been linked to increasing dopamine in areas of the brain associated with reward processing. Although oxytocin levels were increased artificially in this experiment, the authors noted that occurrences can also raise oxytocin, including touch and other positive interactions with others. The authors posit that these positive interactions stimulate oxytocin levels and promote generous behaviours, thus explaining generosity towards strangers.

II. INDIGENOUS PERSPECTIVES DIALOGUE

Greg Cajete, Jongmin Lee and Four Arrows

Four Arrows. I think these studies could be used to support intuitive, universal and Indigenous wisdom as relates to the importance of empathy and trust in human potentiality. The experiment with the infant is difficult to argue with as evidence that generosity is more of a biological imperative than is selfishness and that cooperation is more natural than competition. They do reflect a shift somewhat from the idea about generosity being a more or less selfish act for the sake of future returns. However, I still find the emphasis on reward and punishment to be continuing a misunderstanding about the nature of generosity, whether human or animal. It seems that Huxley, Freud and Wright's contentions that there is no such thing as morality in evolution and only through deception and self-deception do we make believe otherwise, are still operational concepts that cloud the lens of current neuroscience on this topic. From an Indigenous perspective, I believe this reward-punishment and selfish motive is misleading and ultimately not of benefit to humanity. As I hope we will discuss, I also think that animal studies relating to conflict resolution and reconciliation support Indigenous thinking on this topic. Much of this research can be reviewed in Changeux's edited work, *Neurobiology of Human Values* (2005).

Part of the challenge in looking at these experiments has to do with the assumptions and frameworks that are utilized in setting them up. I don't think that using monetary rewards and punishments or thinking in terms of selfishness or non-selfishness as experimental factors or as rationales for behaviour will get us to the deeper truths relating to generosity, no matter how rapidly we identify the related chemicals and neuralpeptides like oxytocin or places in the brain where activity seems to be most pronounced. Nonetheless, I think that observations about empathy and something different happening than happens with "pleasures" like drugs or sex offer a starting place for dialogue in neurophilosophy.

It is understandable how Western scientists, no matter how open-minded, might use a lens of understanding that is colored with Western values. Although most societies claim generosity as an important value, and although the major religions of the world endorse it passionately, the last several thousand years of human existence is characterized largely by greed, competition and selfishness. Whether or not the major developed countries, or their citizens at large, might be identified by the concept of generosity or altruism is not a topic for extensive discussion here. The answer is complicated and controversial. However, sifting through the literature does not cause one to characterize most of countries as being truly generous. Certainly the claim that the U.S. is a "generous country" needs rethinking. In fact, researchers like Sardar and Davies write in their book that the conventional idea that the U.S. is a generous nation is "knowledgeable ignorance" (2003). A *Boston Globe* article entitled, "Global Analysis Dispute Perceived US Generosity" reported that since the Reagan administration U.S. donations fell continually to their current low (Dec. 31, 2004). The Organization for Economic Cooperation and Development has had a long established target of 0.7% GDP that only few Scandinavian countries achieve. Where private and public donations occur, few people give without being asked to do so, and even then giving is closely related to self-interest, tax benefits, social status and donations to one's religious institutions (Kendall, J., 2003). As for the wealthy givers, consider this fact for a perspective. Ebay founder Pierre Omidyar was ranked the eighth most generous billionaire, giving 549 million dollars from 2002–2006. He was ranked the 32nd wealthiest person in the world with 8.9 billion (San Francisco Chronicle, 2008). (Keep in mind that one billion dollars is one thousand million.)

On the other hand, generosity is considered as an identifier of many if not most Indigenous cultures, both today and historically. In fact, the entire philosophy and spiritual understandings revolve around a complex notion of sharing and interconnectedness (Murray, 2000). Noted educator Larry Brendtro claims that virtue in American Indian ways of being in the world is "reflected in the preeminent value of generosity (Brendtro et al, 1990, p. 35). Wells writes that giving in Native cultures is a way of life (Wells 1998). Dagmar Thorpe, the granddaughter of Olympic Gold Medalist Jim Thorpe says the "underlying values, principles, philosophy and world view of giving are universal concepts among Native People" (1997, p. 13). Daniel Wildcat in a book he co-authored with Vine Deloria, Jr., writes, "I find it difficult to discount the impressions of so many non-Native persons, from conquistadores to Harvard anthropologists, who in spite of incredibly ethnocentric, if not racist, assessments of our ancestors, all saw indigenous North American societies possessing something they found admirable and lacking in their own Western societies: generosity and a social well-being (2001, p. 141). Gilliland's research shows that generosity is an inherent aspect in the learning styles of contemporary American Indian students (Gilliland, 1999). Swisher's research came to similar conclusions (1989).

So what is going on Greg? Why in spite of the research pointing to the natural tendency for humans to be generous do we face such a lack of generosity in our world?

Greg. I agree that generosity is the expression of a deep biological instinct connected at the physical level to the way we as humans think. I also liked the neuroeconomic emphasis on studying choice as it relates to reciprocity. Generosity involves a reciprocal mindset based on giving and receiving. Indeed in some ancient languages the word for giving and receiving were one in the same. So what is it in the Indigenous way of giving and receiving that takes the altruist social form of Generosity that we can explore to give some insight into the underlying biological and social value of being generous?

As you have pointed out with your references, to give of oneself, of what one has materially is an Indigenous value rooted in a life oriented dynamic, a spiritual ecology of relationship. To give away what one has to others is to honor that most precious thing that has been given...Life. It is a primal quintessential reciprocal relationship with life that is honored. Giving and receiving, giving and receiving emulates the central animating dynamic of life itself. Indigenous mind mirrors Natural mind. And so, it is the Indigenous way to emulate the ways of Nature in the social ways of community. I think this idea of mirroring nature is missing in neurophilosophy even though I understand that neuroeconomics includes the role of rewards and punishment in animals other than humans.

All Indigenous cultures reflect this central dynamic of life giving and life receiving through both a personal and social forms of "giving away." Indigenous traditions of generosity and its expression through hospitality are intimately tied to the function of sustaining both the life of the individual and the community. Given the pervasiveness of hospitality as a social value in all cultures of the world through time, there is little doubt that there is a bio-social foundation stemming from the way our brains have evolved. Ultimately, one can trace the function of human generosity to the human instinct for survival, but again, survival when considered in Nature's terms is a symbiotic phenomenon with little room for the kind of selfishness seen in the world today.

The exploration of generosity and its expression through hospitality opens a window into the natural process of the mind. The social contexts of giving along with those everyday exchanges of giving and receiving between family, friends and strangers afford both windows and mirrors into the brain itself. The thinking, language, social, situational contexts in which generosity is shown all reflect brain function and more importantly the human meaning and mindful intent of giving. The host and the hosted exemplify a kind of cosmic giving and receiving which belongs to the realm of the first creator and to the manifestations of his first creations in the form of the universe. The ultimate host is the Great Mystery. One might metaphorically say we are all guests, guest of the universe, of our mother earth, of life giving spirit itself. So to be generous to another is to be generous to one's own life spirit. It is an acknowledgement of the Grace that we have been given through our own life and that which we see, acknowledge and honor in another. Of course, as with all things in nature, there is an opposite force, energy or intent that forms the creative tension necessary to define a whole. This dark quality is what is often metaphorically personified in the many Indigenous stories of sacred twins, ogres, monsters and shadows. These teaching stories help us remember our natural ways and relationships and how easily we can risk them or find ourselves out of balance with them.

In Indigenous contexts, giveaways are founded on such guiding stories which tell of sharing the gifts of life with other people, with animals and spirits of nature. The gifts that are shared are many times symbolized by food as the most foundational element of life. The feast as the context for sharing and the context for the expression of generosity appears to be the oldest and most commonly shared cultural ritual expression. The sharing of food reminds us of our personal and collective connection to the sacred sources of life. The sharing of food and other material possessions is a representation of the mutual reciprocal nature of the process of life. The sharing of food reminds us that the first expression of generosity that we must acknowledge is the generosity of the Earth in her sharing of the bounty of life with human beings thereby allowing human life to perpetuate. This is an implicate understanding that seems to be wired into our brains which in turn finds expression in the ways food is culturally symbolized as a primal source of life.

The social and spiritual transactions in Indigenous cultures which surround the giving and sharing of food form the backdrop for the practice of generosity, the sharing of life and material wealth in a way that gives special focus to the importance of sustaining both people and community. All aspects of Indigenous community life involve the sharing of food at some level. In some cases the food is the prime focus of the occasion. In other cases it is a part of the sharing of words, knowledge, history, ritual or fellowship.

In a broader sense these acts of ritual giveaway represent the natural process of giving and receiving at every level of the natural world. The given of food water and clothing symbolically represents the ethic of care for others and these acts reinforce the bond of relationship that is ultimately essential to both the survival of the individual and the group. So this is the payoff of generosity of individuals in relationship to communities. The survival of both individual and community and the imprinting of the mind with the life sustaining ethic of giving through the practice and storying of the giveaway. Sacrifice and giving become valued over self centeredness and hoarding. These are the values which sustain community and mimic in human terms the mutual reciprocal processes of natural communities. For the giver the benefit is a transformation of self from a self centered orientation to a community centered one. This is an essential conditioning for a tribal society for it is one way to perpetuate the tribe through time.

When I was about five, I remember going with my grandmother to visit with her friends and relatives in the Pueblo. I remember those days vividly because each visit was an adventure, a break from the usual routine. I seem to remember everything and every place we visited during that year. It was the year before I started first grade at the local elementary school. I learned so much during that time before school with my grandmother. This was also the time when I was immersed in the practice and process of generosity. This was generosity being practiced not as a concept but as an everyday reality.

In traditional Pueblo life generosity was expressed in a multitude of ways. Generosity was expressed in helping others, with sharing knowledge, work, goods and the fellowship of community. I remember watching my grandma and other women and men of the Pueblo replastering their houses with adobe mud, laughing, and working as if they were "one body". I remember visiting people who were ill and my grandmother taking her "special bundles" of plants to give them and giving special instructions about their use and the proper prayers to say. I remember my grandmother and other aunts baking bread in the special outdoor Pueblo ovens called "ornos". I remember those special feasts when all my relatives would come to my grandmother's home or those times when she would go to help others prepare feasts for weddings, baptisms, and even funerals. All of these events involved the generosity of sharing in community.

Generosity then is intimately tied to family, community and spiritual virtue. There is a saying "as Nature, so as Man" meaning that man is a reflection of Nature and man's nature is formed and informed by the same principles that operate in the natural world. This also means that generosity is both a biological and an ecological principle predicated <u>on</u> the essential activity of giving and receiving that characterizes the central dynamic of living communities. Man's brain and hence man's nature are wired toward expressing behaviour that enhances his own survival and that of the human family and community upon which he depends.

Although I know that neuroeconomics studies the brains of animals to see what happens when they make choices that are considered by the researchers to be either generous or selfish and they do this with some interspecies experiments, I think a missing link in understanding generosity is an emphasis on the idea that hospitality, generosity and kindness are not only the expression of ethical behaviour honored by every human culture in some way but it is also an expression of our instinct for bio-affiliation. There is a kind of associative empathy between humans and other living things which is grounded in the physical nature of our body, mind and spirit.

A Harvard zoologist has termed this empathy, "biophilia" or the innate human instinct to affiliate with other living things. Biophilia may be the biological human instinct which forms the foundation for human relationships of all sorts and the tendency to form the bonds of love and relationship found between human beings in families and communities.

Four Arrows. Greg, do you think that we might better understand what is coming out of neuroscience and contribute to neurophilosophy if we could describe how Indigenous wisdom sees generosity as a spiritual value?

Greg. Yes, I think so. As I've hinted at, the first expression of generosity that is recognized by Indigenous peoples is the generosity which is modeled by Mother Earth. In the various expressions of Indigenous spirituality among American Indians, the active focus on maintaining and/or striving for a harmony between one's self and one's natural environment was the most essential principle for applying knowledge. As a result of this orientation, Indian people determined that there were right purposes, right acts, right ways of approaching and understanding the natural world. These codes of behaviour were in direct relationship to the way that Indian people conducted themselves in a reciprocal relationship to the natural world. When something was taken from the natural world or animals were killed, ceremonies and symbolic ritual acts were performed to ensure the perpetuation of this right balance and attitude toward relationships.

"Mutual reciprocity" was engendered and reflected in all the kinds of acts that Native people experienced within the context of their natural environment. Indeed, ceremony and ritual were primarily social and spiritual mechanisms which maintained and/or re-established harmony with natural processes, if they had been lost. It was also a way of learning how to maintain one's relationship to the natural sources of life which Indian people recognized within their place. The offering of tobacco after taking the life of an animal, such as the deer or antelope or buffalo, was a reflection of this understanding, this environmentally-educated sense of being which Indian people practiced in their everyday lives.

For Indian people, the Earth is alive and had its own sense and expression of consciousness and being. The natural environment is a spiritual reality and the earth entities, living creatures, were not to be used haphazardly and without great respect or reflection on the repercussions of their use and/or abuse. A sense of spiritual ecology, founded on a deep spiritual resonance with the natural world, characterized the process and reflection of environmental education among Indigenous people. This sense of relatedness to the natural world came from a much deeper source than simply intellectual understanding. It came from a spiritual orientation to conscious relationship and direct responsibility for maintaining that relationship with those things which allowed human life to exist and upon which human life depended for survival. This sense of relationship unfolded through the perpetuation of what may be called "natural community", which, in turn, reflected a "spiritual ecology" which connected the People to their Place, their environment and to each other. Since everything was viewed as being mutually dependent, mutually inter-related, nothing in nature could be viewed as purely self-sufficient, including and especially human beings. The idea of a community which included not only the human species, but all species of plant, animal, insect, which were a part of the place that a tribe recognized themselves as being a part of, became an integral foundation and context for expressing Indigenous environmental education. In turn, the understanding that there was such a thing as a "natural community" led in specific ways to the social organizational concept of "natural democracy". Within this context of natural democracy, natural community, there is the idea that plants and animals, and those other entities in the natural world which share their presence and place generously with man, have rights of their own and must be accorded generosity and given similar respect, truthful and honest presence as would be given to any member of a human tribe.

Four Arrows. Yes, and if I may say I worry that without this context neuroscience could lead in the same negative directions that research into the atom has led. Greg, you speak of "a reciprocal mindset" as being behind the emphasis on generosity practiced by most Indigenous cultures. I think you and I understand this as a "returning in kind" in order to maintain balance in the universe. So if we take a branch from a willow tree to build a lodge, we offer hair or tobacco in return to reciprocally acknowledge that each breath or achievement results in a depletion of some other being. I'm not sure if the brain science is being interpreted in this way, however. How do the studies that indicate a reward-punishment based theory of generosity or even an empathy based cause for generosity fit into your idea of a reciprocal mindset? How might we make a connection between empathy, a selfish sense of reward and an Indigenous reciprocal mindset?

Greg. There is a largely unexamined bias of Western Science that is generally ignored by scientists in favor of thinking and saying that science is acultural and objective. On closer examination of the scientific method you will find that it is a creative process of inquiry which reduces our innate subjectivity as human beings to the lowest level of expression. But as long as we are human we will have human subjectivity that is influenced by our personal and cultural history. From this perspective nothing that humans do is totally objective. Therefore, subjectivity (which is the ego conditioned mind) always exists in scientific investigation. The observer affects that which is observed. If you seek the selfish nature of brain function and design, that is what your brain, with the active involvement of the mind, will facilitate you finding. If you seek the communal, empathetic nature of the brain that is what the brain with the mind will facilitate you finding. The mind as an emergent quality of brain functioning is very accommodating. This is the quantum quality of the mind. From my perspective human communities and the cultures that they create can be both selfish and empathic at the same time. Individual self preservation and communal perpetuation are not diametrically opposed. They can and do work in a symbiotic harmonious way with one another. This *both and quality* is exactly how natural communities operate. Human and natural communities are first and foremost complex adaptive systems.

Jongmin. I can agree about both the symbiotic and the adaptive design of our brain functions, but as a scientist who studies brain functions, I probably do tend to give more power to objectivity than does Greg. I believe that the reciprocal mindset can be built up by the brain's summation of long-standing trials and errors, either consciously or unconsciously. Based on much continuous feedback from the results of their behaviour, people can develop a reasonable knowledge for sustaining their environment, either locally or globally. Thus the reciprocal mindset is powered by superego. In addition, the reciprocal mindset can be fortified when the subjects are exposed to some risk of losing their well-being or happiness. In this case, the reciprocal mindset is driven by both unconscious symbiotic instinct and reasonable knowledge.

Four Arrows. So you agree with Greg about reciprocity and symbiosis being a primary function of adaptation?

Jongmin. I think so. An extreme example might be how during the tough army training or battle, soldiers are mentally tied together with great generosity stronger than between family members, to help one another survive. Similarly, humans will work in harmony with the mountain to plant trees so future generations will enjoy the beauty and health of the mountain. Or they will be sure not to hunt young animals so as to maintain a healthy population for future generations. I think this is all about reciprocity.

Four Arrows. But Jon, this is exactly what is NOT happening in our world! The Western way of "thinking" or "unthinking" is destroying the mountain and animals and more for future generations. And the situation with the soldiers is not about survival for future generations, but immediate survival. On the other hand, Greg talked about how his Pueblo re-plastered their houses with adobe mud, laughing and working as if they were "one body." This seems to be the ultimate form of empathy but is more than just empathy. I remember a story about a guy who tried to save someone from jumping off the Golden Gate Bridge. He was holding on to the heavier man's arms with his toes on the rail about to go down with him when the police hauled both men to safety. When asked why he risked his life for a stranger, the man said "For a moment I could not tell the difference between him and me." Is this reciprocity or something else? I tend to think that the Western cultural emphasis on reward and punishment relates to the devastation of life systems on earth. What can we learn from Indigenous wisdom and research on the brain to help us be generous in ways that can bring us back into balance?

Jongmin. The emotional mental function of the human-being is sensitively and quickly activated but shows fluctuation influenced by the other kinds of emotion by time and environment. So perhaps other influences are causing the emotions to move in unreasonable directions and this causes our destructive behaviours. I think that reasonable thinking takes longer to activate and when it does it is coming from our super egos, not our egos. And at the super ego place, the reciprocal mindset, which stems from the reasoning activity of the brain, combines with empathy, which stems from emotional centers in the brain, combine to create appropriate survival adaptation. The example of the brave man who saved a heavier man would be an extreme case of empathy alone, whereas the Pueblo Indian's activity would be a typical case of reciprocal mindset driven by high-level empathy.

Four Arrows. I think the example on the bridge is an extreme example in Western culture but it is not extreme or unusual in Indigenous cultures nor in other animal kingdoms. So such emotional activity as you mention was somehow special in the rescuer but what is it that allows emotional triggers to be so widespread in Indigenous cultures? We know from neuroscience that moral judgments are associated with the stimulation of certain emotions. Perhaps the deep understanding and oneness with all things in Nature and the ways of going beyond fear that Indigenous people employ sets an emotional thermostat in a way that is cultural?

Jongmin. The western reward and punishment principle would efficiently construct the generosity driven by very reasonable and logical thought not by indigenous altruism either emotional or unconscious. However, in the viewpoint of oriental scholar not western scientist, I would like to comment about "karma", which is a very important concept in Buddhism and Confucianism. The basic concept of karma is that all life-forms, which you encounter in your life, have had a special relationship with you in your former life. Of course the species of the life forms can be transformed during the "circulation of life". Therefore, people should not deal with life forms as if they are trivial. With referencing this idea, I would say there is something which cannot be explained only by examining emotion and reason. I think there is something else encoded in the human brain that drives people to give more generosity than simple sympathy to the others in exceptional ways.

Greg. In the broader context of the natural world what at the surface may seem to be a basic punishment and reward scenario in isolation turns into a mutual reciprocal play of events in the broader context of community. Human beings are social beings and we derive meaning as much from our relationship with the world and each other as we derive from our own self exploration. Our brains are wired at one level to facilitate our individual survival and yet at another level to facilitate our bio-affiliation, our group or communal mind and yet at another level our spiritual or transcendent mind. The human brain has evolved this way and indeed is still evolving this way … the emergent mind is the sum of all of these parts of our brain …. But the sum is always greater than the parts and this is what Indigenous cultures, philosophies and traditions of community learned to work with … the emergent quality of the natural mind. This is the ancient ecology that Indigenous cultures are trying to revitalize, perpetuate and preserve.

Re-introducing this quality of mind and natural propensity of brain function into a contemporary context of expression is what Indigenous traditions of thought have to offer to bring balance back to the dysfunctional collective mind of modern society.

Jongmin. From my medical/science view, such generosity is driven by emotional activity. Emotion is a highly complicated brain function which requires abundant cerebral functional resources. This is especially true as relates to the frontal lobe of the cerebrum which is in charge of high-level mental function and emotion. The hypothalamus and pituitary gland, where stress hormones spring out, are activated during emotional events. However, when the brain is operating in balance, in complementary communication with itself, then no evident emotional activity or conflict appears or seems to be required. Due to this fact, the reciprocal mindset would not need strong brain activation. People feel more comfortable when the brain's reasonable function overwhelms the emotional function. There is no apparent stress. So reciprocity as we are describing seems to be the highest, healthiest state of the human brain. Therefore, getting back to what you were asking Four arrows, perhaps the Indigenous relationship that you describe has more to do with a balance between the brain's complementary hemispheres than with some emotional setting.

Four Arrows. Very interesting, Jongmin, This reminds me of the research we did together where the student had people watch a simple sights and sounds of nature film and also a portion of Al Gore's film, "An Inconvenient Truth," while we monitored brain functions under an fMRI. I recall that while watching the latter scary predictions about the future, the brains had much stress and emotional activity, especially from the pituitary, but during the simple sights and sounds of nature film, the brain activity was quiet except along the corpus callosum, where communication between the right and left hemispheres was high. Nevertheless, I want to ask another question. You said reciprocity is the highest, healthiest state of the human brain. But why just the human brain? Although intraspecies cooperation with non-kin is an issue that has attracted substantial attention in neuroscience, it is not at all understood. (See Boyd 2003 and Brosnan and de Waal 2003). In the absence of this understanding, the research thus far tends to conclude or imply that reciprocal altruism is rare in other animal species, with some exceptions. I have trouble with this and wonder if you agree that Indigenous ways of knowing see animals as being generous for largely the same reasons suggested by Indigenous wisdom? And if animals are generous, is it because of an activation of places in the brain that stimulate "good feeling" chemicals and reward feelings that are also served by food, sex, drugs and money?

Jongmin. I believe that only human-beings can perform "genesis," like the replanting of trees or a garden, etc. We seem to take joy in doing this and thus it is a high level emotional function. Due to this kind of behaviour, human-beings play a major role in maintaining the balance of the world. I think this stems from empathy for other parts of the world. However...

Four Arrows. Excuse me for interrupting my friend, but I am recoiling inside at the assertion that humans today have empathy for other parts of the world. I agree we play a large role in maintaining the balance of the world, but it has largely been about upsetting the balance! The Indigenous perspective says over and over in our stories and teachings that the animals are the teachers and the main creatures for balancing the world, whether it is the buzzards cleaning up road kill or bacteria doing what it does.

Jongmin. However, any reciprocal mindset of animal species other than human-beings is based on selfish desire, I think. The emotions of animals are primal and the basic components are 'like' and 'dislike'. If the 'like' component is stronger than the 'dislike' component, the animal will tolerate the 'dislike' variables. For example, Penguins in Antarctic islands show tight gathering together when it is very cold and windy to keep their body temperature and make the kids warmer. During this activity, they have to give up asserting their territory of family or themselves and they seem to be very generous to the others by allowing closeness. But in warm weather especially during egg-laying, they are very strict in keeping their territories.

Four Arrows. We perceive it as selfish with our Western eyes and our belief that competition is the way of the wild, but it is not true and Indigenous Peoples know this.

Jongmin. I think we can compare the behaviours of young animals, especially mammals, with human babies. Human babies, especially during the early infancy, can express their emotion and desire using few behavioural actions such as crying, smiling, wriggling, etc. These behaviours express their emotion of "like" and "dislike" in either simple ways during the newborn or negotiative way during infancy and early childhood. We used to compare the intelligent quotient (IQ) of human and animal. For example, a dolphin's IQ is evaluated as similar as the IQ of a 3 or 4 year-old child. Although I don't have professional knowledge about animal intelligence, I think, this comparison would reflect the ability of negotiation to express their desire and emotion of "like" and "dislike". During this negotiation process, we can observe some generosity which will be compensated by bigger rewards sooner or later. Chimpanzees are regarded as the most intelligent animal and their IQ reaches up to preschool or early school age child. Even we can feel some mind of Chimpanzee in close contact. However, the highest intelligence of animals reaches the level of the child before completion of the 'ego identity.' In human development (or growth), remarkable behavioural advancement occurs at the moment of building up 'ego identity' around 5 to 7 year of age. For human, ego identity is 'acknowledging the existence of himself or herself' and the human starts to think in reasonable and logical ways more than through emotional response. After this level of development, we can talk about wisdom either indigenous or educated. Therefore I would like to comment that the reciprocal mindset with unconditioned generosity is superior to simple empathy and is a property of the human being although we cannot be free from empathy and instinct.

Four Arrows. Study #5 offers support for what you are saying but also offers opposition I think. Recall that the authors speculate that humans' ability to feel attachment or aversion to societal causes may have emerged through the same evolutionary mechanisms that resulted in the reciprocity theory applied to animals. This study supports what you are saying in its conclusion that humans may operate beyond the primate reward, social attachment, and aversion neural systems, allowing humans to directly link value to abstract collective causes, principles, and ideologies. However, keep in mind that the "primitive centers of the brain" are still linked to altruism. So just because we may have a uniquely developed anterior prefrontal cortex that becomes involved when immediate self-interest and moral beliefs are at odds, animals don't have to have this because they do not experience such contradictory behaviours. That's why they are the teachers!

Greg. Jongmin, I respectfully disagree also. I think it is a limited view to reduce animal behaviour to simple reward/punishment oriented stimulus response mechanisms of brain function. My first college degree was in biology with later graduate level training in wild life biology. My early professional training as a "field" biologist, as we were called in those days, involved many hours of field based observation of animals in their natural habitat. This professional field training combined with a lifetime of prior and current "nature watching" lead me to think that brain chemistry may provide an underlying foundation with some indication of certain behaviour patterns of some basic human and animal behaviour, but it is not all that determines behaviour. I have seen many examples of something greater than just brain chemistry operating to determine both human and animal behaviour. Both Humans and animals exhibit an "emergent" quality called Mind. It is the mindfulness nature of humans, animals, plants, places, the Earth and celestial beings and spiritual entities that Indigenous wisdom is keyed into. So, whether animals are truly generous or are just motivated by instinctual drive, I would point to the countless examples of animals acting in altruistic ways toward each other and toward humans.

Interestingly, or one might say synchronistically, while writing this I stopped to watch a Discovery Channel program about the plight of the polar bears as they attempt to survive the melting of sea ice in the Arctic manifesting as a result of global climate change. There are two scenes in the program which illustrate Indigenous perspective that I have presented. In the first scene a large male polar bear has ambushed a colony of walrus sunning themselves on the rocky shore of an arctic island. The male bear has surprised the colony and they are flipping to safety in the ocean. In the frenzy of the colony's flight the polar bear is able to corner a walrus pup by coming between it and the safety of the ocean. The pup screams it's distress call and the sister of the mother of the cub re-emerges from the safety of the water and pushes its way between the cub and the polar bear, giving time for the cub to escape This walrus gives its own life to save the life of the pup which looks on helplessly with its mother as the polar bear ends the life of its relative. Therefore, what is the motivation of this selfless act of self-sacrifice on the part of the older walrus to save the life of this pup. Is it reward and punishment based on brain function or is it something else? In the next scene, as this large male polar bear is devouring its prey, another much smaller female polar bear approaches and tries to get a share of the walrus. This is highly usual for another polar bear especially a female polar bear to approach a male which is eating. The larger male bear could easily kill the female for exhibiting such bold and aggressive behaviour. But the female is starving and if she does not feed she will certainly perish within a few days. The male bear initially charges the female and drives her away but in desperation she persists and continues crying for food. In a brain conditioned scenario the male bear would have killed the female. But the male bear seems to sense the desperation of the female and it an "act of generosity" the male bear allows the female to feed with him on the walrus. These acts of "generosity," cooperation and mutual reciprocal relationship among animals of the same species and among interspecies including humans are what Indigenous hunters observed since time immemorial. It is these kinds of acts which formed the basis for the ethical and mythological construct which form the basis of Indigenous wisdom of fostering life through rightful relationship.

Jongmin. Greg, basically I know about the existence of animal generosity cases that people enjoy watching. But I don't think this generosity works constantly all the time in the animal world because it cannot be based on reasonable consciousness since, in the field of psychiatrics, the superego is described as a specific mental function to the human being.

Four Arrows. But this is just a theory developed by a species that has continually alienated itself from the "other" animals.

Jongmin. Of course empathy, emotional exertion, should exist in animal brain function and it may also be fluctuating by external stimuli as in humans. I tend to think that the empathy might be a core of animal generosity. In addition, I think that the scene of generous animal behaviour would be produced by instinctive brain function including some hormonal and chemical neurotransmitter reaction.

Four Arrows. I agree that empathy is key, but in human generosity as well. The Indigenous idea expressed in the Lakota prayer that asserts "we are all related" is the expression of the spirituality based empathy Greg described.

Jongmin. But without reason, just emotional chemicals is not enough for generosity. It requires reasoning. For example, after feeding period or independence of their offspring, animals might be indifferent to each other or even they cannot acknowledge each other. These behaviours can be explained based on the influence of biochemical reaction in their brain. Even in the case of humans, well-known hormone-related behavioural changes can be observed. For example, during menstruation or pregnancy, some people do violations such as stealing, kleptomania, or fall into a manic-depressive bipolar disorder. Not only in animals but also in human beings, the instinct governs their behaviour of maternity. It is even called "maternal instinct." These examples are also described as hormonal influence in the brain since a remarkable change of hormonal secretion pattern occurs during the period of pregnancy and lactation. But to be generous in these times, only humans with consciousness can do.

Four Arrows. I don't disagree with what you are saying. I'm not saying that any creature is always generous. And I think you and I are really saying the same thing and this is why Indigenous wisdom is crucial. But as you say, there are these similarities between humans and emotions but also there are great lessons to be learned from the animal who eats its young and from a deep understanding of it I contend we truly learn a spiritual, Nature-based generosity.

In my work in the field of character education, I have often written that the great virtues such as generosity, courage, patience, fortitude, etc., are not human created but rather are sourced in the larger animal kingdom. I contend that humans learned these virtues from the animals and that we are not the original creators of these concepts or ways of being in the world. It of course has been quite a controversial contention.

Greg. There is many stories in Indigenous traditions that relate the generosity of animals to humans and to other animals as well. These stories certainly originated from actual observation of animals in their natural environment as they were from the creative imagination of the story tellers. The generosity of animals is either related directly or indirectly in these stories. One of my favorite stories is the Blackfoot story of Scarface. A condensed version goes something like this:

Scar Face lived with his grandmother for his mother and father had disappeared shortly after his birth. His face had a birthmark which set him aside from all others and also became the source of ridicule and shame. Because he was different, he was taunted by the other children and "whispered" about by others in the tribe. As Scar Face grew older he withdrew within himself and spent much of his time alone in the forest befriending and learning the ways of the animals he encountered. It is said that he learned "to speak with them." And through them he learned how to be related with all things.

As Scar Face grew older he experienced all the things of life with humility and great reverence. He even fell in love, as young boys do, when they come of that age and express that facet of their "face". The focus of Scar Face's affection was a young woman, Singing Rain, the chief's daughter. Singing Rain was also "a special person", kind and with a gift of insight. Although all the other young men competed for her affection, it was Scar Face who she came to respect and love because of his honesty, generosity and "good heart". However, when Scar Face asked for her to marry, she revealed her sacred vow to the Sun to never marry as a pledge of spiritual piety in the way of the Blackfoot. The only way she could marry was if the Sun were to release her from her pledge. On hearing this, Scar Face determined to undertake a journey to the "place where the Sun dwells" to ask the Sun to release Singing Rain from her pledge. And so, it is said that Scar Face began his visionary journey to the land of the Star People.

Scar Face did not know where the Star People lived, only that they must live in the direction of where the Sun set every evening, beyond the Great Water in the West. So, Scar Face prepared himself with help from his grandmother and when he was ready he set forth on his journey, a journey to the land of spirit. He first travelled familiar territory, but then began to enter into lands which neither he nor other members of his tribe had ever seen. As the snow of winter began to fall, a hundred paths became open to him and he became confused, he did not know which way to go. He met a wolf on one path and with great humility asked for help and direction. Knowing the goodness of his heart, the wolf spoke to him and guided him to the right path. He travelled that path for a great distance until he came to another series of paths and again he became confused. He stopped, set his camp and prayed. Soon a mother Bear and her cubs appeared on the path in front of him. Again, with great humility he asked for guidance form the mother Bear.

The Bear spoke with great kindness and pointed out him to the right path. Scar Face followed the bears' path for many days until the path ended. Now there were no longer any paths in front of him to follow, only the vast expanse of the great forest. As he stood and pondered in front of the forest, two white snow owls approached him. He called to the owls and they landed in a pine tree above him. Again, he asked for direction and help from the owls. Knowing his heart and the nobility of his quest, they responded with great kindness. They guided him through the forest to the edge of the Great Water, where, exhausted, he made camp. He thanked the birds and he thanked each of the animals which had helped him by offering them a gift of song and tobacco. He could see a twinkling of lights across the Great Water and he knew that that was the land of the Star People.

Scar Face did not know how to cross the water to "that place that his people talked about." But he was determined to find a way. He made camp and then fasted and prayed for three days and nights. On the fourth day, a path of sunlight began to form in front of him leading toward the "that place". He leaped onto the path and followed it as it took him higher and higher into the sky. When he reached the end of this path of sunlight, he came to a beautiful forest and another path, a path of great width as if made by thousands of people travelling on it for a long, long time. As he followed the path he came upon a richly decorated quiver of arrows leaning against a tree. He wondered who they must belong to, so he waited to see. Soon on the path coming from the other direction was an extraordinary-looking warrior dressed in richly decorated white buckskin. As the Warrior approached, Scar Face could see that this man was an image of perfection. He asked Scar Face if he had seen a quiver of arrows. In response, Scar Face showed him where the arrows were. Grateful and curious, the stranger introduced himself, "I am Morning Star." Then he asked Scar Face his name and where he was going. "I am called Scar Face and I seek the lodge of the Sun. Then come with me, Sun is my father and I live with my mother Moon in his lodge."

When Scar Face arrived at the Lodge of the Sun, he saw that the walls were painted with the history of all people of the world. Morning Star introduced Scar face to his mother the Moon and as his father the Sun entered the lodge a great light entered with him. Morning Star introduced Scar Face to his father Sun, the greatest chief. Scar Face was so impressed that he could not bring himself to reveal his reasons for coming to the land of the Star People. Sun and Moon treated Scar Face with great hospitality and asked Scar Face to stay with them as long as he wished. Over the next few days, Morning Star showed Scar Face the many paths in the beautiful land of the Star People. There was one path to a distant mountain that Sun had warned Morning Star and Scar Face never to go near. It was a mountain on the top of which lived a flock of seven giant birds which the Star People greatly feared.

One morning, Scar Face woke to find Morning Star gone. Scar Face arose and quietly left the Lodge of the Sun to take a walk and decide how he might ask the Sun to release Singing Rains from her vow. He thought he might meet Morning Star and ask him for advice. As he walked, he began to feel that something was wrong and the nearer he came to the mountain where the Giant Birds lived thegreater his feeling became. He knew that for some reason Morning Star had gone to the forbidden mountain.

Scar Face set out in search of Morning Star. As he climbed to the top of the mountain of the Giant Birds he found Morning Star engaged in a ferocious battle with the birds. These birds were indeed savage and extremely large. They were about to overcome Morning Star when Scar Face joined the battle. Scar Face fought valiantly and soon turned the tide of battle. One by one, Scar Face and Morning Star began to kill the Giant Birds until all seven were slain and their tail feathers taken by the two warriors.

Tired, yet proud of their accomplishment, Scar Face and Morning Star descended the Mountain and returned to the Sun Lodge to inform Sun and Moon of the defeat of the Star People's most feared enemies. Sun and Moon were very impressed by the courage shown by both young men and were especially grateful to Scar Face for saving the life of Morning Star. In honor of the courage of Scar Face, Sun offered to fulfil any desire that he would request. Yet, Scar Face could not speak his greatest desire and remained silent until Moon, knowing his heart spoke of Scar Face's love for Singing Rains and her vow to the Sun which prevented them from being together, spoke up. Sun immediately responded by saying to Scar Face that he would release her from her vow. Sun touched the cheek of Scar Face and the scar which he had borne all his life disappeared. Morning Star in turn gave him special personal gifts and revealed to him that he was his "spirit" father, confirming the feeling that Scar Face had felt all along. Then Sun and Moon began to sing songs in praise of Scar Face and Morning Star. Sun and Moon then gave Scar Face many gifts, rich clothes and a special shirt. In addition, Sun renamed Scar Face "Mistaken Morning Star" because now without the scar on his face he looked like Morning Star. Sun taught "Mistaken Morning Star" his own special dance, the Sun Dance. He said that if Earth People wished to honor him and bring health and well being to their tribe they should dance the Sun Dance each year when he had reached the highest place in the sky. Then Morning Star led his Earth son to the path called the Wolf's Trail (the Milky Way) and placed a wreath of juniper on his head. In an instant, Mistaken Morning Star was back on Earth and on a path leading to his own village.

Singing Rain was the first to meet Mistaken Morning Star as he approached the village. He told her that Sun had released her from her vow and she knew in her heart from seeing and feeling the magnificence of him that they could now be together, always. Mistaken Morning Star called the people together and taught them the rituals of the Sun Dance. He showed the women how to build the Sun Dance Lodge and he taught the men how to conduct the sweat lodge ceremony and raise the Sun Dance pole. He taught them about the sanctity of their individual "spirit" and the nature of scared visioning. He taught them from "that place that Indian people talk about".

There are profound lessons to be learned from stories like Scar Face. The traditional versions of the tale told in the Native language have a richness and depth of meaning which is difficult to express. Such richness and depth of meaning is true of other similar tales among Indigenous people around the world. They are like the mythical "spirit" deer: they leave tracks for us, beckoning us to follow, if we would but follow. [13] These stories also embedded the understanding that human beings have always been learning from animals and celestial beings. They represent the generosity of animals and other spirit beings in providing human beings, with food, clothing and advice.

Jongmin. I appreciate ending this dialogue with the story because, indeed, it has meaning that is difficult for us to express otherwise. Still, I will try to summarize my final opinion, for I think the dialogue has modified it a little. In this dialogue section, I adhered to the analytical evaluation of generosity, which might be the highest mental function in reciprocal mindset, in the viewpoint of a scientist. I bisected generosity into emotional and reasonable traits to understand bipolar characteristics of generosity, prompt sympathy and consistent and cautious altruism. Animals and human babies express more emotional generosity and grown up humans express more reasonable generosity. Paradoxically speaking, the emotional generosity would be more common and frank whereas the reasonable generosity would be less common and hard to be expressed by common people.

Sometimes, the source of generosity is difficult to differentiate. This would be due to the emotional and reasonable traits of generosity being interlinked and intermixed. In ancient Sumer tribes, they were very cautious when making important decisions. At first they would make a decision with a clear mind and subsequently would make the same decision after drinking wine, or vice versa. This cautious behaviour stemmed from the wish not to make any mistakes about important decisions since they treated both emotional and reasonable ways of thinking with equal weight and even they could not decide which decision was right.

The Buddhist philosophy emphasizes the virtue of 'balance'. The whole world is a single perfectly harmonious world and all life forms including human beings are components of this dynamic world. This concept is quite similar to the concept of "Gaia" in western philosophy. But one distinctive concept of Buddhism not found inwestern philosophy is the "circulation of life". Even this "circulation of life" is included in the whole world as a component. As a component life form, people respect the other life forms as colleagues or siblings. Buddhists think the relationships of all the life-forms are perfectly organized along with the balance of the whole world including this and former life. This concept would deal with the mindsets of human and animal on the same level. In this viewpoint, the externally observed generosity, either human or animal, has similar features. Whether the hidden motivation of the generosity is emotional or reasonable traits, the generosity itself should be respected as a great virtue to keep the balance of the nest which we and our offspring should inhabit forever.

III. CONTINUING THE DIALOGUE FOR UNDERSTANDING

1. After having read the brain research study summaries and the dialogue that followed, where do you see similarities between Indigenous views and Western neuroscience and where do you see differences?
2. Do you believe there is a possible paradox between the idea of a "spiritually" based or Nature based source for generosity and a brain neurotransmitter caused phenomenon? Why or why not?
3. Considering the historical and cultural differences in a widespread practice of generosity/altruism between Western cultures (generally speaking) and Indigenous ones, how would you explain the difference?
4. In Indigenous wisdom, it is understood that the highest expression of courage is generosity. This is why encouraging a young child to give away its favourite puppy might have been a lesson in generosity. How might this kind of cultural understanding of a connection between sacrifice and generosity influence or contribute to neurophilosophy?

REFERENCES

de Quervain, D. J.-F., Fischbacher, U., Treyer, V., Schellhammer, M., Schnyder, U., Buck, A., et al. (2004). The neural basis of altruistic punishment. *Science, 305*, 1254–1258.

Gintis, H., Bowles, S., Boyd, R., & Fehr, E. (2003). Explaining altruistic behavior in humans. *Evolution and Human Behavior, 24*, 153–172.

Hamlin, J. K., Wynn, K., & Bloom, P. (2007). Social evaluation by preverbal infants. *Nature, 450*, 557–560.

Harbaugh, W. T., Mayr, U., & Burghart, D. R. (2007). Neural responses to taxation and voluntary giving reveal motives for charitable donations. *Science, 316*, 1622–1625.

Moll, J., Krueger, F., Zahn, R., Pardini, M., Oliveira-Souza, R., & Grafman, J. (2006). Human fronto-mesolimbic networks guide decisions about charitable donation. *PNAS, 103*(42), 15623–15628.

Rilling, J. K., Gutman, D. A., Zeh, T. R., Pagnoni, G., Berns, G. S., & Kilts, C. D. (2002). A neural basis for social cooperation. *Neuron, 35*, 395–405.

Sanfey, A. G., Rilling, J. K., Aronson, J. A., Nystrom, L. E., & Cohen, J. D. (2003). The neural basis of economic decision-making in the ultimatum game. *Science, 300*, 1755–1758.

Zak, P. J., Stanton, A. A., & Ahmadi, S. (2007). Oxytocin increases generosity in humans. *PLoS One, 2*(11). Retreived December 2, 2008, from http://www.plosone.org/article/info%3Adoi%2F10.1371%2Fjournal.pone.0001128.

CHAPTER 2

HONESTY AND DECEPTION

"None Excel Them in Virtue and Honesty"

(From DeJong, D.H. "Ecclesiastical and Military Descriptions of the Gila River Pima, 1694–1848" in *The American Indian Quarterly* 29.1& 2 (2005) pp. 24–55)

I. NEUROSCIENCE STUDIES OVERVIEW

Joy Welcker and Krista Freece

We have selected and present seven imaging studies investigating the neuroanatomical pathways implicated in deception. In general, the studies support the contention that deceptive behaviour is guided by activity of more highly developed and sophisticated areas of the brain, specifically within the prefrontal cortex. Several studies also implicate the anterior cingulate cortex and the amygdala, which are more primitive structures associated with emotion and reward seeking. However, there exist differences in the particular neuroanatomy associated with deception, across the studies. Changing the circumstances surrounding a deceptive act results in activation of diverse sets of neuroanatomy, including areas implicated in linguistics, impulse control, inhibition, attention, planning, and theory of mind, emotion, and memory. Differences are even found among individuals performing the same task. The cognitive complexity of deception is affirmed by subtle variations in findings among the studies reviewed.

The empirical exploration of deception has been facilitated by the availability of improved neuroanatomical scanning devices, such as functional magnetic resonance imaging (fMRI) and positron emission tomography (PET). According to the research, deception is a common human behaviour, serving as a means to avoid punishment, as in lying about committing a crime; serving as a way to achieve social acceptance, possibly by averting a negative truth; or serving to reduce external stress, by allowing the organism to predict and escape unwanted interactions. Spence et al. (2004) affirmed that the purpose of lying has roots in cooperative social interactions among members of the human species. Limited disclosure and tactfulness serve to promote healthy social relationships that aid in survival. This may facilitate protection, communication, and promotion of knowledge among humans. Deception is also present in more pathological forms, exemplified by such mental health disorders as Factitious Disorders, Somatization Disorder, Conversion Disorder, Pathological Lying, and Malingering (Hughes, et al., 2005). Spence et al. (2004) also hypothesized that lying requires multiple cognitive processes within prefrontal systems, and that truth-telling can be used as a baseline measure for neuroimaging of deceit. Thus, a main feature of telling a lie is the cognitive ability to suppress the truth (Langleben, et al., 2005; Spence, et al., 2004). Lying also involves using context to make it believable, and remembering the difference between what information is real and what information is fabricated. In the studies below, honesty (or truthful responding) is used as a control mechanism by which to compare neural activity generated by deceptive acts. However, it is argued that using this method alone may be problematic (Spence, 2008).

Deception can be viewed from an evolutionary perspective. Previous research speculated that the cognitive ability to lie probably emerged within the primate brain, prior to the evolution of man. For example, Byrne and Corp (2004) found that "the size of the neocortex in a modern primate species predicts the extent to which individuals of that species use deceptive tactics for social manipulation" (p. 1696). Deception eventually evolved into "an integral part of human social interaction" (Hughes et al., 2005, p. 278). Hughes and colleagues (2005) also suggested "deception has evolved in later, more sophisticated organisms, and … it persists for a reason" (p. 273). Effective use of deception requires theory of mind, or the ability to infer one's own mental state as well as the mental state of others. Further, Lee et al. (2002) precisely defined lying as "the recognition of, and attempt to manipulate, the mental states of others" (p. 163). This requires one to be able to know what one is thinking, suppose what another is thinking, and premeditate a way to manipulate another's train of thought. Hence, lying involves the complex activation of prefrontal areas of the brain, which direct executive function. Further, the idea that propensity for deception exists among higher-order species as an innate behavioral characteristic that is influenced by culture, is supported by current lexical research suggesting that honesty should be considered a sixth factor of human personality development (Ashton, Lee, & Son, 2000).

Deception may also be viewed from a developmental perspective. Ford, King, and Hollender (1988) speculated that the act of deceit serves to create a boundary between "self" and "other", particularly between a young child and mother. The authors asserted that lying is a skill that naturally arises during childhood and constitutes "normal" human behaviour. From a biological standpoint, children develop the cognitive capacity to lie because it benefits them as adults in society. Hughes et al. (2005) also reported that studies of children have acknowledged the natural development of deceptive strategies. In fact, they asserted that "from a cognitive neurobiological perspective, deception resembles an executive task," (p. 274) suggesting that the inability to successfully deceive another may be the result of neurological dysfunction.

The act of deception encompasses a broad range of mental activities, whose activation is dependent on the exact set of circumstances that bring about the need or desire to lie, thus a human's propensity to lie is a well-developed, complex, and sophisticated skill. According to Mohamed et al. (2006), numerous areas of the brain are involved in deception as a broad concept, including the following: lingual gyrus of left hemisphere (differentiating language), anterior cingulate gyrus (attention and response inhibition), inferior parietal lobe of right hemisphere/ inferior frontal gyri of left hemisphere (mirror neuron system enabling theory of mind), hippocampus (memory and emotion), and amygdala (fear and anxiety). Ganis, Kosslyn, Stose, Thompson, and Yurgelun-Todd (2003), found that different patterns of brain activation are present when people tell lies than when they tell the truth. The parietal lobes (bilaterally) are associated with truthful responding (Langleben et al., 2002), while deception is associated with frontal lobe activation, particularly the ventrolateral prefrontal cortex, anterior cingulate cortex, and the amygdala. However, as the following studies will show, the neural processes that underlie deceit seem to vary among individuals, likely because each person's qualitative experience during deceit is individualized. This makes detection and measurement of deception an imperfect science.

Current methods of detecting deception include polygraph (using electrodermal activity to measure anxiety, supposedly resulting from guilt), Guilty Knowledge Test (GKT) in conjunction with polygraph (uses multiple choice questions to elicit electrodermal changes when a guilty subject sees the correct answer, thus the test targets change in heart rate, respiration, and blood pressure), event related potentials (ERP) (a measure of response latency), and most recently neuroimaging, including fMRIs and PET scans (Hughes et al., 2005). The GKT has been shown to be a relatively effective measure of psychophysiology (Ben-Shakhar & Elaad, 2002) and the polygraph is routinely used to determine if a person is being truthful. However, neuroimaging techniques and ERP to date have been used to measure deception and response times primarily in a research setting because their efficacy has not been standardized. But it can be inferred from the literature that fMRI and PET scans may be used in the future to enhance the detection of deception, by pinpointing the activation of particular neural processes, associated with deceptive acts. Following is a summary of studies that explored various circumstances involving deception; the differences among the findings should alert the reader to the multi-faceted nature of the cognitive processes underlying this broad concept.

Study 1: "Correlates of Deception in Humans"

Spence and colleagues (2001) believed that lying is a "normal component of human social interaction" and its development can be traced through the evolution of the primate species (p. 2849). They proposed that deception is achieved through a series of cognitive processes, including the ability to determine what another is thinking (theory of mind). Current methods of detecting deception may be too simplistic and fail to capture the gestalt of the cognitive processes that activate during intentional lying.

Using 30 subjects, Spence et al. (2001) found consistent behavioural and neurological output during a simple lying task (using dichotomous yes/no responses). During lying, response times were longer than during truth-telling, and areas of the prefrontal cortex were activated. This study sought to identify differences in cognitive processes during lying behaviour using visual versus auditory tasks.

Thirty healthy subjects completed a 36-item questionnaire of yes/no questions. Next, the questions were read from a computer screen (visual administration) and the subjects were prompted to lie in accordance with a "color rule" (red or green).

In the visual condition, the series of questions was administered twice, and over the course of the two runs the subject provided a true and a false response for each question. This format was then duplicated for two voice-automated presentations of the questions (auditory administration). Finally, ten males were selected from the original 30 subjects for scanning (BOLD fMRI). Data was collected on both the non-scanned and scanned samples.

Data collected from outside the scanner revealed significantly longer response times for lying behaviour in both the visual and the auditory conditions. Similar results were found for the smaller sample inside the scanner. While subjects exhibited consistent fMRI responses within some areas of the PFC, there were differences observed in the sites of activation for the two conditions. During the visual administration, the ventrolateral PFC and the medial PFC were activated during lying. But during the auditory administration, the ventrolateral PFC and the medial premotor region were activated while lying.

These findings suggest an inhibitory function (withholding the truth) while lying; it is speculated that this cognitive function may be absent in the autistic population. This particular study required both suppression of the truth and production of a lie, thus it did not allow for investigation of differentiation between response inhibition and response alternation.

Study 2: "The Complexity of Deception"

In this study, Ganis and colleagues (2003) conclude that lying should not be treated as a single category of behaviour because it requires the activation of several different neural systems, based on the specific conditions underlying the deception. They stressed that future research on lying behaviour must recognize different types of lying conditions and treat them independently.

More specifically, various types of deception require the activation of specific sets of neuroanatomy within the PFC. Ganis and colleagues (2003) explored two different types of lying: spontaneous lies (which require the integration of stored info) and memorized lies (which require only retrieval from memory), with the assumption that different types of lying will elicit activity within distinctly different areas of neuroanatomy. First, they hypothesized that retrieving a deceptive memory is more difficult than retrieving a truthful memory. Second, they hypothesized that there would be differences in neural activity between isolated lies (about a simple event) versus coherent lies (must fit into a scenario). Third, they expected that working memory must play a greater role in the creation of coherent lies. The study investigated neural activity using fMRI for three conditions: truth, memorized lie, and spontaneous lie.

Ten subjects (ranging in age from 20 to 30) were required to write about their most memorable work experience and their most memorable vacation experience. One week later, the subjects returned and their stories were reviewed. The subjects were then asked to create an alternate (untrue) scenario of one of the situations; this story served as the Memorized/Scenario (MS) lie. The subjects were then placed in the scanner and asked to recreate the MS lie. Next the subjects were asked to recreate their story about the other scenario; this served as the Spontaneous/Isolated (SI) lie (for which they were unprepared). Finally, the subjects were asked to provide honest responses, based on their initial stories.

Results revealed differences in cognitive activation between the truth condition and the lie condition. Also, different areas of the brain were activated under the two distinct lie conditions. MS lies activated the middle frontal gyrus, while SI lies activated the anterior cingulate gyrus, the premotor cortex, the precentral/post central gyrus, and the right cuneus. Brain regions activated by both conditions included the middle frontal gyrus, fusiform/parahippocampal gyrus, right precuneous, and the left cerebellum. In sum, "different patterns of brain activation arise when people tell lies than when they tell the truth, and the type of lie modulates these patterns" (p. 833). These results also support the contention that the cognitive act of deception is multifaceted, and lying in different scenarios creates experiences that are qualitatively different.

Study 3: "Measuring Brain Activity During Deception"

Because deception is associated with numerous medical and mental health disorders, Kozel et al. (2004) asserted a need for measuring deception in a manner more reliable than the current methods, including peripheral measures of deceit, such as the polygraph. They suggested that using fMRI and PET scans in the future to detect deception by revealing brain activity associated with lying behaviour, may offer a more dependable measure to aid in patient diagnosis and legal decisions. Kozel et al. used blood oxygen level dependent (BOLD) fMRI and electrodermal activity (EDA) to identify brain regions, specific to deception. Since no prior studies of this nature (using the same two measuring techniques) were available at the time, the authors investigated the whole brain, while hypothesizing that activity in the orbitofrontal cortex, anterior cingulate gyrus, and amygdala would be heightened during deception. These brain regions were selected due to their suspected involvement in response inhibition, divided attention, and anxiety.

Eight males, ranging in age from 21 to 28 years, were given the opportunity to earn up to $100.00 each for participating in the study. Each participant was directed to find the object beneath which a $50 bill was hidden, remember the location, and leave the money in place. All participants were then randomly assigned to either the "truth room", where they were instructed to accurately report the location of the money, or the "deception room", where they were asked to respond in opposition to the truth. Participant groups took turns in each room so that each participant provided both truthful and deceptive responses. All responding resulted from nonverbal gestures requiring the participant to hold up one finger to signify "yes" and to hold up two fingers to signify "no" in response to the investigators' standardized question set. Brain scans acquired from the "truth room" were used as a control against which to compare responses generated from the "deception room". Participants were motivated by the opportunity to earn $50 for correctly reporting the location of the money in the "truth room", and an additional $50 for being able to deceive without being recognized in the "deception room". Both group and individual analyses were performed.

Group analysis of EDA changes and BOLD fMRI changes confirmed the presence of statistically significant activity in the orbitofrontal cortex and the anterior cingulate gyrus during deception (as hypothesized), but failed to confirm statistically significant activation of the amygdala. Other brain structures that were not included in the original hypothesis were also found to be significant, including the superior temporal gyrus, cerebellum, and the frontal gyrus.

Individual analysis of EDA changes and BOLD fMRI changes revealed that no specific regions of the brain were activated for *all* subjects during the deception task. However, six out of seven subjects showed significant right orbitofrontal activity, and five out of seven subjects showed significant right anterior cingulate activity. Also, no additional brain regions (outside of those in the original hypothesis) revealed significant activity in response to the deception task consistently across individuals.

Study 4: "Neural Correlates of Telling Lies"

Phan et al. (2005) pointed out that deception is a common human behaviour that can be used as a positive social adaptation or a means to evade the consequences of violating societal law. As such, it is important to be able to determine with accuracy who has broken the law and who is innocent of offense. Because deception employs several semi-independent neural systems, including those responsible for theory of mind, constructing lies, telling truths (pre-potent responses), monitoring tasks, and motivation, the endeavour to predict deceptive activity becomes convoluted. fMRI was used to simulate conditions similar to that of polygraph testing in order to examine neurological activity during deception. This was achieved by replicating a study design by Langleben et al. (2002). Initially, 14 subjects, ranging in age from 23 to 48, were given two playing cards (a five of clubs and a two of hearts). They were asked to memorize the cards and place them in a pocket. The subjects were then asked to lie about one card and to tell the truth about the other card (half the subjects were asked to lie about one card and half were asked to lie about the other card). Subjects used a button press to respond "yes" or "no" to questions about the cards.

For the actual study, an entire deck of cards was used. Subjects were placed in the scanner and told that their performance was being monitored (similar to a polygraph situation). The five of clubs served as the lie/truth condition, the two of hearts served as the truth/lie condition, the ten of spades served as the control condition, and the remaining cards in the deck were "non-target responses" always answered with "no"; they served to sustain attention to the task. The subjects were given one card at a time and they were asked questions, such as "Do you have this card?" and "Is this card the ten of spades?"

Results revealed activity across several prefrontal cortical regions during the telling of a lie; these areas included ventrolateral PFC, superior temporal sulcus (associated with malingering, but not other types of deception), dorsal medial PFC (associated with awareness of one's own emotions and theory of mind), and dorsal lateral PFC (associated with impulse control). The medial PFC was the area most consistently activated across subjects; therefore, it could be viewed as a "neural signature for the generation of lies, suppression of the truth, or both" (p. 169). These results support the idea that, in fact, very precise areas of the prefrontal cortex are involved in deceptive behaviour. The authors also asserted that lesions within these areas are likely to result in specific patterns of cognitive dysfunction in rodents, primates, and humans. In the future it may be possible to use fMRI scanning in conjunction with polygraph-like instruments to enhance the reliability of lie detection.

Study 5: "Types of Deception"

Abe et al. (2006) discuss that humans deceive each other for various reasons, both trivial and serious, citing deceptions between husband and wife as an example of trivial deception, and deception between nations as serious deceptions. Further, they consider the powerful effect deceptive acts can have on the lives of self and others, prompting an interest in "why people tell lies, when and where they do, how they do, and whether or not we can detect the deceptions of others" (p. 192). In this study the authors examined two types of deception: "experienced" events in which the participant pretended not to remember performing a task, and "unexperienced" events in which the participant pretended to remember performing the task, although he/she did not actually perform it.

Fourteen male participants, ranging in age from 18 to 23, were asked to perform twenty tasks (e.g., coloring a picture, shaking maracas, solving a puzzle) in a randomized order, during an "experience" phase. During the PET scan experiment, the participants were shown pictures of both tasks they had performed and those they had not. The participants were asked to respond to the pictures by sometimes telling the truth and sometimes lying. This created four conditions: truth-old task (TO), in which they truthfully responded to a task they had performed; lie-old-task (LO), in which they lied about a task they had performed; truth-new-task (TN), in which they told the truth about a task they hadn't performed; and lie-new task (LN), in which they lied about a task they hadn't performed. The authors found that the lateral PFC and the medial PFC were activated during deception. Additionally, the anterior cingulate cortex was activated only during the "pretending not to know" condition (LO). They also concluded that "the cognitive processes associated with deception are more complex that those associated with truth telling", as evidenced by measuring reaction times (p. 196). Overall, these results suggest the "possibility of dissociable roles of the prefrontal and anterior cingulate cortices in human deception" (p. 197).

Study 6: "Emotional Aspects of Deception"

According to Abe, Suzuki, Mori, Itoh, and Fujii (2007), deception consists of not only the inhibition of truthful responses and the production of untruthful ones, but also the intention of deceiving someone. Thus, emotional regulation and social processes are thought to be involved. The intent of their study was to determine whether different regions of the prefrontal cortex were activated during two deceptive activities, producing untruthful responses and attempting to deceive someone, by asking questions during a PET scan. The authors used a 2 X 2 factorial design to measure the main effects of the truthfulness of responses to the questions (truth versus lie) and attitude toward the questioner (honest versus dishonest), as well as any interaction effects.

During the course of the study, each participant was asked a total of 12 autobiographical semantic questions; four related to elementary school, four to junior high and four to high school. Each answer was a one word verbal response. In one task, the participants obeyed the interrogator and told the truth in response to questions (honest-truth; HT). In the honest-lie (HL) task the participants obeyed the interrogator and told lies in response to questions. During the dishonest-truth (DT) task, the participants deceived the interrogator and told the truth in response to questions when they were asked to lie. In the dishonest-lie (DL) task, the participants deceived the interrogator and told lies in response to questions in which they were instructed to tell the truth.

Before each of the DT and DL tasks, during a ten minute break, a second experimenter had entered and asked the participants to deceive the first experimenter by doing the opposite of what the first experimenter asked. The participants were told that the first experimenter did not know they were being asked to do this, and that deceiving the interrogator was the most important purpose of the study. In addition, participants were asked to make sure that the first experimenter did not discover their deception.

The results indicated a main effect for lying in the left dorsolateral PFC, whereas the right anterior PFC showed main effects of both lying and dishonesty. The ventromedial PFC and amygdala showed a main effect of dishonesty only. In summary, each of the deception conditions in this study affirmed activation of areas within the prefrontal cortex, but only the condition specific to dishonesty revealed activity in the amygdala.

Study 7: "Affective Response of Self to Moral Violations"

Berthoz and his co-researchers (2006) suggest that honesty is a component of morality which "depends on a set of cultural rules that regulate interpersonal behaviour and provide a basis for social cohesion" (p. 945). They explain that a person's affective response to a violation of these cultural rules depends on if the event was accidental or intentional, and whether the individual committed the transgression or witnessed the event. Consistent with their hypothesis, the authors found that the amygdala was activated when individuals described stories of their own intentional violation of cultural rules.

The participants of the study were twelve males, ranging in age from 19 to 36. The study design was a two-way factorial in which intentionality (accidental, intentional) and agency (self, others) were factors. The participants were asked to read four types of stories: self-accidental (SA) (subject engaged in an accidental violation of social norms), other-accidental (OA) (someone else engaged in an accidental violation of social norms), self-intentional (SI) (subject purposefully engaged in a violation of social norms), and other intentional (OI) (someone else purposely engaged in violation of social norms). The stories for self and other were identical except for the protagonist of the story. The severity of the accidental and intentional violations of cultural rules was judged to be equivalent. Neural activation for each type of scenario was measured using fMRI.

When comparing intentional violations to accidental ones, the areas of the brain showing a significant differential pattern of activation during intentional violations included the left dorsolateral cortex, superior frontal cortex, anterior cingulate gyrus, left inferior parietal cortex, left superior occipital gyrus, left amygdala, right cerebellum and bilateral precuneus. When comparing accidental to intentional violations, the only significant activity occurred in the right temporal pole. The main effects of agency showed significantly different activation of the left precuneus and the right cerebellum, specifically when the participants read the "self " stories, rather than when the violation was committed by another. In the SI condition, significantly different bilateral amygdala activation was seen when compared to the other conditions. The authors suggest that further research is needed to determine whether the activation of the amygdala "reflects the anticipation of punishment" (p. 949). Overall, precise areas of prefrontal activation differed among the various tasks.

II. INDIGENOUS PERSPECTIVES DIALOGUE

Greg Cajete, Jongmin Lee and Four Arrows

Greg. These studies seem to reveal that deception is a higher order brain function that evolved to help humans survive. This does not make much sense to me. In Indigenous ways of thinking, we learn to observe and listen carefully so as to understand physical reality and experience, not to find ways to misrepresent it! There can be little doubt that deception has "evolved" to play a large role in the world today, but this says something different. Indigenous Peoples have always believed that it is important to see what is real about a situation, a thing or an entity. If something did not occur in the physical plane, it did not occur. Our languages help in such understanding because they are rich with descriptive terms and action verbs that minimize reductionism and abstract generalizing.

At the same time, Indigenous thinking honors the reality that there are always two sides to the two sides, that there are realities and there are realities. Learning how they interact is real understanding. Our knowledge comes from our stories, stories that mirror the way the human mind works. They echo a truth lived and remembered because their roots go beyond the context processes of the brain. They stem from the heart of the human psyche. Thus understanding what is true is a matter of heart and mind and this also helps one know what cannot be comprehended or articulated. If it were otherwise, if deception, not right thinking and remembering were tools for social cohesions, as these studies seem to conclude, it seems that survival would be compromised, not enhanced. Moreover, Nature is the first and foremost teacher of how things are in the world. This is why animals and plants are considered to be teachers for us. Neither Nature nor animals lie about reality. Animals may have instinctive ways of hiding food or playing dead or stalking prey, but these are not examples of misrepresenting reality in the ways human deception does. I think deception is not a cultural adaptation for survival and social cohesion but rather a moral failing and thus agree with David Putman's ideas that self-deception, like greed, is a vice that is justified in Western culture on utilitarian grounds (Putman 1987, pp 549–557).

All of this is to say that, as a virtue, honesty is extolled upon metaphorically and symbolically in many aspects of Indigenous cultures. This is why it is highlighted or alluded to in many Indigenous stories, especially Trickster stories, and is a part of the central teachings of Indigenous spiritual traditions. But why have people who have lived on the Earth for so long and in such close harmony with her come to view honesty so intently?

A key to understanding the origins of honesty in the human psyche and in human society is to view it as one of the traits which supported a group oriented way of life that placed value on belonging to a group and to a community. Human beings are after all social animals. Our brains and subsequently our behaviour are conditioned by our social instinct for living and relating in intimate groups. Early human evolved in groups whose way of being in the world did not place value on amassing material goods, avarice, self-centeredness or aggression. It was belonging to a group and the complex of values that supported such belonging that were valued. Honesty supported good long term relationship and facilitated the cooperation and adaptation so essential to maintaining human social groups. In other words, valuing honesty which in turn reinforced trust provided the first human families with the edge that was the essence of early man's survival. In the development of early human societies a single isolated individual had no chance at long term survival. Of course, this perspective, as we have seen, stands in opposition to many Western academics view on the value of deception in survival.

Still, it was the "group mind" that developed first among human beings. This "group mind" was rooted in the interdependence and mutual reciprocal behaviour which paralleled the symbiotic relationships found in natural communities. The dynamic process of human adaptation to ever changing environmental conditions that is so much a part of the "genius" of human evolution is based on our singular ability to evolve social environments conducive to the needs of our group. Honesty is both a value and a way of behaviour which is required for the development of "trust" with in a group. Honesty reinforces "trust" between members of a community which in turn fosters the cooperation necessary to sustain the group. Human adaptive values are those that encourage individual and family relationship, love, honesty, cooperation, collaboration, compassion, generosity and self-lessness. These are the values that keep a group working and living together for mutual benefit. Pre-agricultural humans cultivated these values of group cohesion because the survival of the group was the first and foremost priority. For our pre-agricultural ancestors belonging to a group mattered and belonging to a place mattered. Values that reinforced belonging to a group form a deep part of human consciousness. Psychologically, pre-agricultural people did not see themselves as separate from their group or the natural place in which they lived. The community or group mind and its affective orientations of belonging, interdependence, mutual - reciprocal behaviour characterize all tribal societies. Some socio-biologists would refer to this deeply embedded sense for belong as an expression of our human instinct for "biophilia," the predisposition to relate or affiliate with other living things particularly other humans. This instinct might be said to be the biological basis for sociability, relationally and community.

In hunter-gatherer communities there was a general absence of stealing. Richard Erdoes writes in his book, *The Sun Dance People:*

> Among a people without locks, keys, or money there were no thieves...Without lawyers, no contracts, or anything in print, men found it impossible to cheat. Without any jails, there could be no criminals.

Invariably the practice of horse theft, theft of women and children during raids on other tribes comes up. And why does the theme of theft come up in a variety of Native American stories, especially related to the exploits of tricksters which abound in stories from all tribes.

According to Erdoes:

> Ideas of acquiring more wealth and personal property than one truly needs were foreign to Native Americans. This is not to say that they were not concerned with self-image. Quite the contrary, it is hard to imagine people more aware of honor, their status and their place in the eyes of peers, than Native Americans, past and present. But the orientation was towards people rather than the individual. A man of great wealth who did not share freely was not well respected... If someone did something purely for himself – such as stealing another tribal member's property – he committed a double transgression. Not only had he stolen, he had placed his own interests above that of the people. Punishment for such an offense was usually the most devastating sort of treatment imaginable to the group-oriented Native American – to be exiled or completely ignore. (Stealing Horses, Joseph Bruchac in Parabola. pp. 54–59. Vol. IX. No. 2. April 1984).

Stealing horses [from enemies] on the other hand was an act of great courage and a great service to one's people. It served to benefit the people and to extend the survivability of the people from the standpoint of Plains Indian society. In terms of individuals it bought honor as a warrior. Stealing for the good of the people brought honor in Plains Indian society. The deed of stealing horses showed the individual warrior to be a person of character, willing to face danger for the good of the people. It showed the person to individual to be a person worthy of trust, a person that could be depended on to work for the good of the people. Honesty as a value that promoted trust within the group was actually mirrored by the "stealing" of horses as an act for the benefit of the people which also engendered trust in the individual. Horses were considered sacred animals and possessing them brought not only honor but great luck as well. All the Indian groups who encountered the horse early on such as the Plains Indians, the Apache and Navajo created a place for it as a spirit animal in their story and spiritual traditions. This was because its introduction and use for transportation, hunting, trade and warfare transformed their cultures. In short, it was a gift of the spirits which "revolutionized" while at the same time sustained their cultures. Bruchac gets right to the heart of what at first glance might seem like a paradoxical relationship of theft to the adaptive value of honesty in Indigenous societies.

> If there is one evil which is greater than all others to Native American people, it is selfishness. When someone owns something which can benefit others and does not share it, it is a great wrong especially when that something is one of the great gifts of the Creator such as Tobacco or Fire o or Light… or the Horse. (p. 59).

The theme of "theft" for the greater good of the people may be said to be a kind of "mirror" value to honesty in that it mirrors the importance of trust in a group. Theft for the greater good was often intertwined with lessons of the importance of honesty in trickster stories. Native American Trickster stories allude to or directly present the value of honesty as an antithesis to the behaviour of Coyote. By extensively representing the less than honest nature of Coyote these stories reflect on why honesty is important as a value and as a way to conduct one's life. In stories where theft is a theme, Coyote's propensity for trickery and deceit ultimate benefits others. In these stories, theft becomes an acceptable outcome because it improves the life of the people in some way.

Four Arrows. I agree Greg. All of these studies tend to support the idea that deception may be an evolutionary survival mechanism and this does not make sense to me either. Yet this seems to be one of the major conclusions in neuroscience. For example, in his book, *Why We Lie*, David Livingstone Smith, Director of the Institute for Cognitive Science and Evolutionary Psychology at the University of New England, says, "Deceit is and probably always has been a major concern of human culture (2004, p. 12)." He contends throughout the book that "the very structure of our minds has been shaped from our earliest beginnings by the need to deceive (backcover)." He even refers to hunter-gatherer populations, past and present, and asserts that "It would be a grave mistake to draw the sentimental conclusion that these people are "noble savages," innocent of a thirst for power" and speaks to his presumed "fact" that warfare was common among Indigenous Peoples as one source of evidence, p. 174). Of course, his claim about the prevalence of Indigenous warfare is itself is a deception, as shown, for instance, in my book, *Unlearning the Language of Conquest*, and more thoroughly in Johan M.G. van der Dennen's 2005 dissertation, *The Politics of Peace and War in Preliterate Societies*, that begins, "Peaceable pre-industrial (preliterate, primitive, etc.) societies constitute a nuisance to most theories of warfare and they are, with few exceptions, either denied or 'explained away'." http://dissertations.ub.rug.nl/FILES/faculties/jur/1995/j.m.g.van.der.dennen/OW_APP.pdf

I think what these researchers reveal is a Western worldview that comes from having for too long used the kind of "abstract generalizations" that you mentioned to make sense of the world. Robert Lawlor says it well in *Voices of the First Day:* "In Western thought, generalities are used to make sense of the world around us, but they impose an order on reality rather than connecting us to the world's living presence and the metaphysical dimensions from which it arose (1991, p. 271)." He explains how this has led to stereotyping, making assumptions, deception, and totalitarianism. He even ties this to the brain, saying that the practice of reducing and generalizing actually reinforces a filtering mechanisms in the lower brain stem called the reticular formation causing us to be less able to perceive direct reality. This is supported by the pioneering work of cellular biologist, Bruce H. Lipton, whose work reveals that thought patterns act formatively on the brain ((2008).

Jongmin. Before I speak in my capacity as a neuroscientist, let me join this dialogue with an idea from my Buddhist perspective that tends to support where I think Four Arrows is going with his comments about how a certain way of thinking might change the brain. In Buddhism, in the "Eight Fold Path, there are eight paths of righteousness. "Right speech" is the first principle of ethical conduct. This precept is about avoiding words that are spoken with the intent of misrepresenting truth. It tells us that such a practice can deteriorate the mind, and vice versa in a vicious cycle. This is another way of saying, as Dr. Lipton does, that words and thoughts can change the brain perhaps. It at least explains the addictive quality in which those who practice deception tend to repeat it over and over again. The goal is for right speech that will lead to right speculation and right behaviour and perhaps this too can become a biological tendency of the brain. Whether a particular worldview can cause such changes is an interesting question.

Four Arrows. Jongmin, let's stay with this question about worldview then. Indigenous wisdom seems to be sourced in the emotion of compassion self and all others. Emotive power is related to the authentic respect for and knowledge of the social and environmental surroundings that range from family and community to plants, animals, rivers, rocks and trees. It is not really organized around the brain in the kind of hierarchal control system that we might be accepting in a book such as this that is about brain research. Greg, am I stating this right, because I want to be sure you agree with me on this before I go on?

Greg. Yes, I think compassion for all of life is a requirement for or goes hand in hand with believing in the sacredness of relationships, a belief that defines Indigenous culture. And although I'm not sure where you are going, I'm happy you brought it up in this talk about deception because learning about self-deception, perhaps the beginning for all deception, is a key aspect of Indigenous preparation for learning about life. This begins with understanding the purpose of learning and this purpose begins with compassion and sacred respect for all things. Learning and acting truthfully requires an awareness that ambition, self-gratification, power and control as purposes for learning are forms of self-deception and have to be avoided because they lead to misuses of knowledge and further perpetuation of self-deception. And yes, to get back to your question, I think compassion, authentic, empathetic care for others, respect for others, giving significance to others, is the opposite of the kinds of emotions behind greed or lust for power.

Four Arrows. OK, so here is where I'm going I think and what Greg says here really helps. What I want to ask Jongmin is this: Referring back to the "heart-mind" holistic approach to life typical in traditional Indigenous life, I believe that emotional-rationale phenomenon that lead to honesty and away from deception require a balanced and complementary relationship between right and left hemispheres, medicated along the corpus callosum. Cultural values and practices shape the circuits in ways that promote or do not promote an absence of deception. A culture that does not create brain activity that moves away from a perceived need to deceive is dysfunctional.

In accordance with Indigenous wisdom I believe that emotions are a precursor to appropriate ways of perceiving and representing the world when the primary emotion is compassion and feelings related to it like empathy and respect. Furthermore, naturalistic and spontaneous trance states allow beliefs, whether based on compassion and respect or on fear and narcissism, continually use words to shape our neural circuitry until our integrity or our deception become both conscious and unconscious operations.

And if what I'm saying is so, if compassion for the well being of others is the dominant emotion, rather than say, fear, or some other ego-centric driven emotion, then might this admittedly simplistic idea offer some explanation of the difference in thinking about deception between Indigenous and Western conclusions about the role of deception in human nature?

There seems to be some Western science that supports what I am saying in addition to different interpretations of the studies that began this chapter. For example, Eisenberg's work showed that when empathy and compassion are primary cultural worldview based emotions, integrity and altruism tend to emerge over deception and greed (2002, pp 131–164.) Antonio R. Damsio's work also has demonstrated that emotions are essential to rational thinking (1994). Westen's work on emotional bias at Emory University also comes to mind and has relevance to what I am saying.

Westen showed that when people were supposed to be making a rational, truthful conclusion about a political candidate's obvious, evidence-based deceptions, a network of emotion circuits lit up when they reflected their bias as opposed to the truth. When their lies were concluded, and I'm calling their irrational biases lies, then reward circuits lit up. Yet none of the circuits involved in conscious reasoning were engaged, no activation of the dorsolateral prefrontal cortex involved with reasoning (LiveSciene, 2006). And what about Joo-Yeon's experiment about stress and the activity of the corpus callosum you and I were involved in, how it might relate? It seems that the spiritual precept of Indigenous wisdom relating to everything being related and everything, from rocks to birds deserving respect and compassion, in addition to Indigenous use of ceremony, dance and music to induce trance, is at the heart of what is happening in the brain (no pun intended).

Jongmin. I think I understand what you are saying Four Arrows. As we can see from the studies, the prefrontal cortex is regarded as the main brain center for deception. However the prefrontal cortex is not specific center only for deception. Any kind of high grade mental function can be generated from prefrontal cortex. For example, during deep speculations in fields of theoretical physics, criminal investigations, philosophic discussion, or even designing your own house, the prefrontal cortex should be activated. And, to get to your point, it is also involved significantly in the processing of emotions. The ventromedial prefrontal cortex has reciprocal connections with other regions involved in emotional regulation.

In the literature, lying is reported to provoke the brain more than telling the truth. We can explain this fact with the level of anxiety that activates higher mental functions. So emotions tend to force the brain to work with some degree of stress, such as might be seen from activation of the pituitary gland. Lying seems to cause such stressful activity in the brain. Areas of the brain associated with emotion, conflict and cognitive control, like the amygdale, the rostral cingulated, caudate and thalamus light up during deceptive thinking but not when telling the truth. During telling the truth, you can be comfortable without any anxiety or conflict. as if my mind had to work harder to generate the fictitious narrative.

Four Arrows referred to Joo-Yeon's study for her dissertation, *The Last Leaf* (2009). Well, there we saw that emotional reactions to watching the frightening possibilities for human survival in Al Gore's film, "An Inconvenient Truth," while monitoring the brain via fMRI, caused much stress in both hemispheres with little activity in the corpus callosum. Yet, when the subjects watched her simple "sights and sounds of nature" film, there was no stress indicated and the corpus callosum was highly active, indicate a balanced and cooperative communication back and forth between both hemispheres. The mental stress should be the key to activate high grade mental function in prefrontal cortex either with or without emotion centers being activated. Perhaps the emotion you refer to as compassion, as one of the positive emotions, creates a mental state in which there is no need for deception and thus the viscous cycle I referred to earlier is stopped or is replaced by ways of thinking that de-emphasize deception. There was a study at the University of Wisconsin using fMRI scans that showed that brain circuits involved in emotional responses were actually changed in Tibetan monks who practiced compassion meditation. So this goes back to Lipton and his biology of belief work.

It is interesting to consider the possibility that the abnormal findings of deception in neurofunctional imaging might be a simple reflection of various mentally stressed situations relating to the deception, rather than specific features of deception itself. Just as happens to the muscular structures during rigorous physical activity, the brain would fatigue with the kind of complex workload brought on from deception. Maybe this explains much of the illness in our world today. I agree with both of my colleagues that the deceptive behaviours are against the natural functioning of the brain. Perhaps understanding this secondary gain of health could be a key improving the deceptive behaviours of human beings, whether they are related to Western materialism and self-centered thinking or not.

As for the studies that represent current research in this area, I agree with the conclusions that we are talking about a complexity here that is not easily understood. Deception comprises of various grades of dishonesty such as simple dishonesty, simple lying, tied lying, pathological lying, intentional lying, and criminal lying such as swindle. Higher grade dishonesty requires higher grade mental function with stronger brain activation especially in prefrontal cortex. This fact may paradoxically support the phenomenon that simple dishonesty shows higher activation in cingulated gyrus and amygdala in basal ganglia which is more primal brain than prefrontal cortex in a viewpoint of evolution. This complexity increases because the activated cerebral cortex by deception varies time to time by environment. Based on this reports we can infer that deception has various optional components over basic higher grade mental function. During telling a lie the prefrontal cortex, the center of high grade mental function, activates constantly in functional MRI. In addition, various additional activations are demonstrated by the optional components of deception. For example, if you are telling a lie about food, your olfactory, taste, and salivary centers would be activated in addition to the constantly activated prefrontal cortex. If you are lying in emotionally upset state, the emotion center such as amygdala would be additionally activated. If you are focused on telling a lie itself, your linguistic center activation would be conjoined. Such multiple factors force me to acknowledge the fact that the deception is not simple mental function but the integration of highly complicated and variable mental functions. The scientific trials to reveal the brain cortex specific for deception or to identify the contents of deception in functional MRI or PET are very limiting in their accuracy since our scale to measure deception is too simple to understand it thoroughly. Perhaps Indigenous wisdom and Buddhist philosophy that reinforces the Indigenous worldview (They share the "ubiquity of the sacred, the expressiveness of nature and the nonduality of matter and spirit" (Routledge Encyclopedia of Philosophy), ultimately will be better indicators of the natural place deception has in human nature than our machines.

Four Arrows. It is indeed interesting to speculate, as we will throughout this book, on the possibility that the lens through which we attempt to understand human interactions by looking at the brain and its measured activities might take us further away from what may be true rather than closer. In his book, *After Babel*, author George Steiner argues that deception was at the root of the development of human language. Perhaps, even though I disagree with his idea that deception is fundamental to human behaviour, his assertion has some validity as it relates to the kinds of languages that dominate Western culture, languages that work well with categorizing, generalizing, reducing, labelling and asserting. They tend to stimulate more left brain activity and less right brain. But let's save this related issue for the chapter about "balance." What I'm getting at is this: I believe that Indigenous wisdom has long understood a way to activate right-brain/left brain balanced learning and that such learning, accompanied by the obvious realization that group survival depends more on trust and assumptions that people describe reality truthfully than on any possible range of deceptions, represents the "natural" design of human nature and brain functioning. Such learning creates implicit attitudes and regulates them so they are in synch with values that relate to compassion and a sacred interconnection with all things. Thus deception and self-deception are cultural phenomenon that is not evolutionary, but de-evolutionary. If we re-look at all the studies at the beginning of the chapter with this perspective in mind, a different set of interpretations emerge from what we see. For example, in Study 2, where we learn that retrieving a deceptive memory is more difficult than retrieving a truthful memory, we can see that it is less likely that evolution would create such a condition for survival!

In his wonderful book, *A Time Before Deception: Truth in Communication, Culture and Ethics*, Cooper writes about how Native peoples' first reactions to European habitual lying was believing that the invaders must be insane because in their cultures only insane people who had lost touch with reality spoke in ways that misrepresented it. His research also shows that lying can become a deviant strategy. The strategy may, like the use of weapons of mass destruction, lead to some temporary benefits for a small number of individuals, but in the long run they are not an evolutionary boon to humankind at all.

Cooper also details a research project where when Indigenous individuals and Western individuals suggested and ranked various aspects of cultural values that might have an impact on integrity, Native peoples ranked "respect" above all else but it did not even make the Western list. He shows how the concept of appreciation for life and the recognition of spirit in all things pervades traditional Indigenous thinking and that such perception informed all communication in ways that are incompatible with deception. In reading his book I was reminded of Vine Deloria, Jr.'s famous book, *Red Earth, White Lies: The Myth of Scientific Fact* (1995) and how it might shed light on the implausibility of Smith's contention in *Why We Lie* that "Mother Nature has seen to it that the conscious mind is relatively blind to the nuances of social behaviour (p. 146)." I think it is vital for neurophilosophers to consider Indigenous ways of knowing and the histories of Indigenous Peoples before drawing conclusions too quickly from the kinds of studies and scientific conclusions that have been reported here.

III. CONTINUING THE DIALOGUE FOR UNDERSTANDING

1. Choose one of the studies in Part I and specifically use it to:
   a. Support the Indigenous perspective relating to deception and human nature
   b. Challenge the Indigenous perspective relating to deception and human nature
2. Explain the main differences between the conclusions about deception and honesty offered by the Western researchers compared to those presented by the Indigenous scholars.
3. Name an idea or an observation that is common to at least four of the seven studies in Part I.
4. In what ways does your own worldview support the idea that deception is a higher order evolutionary development for humankind or that it is a natural and unavoidable function of the human brain. Defend your answer.

5. Do some independent research on the phenomenon of hypnosis and describe it in a way that makes a connection between this state and the predominance of deception in Western culture.

REFERENCES

Abe, N., Okuda, J., Suzuki, M., Sasaki, H., Matsuda, T., Mori, E., et al. (2008). Neural correlates of true memory, false memory, and deception. *Cerebral Cortex*, 1–9.

Abe, N., Suzuki, M., Mori, E., Itoh, M., & Fujii, T. (2007). Deceiving others: Distinct neural responses of the prefrontal cortex and amygdala in simple fabrication and deception with social interactions. *Journal of Cognitive Neuroscience, 19*(2), 287–295.

Abe, N., Suzuki, M., Tsukiura, T., Mori, E., Yamaguchi, K., Itoh, M., et al. (2006). Dissociable roles of prefrontal and anterior cingulate cortices in deception. *Cerebral Cortex, 16*, 192–199.

Ashton, M. C., Lee, K., & Son, C. (2000). Honesty as the sixth factor of personality: Correlations with machiavellianism, primary psychopathy, and societal adroitness. *European Journal of Personality, 14*, 359–368.

Ben-Shakhar, G., & Elaad, E. (2002). The Guilty Knowledge Test (GKT) as an application of psychophysiology: Future prospects and obstacles. In M. Kleiner (Ed.), *Handbook of polygraph testing*. San Diego, CA: Academic Press.

Berthoz, S., Grezes, J., Armony, J. L., Passingham, R. E., & Dolan, R. J. (2006). Affective response toone's own moral violations. *NeuroImage, 31*, 945–950.

Byrne, R. W., & Corp, N. (2004). Neocortex size predicts deception rate in primates. *The Royal Society, 271*, 1693–1699.

Ford, C. V., King, B. H., & Hollender, M. H. (1988). Lies and liars: Psychiatric aspects of prevarication. *The American Journal of Psychiatry, 145*(5), 554–562.

Ganis, G., Kosslyn, S. M., Stose, S., Thompson, L. W., & Yurgelen-Todd, D. A. (2003). Neural correlates of different types of deception: An fMRI investigation. *Cerebral Cortex, 13*, 830–836.

Grèzes, J., Frith, C., & Passingham, R. E. (2004). Brain mechanisms for inferring deceit in the actions of others. *The Journal of Neuroscience, 24*(24), 5500–5505.

Hughes, C. J., Farrow, T. F. D., Hopwood, M., Pratt, A., Hunter, M. D., & Spence, S. A. (2005). Recent developments in deception research. *Current Psychiatry Reviews, 1*, 273–279.

Kozel, F. A., Revell, L. J., Lorberbaum, J. P., Shastri, A., Elhai, J. D., Horner, M. D., et al. (2004). A pilot study of functional magnetic resonance imaging brain correlates of deception in healthy young men. *Journal of Neuropsychiatry and Clinical Neuroscience, 16*(3), 295–305.

Langleben, D. D., Loughead, J., Bilker, W. B., Ruparel, K., Childress, A. R., Busch, S. I., et al. (2005). Telling the truth from lie in individual subjects with fast event-related fMRI. *Human Brain Mapping, 26*(4), 262–272.

Langleben, D. D., Schroeder, L., Maldjian, J. A., Gur, R. C., McDonald, S., Ragland, J. D., et al. (2002). Brain activity during simulated deception: An event-related functional magnetic resonance study. *NeuroImage, 15*(3), 727–732.

Lee, T. M. C., Liu, H. L., Tan, L. H., Chan, C. C. H., Mahankali, S., Feng, C. M., et al. (2002). Lie detection by functional magnetic resonance imaging. *Human Brain Mapping, 15*, 157–164.

mapping of deception and truth-telling about an ecologically valid situation: Functional MR imaging and polygraph investigation - Initial experience. *Radiology, 238*(2), 679–688.

Phan, K. L., Magalhaes, A., Ziemlewicz, T. J., Fitzgerald, D. A., Green, C., & Smith, W. (2005). Neural correlates of telling lies: A functional magnetic resonance imaging study at 4 Tesla. *Academic Radiology, 12*(2), 164–172.

Spence, S. A. (2008). Playing Devil's advocate: The case against fMRI lie detection. *Legal and Criminological Psychology, 13*, 11–25.

Spence, S. A., Farrow, T. F. D., Herford, A. E., Wilkinson, I. D., Zheng, Y., & Woodruff, P. W. R. (2001). Behavioural and functional anatomical correlates of deception in humans. *NeuroReport, 12*(13), 2849–2853.

Spence, S. A., Hunter, M. D., Farrow, T. F. D., Green, R. D., Leung, D. H., Hughes, C. J., et al. (2004). A cognitive neurobiological account of deception: Evidence from functional neuroimaging. *Philosophical Transactions of the Royal Society London, 359*, 1755–1762.

Yang, Y., Raine, A., Lencz, T., Bihrle, S., Lacasse, L., & Colletti, P. (2005). Prefrontal white matter in pathological liars. *British Journal of Psychiatry*, *187*, 320–325.
Yang, Y., Raine, A., Narr, K. L., Lencz, T., LaCasse, L., & Colletti, P. (2007). Localisation of increased prefrontal white matter in pathological liars. *British Journal of Psychiatry*, *190*, 174–175.

CHAPTER 3

FEAR AND COURAGE

The courage Indigenous Peoples show is quite amazing. It's a very moving and inspiring experience, and brings to my mind some contemptuous remarks of Rousseau's on Europeans who have abandoned freedom and justice for the peace and repose they enjoy in their chains.

– Noam Chomsky (1992, *What Uncle Sam Really Wants,* p. 101)

I. NEUROSCIENCE STUDIES OVERVIEW

Angela Enlow and Jessica B. Diamond

Five articles are summarized to present evidence that neurological mechanisms lie at the core of the fear response. The most prominent neurological structure involved in fear is the amygdala. However, it is argued that since fear can be learned, and that extinction of fear can also occur, there must be underlying neurological processes involved to counter the fear response, thus altering neurological mechanisms to create courage. The articles summarized here flow to inform the reader that 1) the amygdala is central to conditioned fear, demonstrating its importance of learned behavioural responding, particularly the generation of aversive conditioned responses, 2) the amygdala reacts strongly to viewing fearful faces, but not angry or neutral ones, and this may demonstrate that threats that remain vague intrigue the amygdala until the source of the threat is determined, 3) the amygdala is specifically geared toward processing arousal of stimuli while other brain structures assist in processing the valence of stimuli, 4) the amygdala is highly activated when stimuli are detected, but remain outside of conscious awareness, demonstrating an early detection function of the amygdala, and 5) that courage can be defined as the behavioural approach in the presence of a feared stimulus.

Study 1: "Fear Conditioning as Stimulus versus Response Expression"

Cheng and colleagues conduct D.T., Knight, D.C., Smith, C.N., Stein, E.A., & Helmstetter, F.J. (2003). Functional MRI of human amygdala activity during Pavlovian fear conditioning: Stimulus processing versus response expression. *Behavioural Neuroscience, 117,* 3–10.

Summary. Cheng and colleagues (2003) determined in their research that the amygdala appears to be a critical component in a distributed network essential for associating emotional responses and environmental stimuli, and that it is an integral part of Pavlovian fear conditioning, especially in the expression of learned behavioural responses.

Description. The authors sought to "more closely examine the relationship of dynamic changes in activity within the amygdala to its role in the expression of conditional fear by correlating multiple reference functions with amygdala activity." Many animal studies have established the importance of the amygdala in the learning and expression of conditioned fear, but few human studies have been conducted. Additionally, a lack of agreement in previous neuroimaging studies on the acquisition of fear conditioning motivated this study, as the authors hoped to better understand the various potential roles of the amygdala during Pavlovian fear conditioning.

Participants were 20 healthy, right-handed subjects (8 men, 12 women). Participants underwent a 20-minute anatomical scan (in the absence of visual or electrical stimulation) and were then equally assigned to either a paired or control group. Apparatuses used were a whole brain imaging scanner and thermal monitoring system (GSR, measuring skin conductance). The CS was a flashing red light, while the UCS was electrical stimulation. Subjects rated the level of electrical stimulation on a 0 to 5 scale (0=no sensation, 5=painful, but tolerable) prior to training, and a stimulus intensity that elicited a response of 5 from the participant was then presented intermittently throughout the study. Subjects were exposed to four, five-trial blocks of CS-UCS presentations, during which time functional images were obtained. The paired group received CS-UCS presentations that simultaneously terminated, while the control group received unpaired CS-UCS presentations in which the UCS presented 15 seconds after the CS terminated.

Subjects in the paired group showed learning-related changes, in that they "maintained or slightly increased their autonomic response amplitude over trials," whereas the control group showed a gradual decrease in amplitude over trials (though they initially showed "large evoked responses"). These learning differences were evidenced in the visual cortex (stimulus-based activity), but not in the amygdala (response-based activity). However, the paired group also showed significantly stronger activity in the right amygdala.

The authors "were able to demonstrate clear patterns of activation that may reflect brain activity related to learning-induced changes in stimulus processing versus expression of behavioural responses." This indicated that Pavlovian fear conditioning includes regions of the brain that "process environmental danger signals and those that control the expression of autonomic and behavioural fear responses."

Differences in activity in the visual cortex were noted between the groups. This was likely due to the predictive value given to stimuli by participants in the paired group (in that the paired subjects viewed the UCS as more biologically significant than the control group). This indicated processing differences between the groups based on the predictive value of environmental signals.

Overall, results indicated that the amygdala is important for the **expression** of learned behavioural responses during Pavlovian fear conditioning, particularly the generation of aversive conditioned responses. However, it is possible, due to the short length of time that the amygdala neurons respond during the **acquisition** of fear conditioning (a matter of milliseconds), that the amygdala plays other roles in the development of conditioned fear, but they are simply difficult to observe using an fMRI.

Study 2: "Responses to Facial Expressions of Fear versus Anger"

Summary. According to Whalen et al (2001), viewing fearful facial expressions results in greater activity in the amygdala, the area of the brain that is thought to play a primary role in the processing and memory of emotional reactions, than viewing either angry or neutral expressions.

Description. The authors were inspired by a working hypothesis that "the amygdala functions to resolve biologically relevant associative ambiguity and this role explains its greater processing of fearful facial expressions." It has been assumed that the amygdala is activated when an individual is confronted with "threat-related social signals". If this is the case, both angry and fearful stimuli would elicit activity in the amygdala at comparable levels. However, research has shown that expressions of fear result in greater levels of amygdaloid activity than expressions of anger. Therefore, the authors hypothesized that "the amygdala would exhibit greater BOLD (blood oxygenation-level dependent) signal intensity to expressions of fear than to expressions of anger and that no areas of the amygdaloid region would exhibit greater BOLD signal intensity to anger versus fear".

To determine the type(s) of facial expressions that result in the highest levels of amygdaloid activity, the authors conducted fMRI on 8 healthy, right-handed participants (4 men and 4 women) and recorded their BOLD signal intensity in the amygdala. Participants were shown pictures of 48 faces (8 presentations of the same 6 individuals in each category) during 24-second epochs. During each epoch, pictures shown to each individual participant were all from the same emotional category (some participants viewed 48 fearful face stimuli, some viewed 48 angry, and some viewed 48 neutral). Each individual participated in two scans made up of ten 24-second epochs. Presentations of fearful and angry epochs were bracketed by neutral face epochs, which served as the baseline comparison, and all participants viewed the same amount of epochs from each category. When exiting the fMRI, participants were asked to describe the stimuli.

Results showed significant activation of the dorsal (toward the top) amygdala in the fear versus anger contrast, and in the ventral (toward the bottom) amygdala in the fear versus neutral contrast. The anger versus neutral contrast also indicated activity in the ventral amygdala, but only showed comparable intensity to fear during the first epoch. Greater responsiveness was observed when participants were viewing the expressions of fear in comparison to expressions of anger.

Consistent with previous studies, results indicated "the amygdala demonstrates considerable preference for the facial expression of fear." The amygdala may be an essential component of the brain system that processes fearful facial characteristics. However, research has shown the amygdala to be of importance in responding to various facial expressions, it is likely that there are "more subtle biologically relevant learning situations in which the amygdala has also been shown to play an important role." In other words, fear may be one of many states in which the amygdala is a significant component. In response to greater amygdaloid activity to fearful stimuli, the authors hypothesize that fearful faces require more processing within the amygdala than the angry ones because the fearful faces are more ambiguous. Whereas angry facial expressions provide information about the source of threat, fearful expressions require an attempt to gain information about the source of threat. The amygdala shows more responsiveness when "biologically relevant events remain unclear." Therefore, "amygdala function can transcend detection of valence to monitor unclear predictability."

Study 3: "Processing Valence and Arousal in Affective Words"

Summary. Lewis et al (2007) found that the orbital frontal cortex processes valence, while the amygdala processes arousal. Thus different functions are needed to process stimulus and reaction to it.

Description. The authors sought to "characterize functional neuroanatomy supporting processing of valence and arousal in abstract word stimulus." It is assumed that emotion results from the valence, extent of pleasure or sadness experienced from a stimulus, and arousal, the extent of calmness or excitation that results from a given stimulus. To determine which brain areas respond to valence and arousal, the authors conducted fMRI on 19 participants. 9 were female with a mean age of 30 years. The participants were shown words that were selected from the standardized list: Affective Norms for English Words (ANEW). Words from this list are given valence scores which range from 1 (very unpleasant) to 9 (very pleasant), and arousal scores ranging from 0 (not arousing) to 9 (very arousing). Words were displayed to participants in random order. 124 words were shown with a valence rating greater than 7 (positive or pleasant) and 124 words were shown with a valence rating of less than three (negative, or not pleasant). Words were chosen from all levels of arousal. Words were presented for 1 second, with a 2 second inter-stimulus interval between word presentation.

Data was gathered to determine neuroanatomical areas that responded to valence alone, arousal alone, a conjunction of arousal with both negative and positive words, and an interaction between arousal and valence. During words of increased **valence** in positive words, the right lateral orbitofrontal cortex (this area receives information about the environment and plans being made by the frontal lobes. It produces efferent connections that affect behaviour and physiological responses, including emotional responses organized by the amygdala. The OFC serves as an interface between brain mechanisms involved in automatic emotional responses and the control of complex behaviours) and anterior insula (The insula is believed to process convergent information to produce an emotionally relevant context for sensory experience) became activated. With increased valence of negative words, the right posterolateral orbitofrontal cortex (OFC is involved in sensory integration. The OFC is thought to regulate planning behaviour associated with sensitivity to reward and punishment), the right medial orbitofrontal cortex, and the medial subgenual cingulate (emotion formation and processing, learning, and memory) became activated.

With increased **arousal** with positive words, the ventral striatum (striatum is activated by stimuli associated with reward, but also by aversive, novel, unexpected or intense stimuli, and cues associated with such events) and subgenual cingulate became activated. During presentation of increased arousal with negative words, the midbrain, left insula, left dorsal amydala, and putamen (involved in motor skills and learning) became activated. With the conjunction of increased arousal in both positive and negative words, the ventral striatum, pallidum (filtering out external stimuli so brain can focus on relevant stimuli), left lateral anterior insula, and left dorsal amygdala became activated.

Finally, the **interaction** of valence and arousal was tested for positive words, negative words, and their conjunction. Interactions were found with negative words alone in the left medial orbitofrontal cortex and striatum.

"Significant modulation of the amygdala was found in response to increased arousal in both positive and negative words, but with preferential response to negative words." The assumption has long been that the amygdala responds to fear, but it is more accurate to state that the amygdala responds to stimuli with increasing arousal, both positive and negative.

Study 4: "Conscious Awareness of Fear"

Summary. Carlsson and co-researchers (2004) concluded from their study that the amygdala responds to fear-relevant and phobic stimuli even when there is no conscious awareness of the stimuli. The authors suggest this is evidence that the amygdala responds to anything that might turn out to have important consequences for safety and survival. It may be therefore be prone to false positive responses rather than false negative responses.

Description. The purpose of the study was to identify brain regions involved in processing conscious and unconscious fearful stimuli. The authors identified 16 participants (right-handed females, mean age=26, SD=5 years) who were phobic of either snakes or spiders, but not both. First potential participants were identified by a questionnaire and then seen by a psychologist to confirm specific phobia diagnosis from DSM-IV. 8 subjects phobic of spiders and 8 phobic of snakes. They had no other neurological or psychiatric illness, no past history of head trauma, taking no medications, no drug use, and no nicotine use.

Each subject viewed pictures (9 pictures of phobic stimulus, 9 of fear-relevant, but non-phobic stimulus, 9 of neutral stimulus, and 3 masked pictures). PET scans conducted to record rCBF at various brain areas to determine brain activity when viewing these 3 types of stimuli. Specifically, the subjects viewed the stimuli in 2 different ways. A short-exposure trial had participants view the target stimuli (phobic, fear-relevant, and neutral pictures) for 14ms, followed immediately with 56 ms of a masking stimulus (photo that was a randomly assembled picture made from target stimuli, but without a recognizable central object—no snake or spider could be seen). The long-exposure consisted of a 14ms exposure to the target stimulus with 56ms of a masking stimulus occurring 294ms after the target stimulus offset.

During the short exposure, PET scans showed significant increases in activity of the left amygdala and anterior medial temporal lobe. Significant activation levels were found during the phobic-short versus neutral-short and the fear relevant-short versus the neutral short exposure conditions. During the long-exposure conditions, both the left and right side of the amygdala was significantly activated in the phobic-long versus neutral-long conditions. However, no significant in activity was found in the fear relevant-long versus neutral-long conditions.

During the longer exposure time to the target stimulus in the phobic conditions, the amygdala response is enhanced and associated with activation of the affective processing network [anterior cingulate cortex (associated with affect related tasks/situations and emotional salience), anterior insula (interoceptive stimulation, autonomic activity, emotional states, pain), orbitofrontal cortex (described above in article 1), and periaqueductal gray (defensive responses characterized by freezing immobility, running, jumping, tachycardia and increases in blood pressure and muscle tone. However, in the fear-relevant conditions, the right and dorsolateral prefrontal cortex (which orchestrate thoughts and actions according to goals, planning complex behaviours), and lateral orbital frontal cortex (prepare and apply goal-directed selection for stimuli and responses) were activated during the fear-relevant conditions. The authors conclude that when phobic stimuli are completely processed (longer time exposure), the fear network including subcortical and cortical nodes are recruited as fear is accelerated. When non-feared stimuli are processed, the initial amygdala response to the stimuli is disengaged and cortical areas are never recruited.

The researchers suggest that stimuli that have survival relevance are "tagged" to automatically evoke an emotional response and they get priority for further processing. The role of the amygala is to monitor the outside world for emotionally relevant events relatively independent of the current focus of attention. The amygdala responds to anything that may have important consequences for safety and survival.

Study 5: "Courage and Behavioural Approaches for Fear Situations"

Summary. Norton and Weiss (2009) studied the role of courage in a fear-eliciting situation and found that is measurable, can be self-reported and is predictive of actual behavioural reactions in the presence of a feared stimulus. The study was conducted to assess courage in the face of fear so as to better understand its relationship with anxiety and behavorial approaches.

Description. Thirty-two participants who completed a measure of courage and reported the authors sought to assess courage in order to understand its relationship with fear, anxiety, and behavioural approach. Behavioural approaches study primarily stimuli response phenomenon but also allow for inclusion of cognitive processes. The purpose of the study was to assess whether self-reports of courageousness could reasonably predict a subject's behavioural approach to a feared stimulus. It was assumed that being able to predict a subject's level of courageousness could be helpful in determining treatment strategies for anxiety disorders. Two relationships between the variables (courage, fear, and behavioural approach) were tested: (1) the variance in behavioural approach "above-and-beyond that accounted for by pre-existing levels of fear" (courage was hypothesized to account for such variance) and (2) whether courage could moderate the relationship between fear and behavioural approach.

31 undergraduate female psychology students, with elevated fear of spiders, were used as participants. The Spider Questionnaire (SPQ) was used to assess potential subjects' fear of spiders. To assess self-perceived courageousness, the authors developed a courage measure (CM) comprised of 12 "rationally derived items", using a Likert-type scale in which subjects self-rated themselves on a scale from 1 (never) to 7 (always). The CM uses an operational definition of "persistence or perseverance despite having fear". The CM was given to participants three weeks prior to a behavioural approach test (BAT), and again just before beginning the BAT. Levels of general anxiety were assessed using the State-Trait Anxiety Inventory-State form (STAI-S). Peak anxiety was assessed using a Subjective Units of Distress Scale (SUDS), which ranges from 0 (no fear/anxiety) to 100 (worst imaginable anxiety or highest anxiety ever experienced).

Results indicated that, when courage is measured in the "phobic context," it is predictive of behavioural approach "above-and-beyond scores on measures of spider fears." The "phobic context" was referring to scores on the CM obtained immediately preceding the BAT. Scores on the first administration of the CM (three weeks prior to the BAT) were not significantly predictive of behavioural approach.

Differences in the courage scores led to debate on whether courage is best conceptualized as a state or trait construct. It is possible that inaccuracies occur when self-reporting courage in different situations (non-fear vs. fear-producing). Demand characteristics might also influence scores. Furthermore, courage may not be a single trait-related characteristic, but rather a combination of context-dependent characteristics. Additionally, the CM itself may have contributed to the variance in scores.

Regardless of whether courage is viewed as a state or trait construct, the results of this study "support the ability to quantify courage, as measured by actual behavioural approach to a feared stimulus, using a self-report instrument incorporating an explicit behavioural definition." This research may assist in understanding the relationships between courage, fear, and behavioural approaches to managing fear and anxiety. Being able to assess a patient's pre-existing levels of anxiety and courageousness could help identify appropriate treatment strategies, (e.g. identify which patients would be good candidates for exposure-based treatments and which would benefit from strategies to increase courageousness before engaging in exposure).

II. INDIGENOUS PERSPECTIVES DIALOGUE

Greg Cajete, Jongmin Lee and Four Arrows

Four Arrows. In my 1998 book, *Primal Awareness,* I have a chapter entitled, "Becoming Connoisseurs of Fear" in which I refer to Indigenous cultures as experts on the many faces of fear and courage. Early education focused on instilling courage and respect into children. This expertise included an understanding of the emotions, the personality traits of individuals and the role of spontaneous and induced trance and visualization. The emotion of fear, in addition to its self-preservation role in activating fight or flight mechanisms, also may be designed to help with social regulation in the pursuit of maintaining homeostasis. In effect fear operates, according to my understanding of Indigenous histories, in four important ways. First, for the individual it offers a catalyst for practicing moral behaviours such as generosity, courage, patience and other values important for social harmony and personal transformation. Second, it helps us learn empathy for the emotions of others in ways that can inspire caring for others. Third, it offers a rapid induction opportunity for trance states. We'll save talking about the hypnotic aspects for the last chapter on balance, but it is important to realize that all creatures become hypersuggestible to the signals of a perceived trusted authority figure during times when fear is a prominent emotion. Indigenous peoples used an awareness of this to create ceremonies for self transformation. Western leaders have used it to manipulate the masses. Fourth, I think that a study of how courage and fear plays out in Indigenous stories reveals that it offers a way avoid thinking in the duality common to Western thinking that envisions two categories of things; those to be fearful of and those to embrace. As far as the studies just presented, I was happy to se in Carlson's study that the brain research showed that fear manifested in different and complex ways. At least this opens the door to Western neurophilosophy for considering these four ideas I've offered about the conscious and unconscious possibilities surrounding this particular emotion.

Jongmin. If I may jump in, I think it is important to clarify that current studies like some of these that make a distinction between state and trait anxiety no longer dismiss cognition. The distinction though is commonly understood since the publications and psychometrics developed by Spielberger (1983). States of fear or apprehension relate to unpleasant emotional arousal in response to a fearful stimuli. Trait based bear is about consistent individual differences in how people respond to frightening situation. And like one of the studies showed, people can often self-report and predict their reactions to certain stimuli. So maybe we are all connoisseurs in a way.

Four Arrows. Not according to how I mean it though. Just knowing that one is afraid of spiders does not make one an expert in the many nuances that relate to the fear, its source, and ways to overcome it or use it or control it. I think the most important difference between Western notions of fear and courage and Indigenous is that in the former fear is usually avoided with great effort and courage, when it appears, is intended to conquer the fear for accomplishing some goal. I have suggested in my previous work, especially in *Primal Awareness* (1998) and in *Teaching Virtues* (2002), that a major understanding of fear among Indigenous Peoples is that it serves as a catalyst or an opportunity for practicing a virtue such as patience, courage, generosity, fortitude, etc. This is why fear tests were so commonplace in teaching and learning throughout American Indian societies.

Jongmin. A well- known Buddhist teacher, Daisaku Ikeda, says that one who has the courage to speak the truth lives a good life. Without courage happiness is impossible. It seems that many religions and philosophies teach the importance of courage in the face of fear or worry or difficult times. So don't all culture's ultimate work toward such expertise and understanding about fear and courage?

Four Arrow. I don't think so. In Western cultures, generally speaking, the individual is the basis for such courage talk. Even morality centers on the individual. I think religion, including Buddhist philosophy exaggerates individualism, even as relates to death and the concept of reincarnation. When courage is about "happiness" or "living a good life," and when one believes in the continuation of one's ego after death, then there is, I believe, more likelihood for fear and courage is less about practicing virtues for the sake of community than about some form of salvation. And it is why there is such a focus on the virtues and courage of individual teachers. Indigenous courage is based on a deep understanding about giving back, reciprocity, and even in death a sharing back of the energies of the self to the world.

Greg. The five studies summarized by our neuroscientists tend to confirm that fear responses and courage are learnable but keeping the subject in the realm of stimulus/response and not looking at the deeper issues of worldview you two are discussing makes our conversation all the more important. Realizing that fear and courage have a direct affect on human behaviour and on reciprocity, Indigenous Peoples have created their stories, art, rituals and ceremonies to assure that courage becomes a common trait and that fears are respected as opportunities for survival and growth. It is not surprising that courage to respect and face fear has played a role mythically, psychologically, socially, and spiritually in our many Indigenous cultures. We created in our stories images of fear which are deeply rooted in the cultural psyche. These images embody traits that are deemed fearful from a cultural view point. They may be ogres who devour human flesh, monsters who destroy all in their path, sirens who entice and steal.

We created in our stories images of fear which are deeply rooted in the cultural psyche. They may be ogres who devour human flesh, monsters who destroy all in their path, sirens who entice and steal the soul. For example, the stealer of souls has many names in American Indian traditions, Windigo in the Great Lakes, Koklimalayas in the Northwest, Bone Manin Modoc to name just a few. Historically, we name and image our fears in personal and cultural ways. In modern times, we have incorporated a political aspect as well. In all cases, we advise and devise ways for dealing with fear in our stories, ceremonies and politics. The themes of fear present themselves in our stories as fear for the end of our lives, our people, our ways of life, the earth, etc. The worst fear of all is the psychological one of losing of one's sense of identity, of who we think we are, of our true sense of ourselves In these stories not only is fear named but the ways for dealing with it, for overcoming it are also described. Stories of would be warriors and their adventures through which they overcome their fears are some of the most popular versions of the heroes journey.

What are the essential fears presented in these stories? There is primal fear of death. There is the fear of loss of those that we most cherish, our family, our friends, our community, our way of life. There is the fear of war, of disaster, of the other over the hill or over the waters. There is the fear of losing one's land or one's status or one's possessions. But probably the worst fear of all is the psychological one of losing of one's sense of identity, of who we think we are, of our true sense of ourselves. Any one of these themes could form the exploration of "fear and Indigenous philosophy." What I wish to explore is how Indigenous people dealt with these forms of primal fear by creating ways to engage it in ways which formed both the sense of true self and the warrior within. In many tribes this was accomplished through Indigenous group games.

Although personal recognition was a part of the social context in which Native Games unfolded, at a deeper level participation focused on the greater goal of confronting one's fears and thus fulfilling one's human potential and destiny within the context of Native cultural ideals and values. The development of physical endurance, skill, courage, mental focus combined with emotional and spiritual development characterized the training of the Native player.

Native players strove to achieve the "highest thought" in their training and game playing. This ideal of the "highest thought" is a generic term for a commonly held set of values and belief for guiding the alignment of mind, body and spirit with high ethical and spiritual standards for training and participation in Native games. It was akin to the ideal of "sportsmanship" today but went much deeper in its personal and cultural implications. As an ideal it was something to be sought amidst the human challenges given the propensity of human beings to be also egotistical, vengeful, jealous and argumentative, as well as adaptive, persistent (games often lasted days), and in-balance. Through alignment with such an ideal for developing physical, mental and spiritual prowess, it was thought that the Native player could create the "luck" and attract the attention of the "spirits" that would ultimately help connect them to the creative elements within themselves and the Cosmos.

Four Arrows. Greg, I want to hear more about exactly how the games maximized the ability to create a co-consciousness that was and is in alignment with how we think the brain works according to current neuroscience. From what you have said thus far, it seems that Indigenous Peoples, for the sake of survival and in light of their close observations of Nature, including their own inner natures, understood that:

- (From Study 2) The emotional processing of fear is somehow different than that of anger.
- (From Study 3) Words can create specific arousal levels that stimulate either fear or courage behaviours. The arousal levels play a role in fear interpretation.
- (From Study 4) There is an internal response to fear-relevant stimuli at an unconscious level, so it is prone to false associations.
- (From Study 5) Courage, whether a state or a trait phenomenon, can be learned and evaluated.

I contend that Indigenous Peoples see fear not as something to avoid but as an opportunity to use fear as a catalyst for learning an important virtue, like the ones you mentioned are important in Native Sports, such as persistence, patience, generosity, honesty and, of course, courage. Interestingly, by the way, I know many Indigenous people who have talked about generosity being the highest expression of course. For example, Charles Eastman Eastman, in his book, *Indian Boyhood* (1902/1993) told of his grandmother teaching him to give away what he cherished most, his puppy, so that he would become strong and courageous. I know this at least ties to Native Games because I remember stories about how frustrated Western coaches were when they saw Native teams waiting for the other side to score before it was their "turn" to score again.

Greg. Indigenous cultures used fear as a character builder as opposed to a controlling device. Ultimately, such cultures have made humans afraid of nature and giving us comfort in safety and conveniences instead. I am considering your idea that Natives use fear as a catalyst for practicing a virtue, so any frightening stimuli in nature, a bear or lightening, could well have served as a catalyst to remain one with Nature. As was true with many other aspects of Native education, Native players applied the principles and lessons learned through generations of observation of Nature, particularly animals at play. Indigenous wisdom, at its core is wisdom drawn from intimate relationship with the natural world. Therefore, the practice of learning from Nature and applying natural principles was an integral focus in training for Native Games. Watching animals, particularly deer and antelope, birds such as eagles and hawks, wolves, mountain lions and other predators helped Native players gain an understanding of dynamic movement. Indeed, it is no accident that many references are made to animals in Native Myths about games. The stories of how certain games originated among animals are a reflection of this close observation. The development of many Native games and the techniques used by Native players are adaptations of human movement to parallel or other wise mimic animal movement. Observing how certain animals such as deer and antelope seem to "flow" with the landscape as they move provide cues on how Native players could mimic such flow in their own play in Native games.

This "moving with the flow might be considered the first natural principle applied in Native games. Moving with the natural flow of the game was viewed as akin to a deer running, lion or bear cubs playing naturally, a fish swimming effortlessly in a stream, or an eagle gliding through the air. Going with the flow of the process of the game is what characterized the best Native players. Intuitive use of your environment or circumstances of play in a game facilitates the integration of mind, body and spirit. To flow with the circumstances, with other players, with the ball in motion, was the level of play which was sought after and simultaneously through its attainment the realization of a connection to the greater play of the world of spirit and the cosmos. A play that demands an emphasis on courageous and respectful engagement with that which might be a risk that otherwise invokes only fear.

Another way Native games might illustrate the courage to become one with the great mysteries and powers in Nature relates to the circle movement in Native Games. Everything in Native Games moves in a circle toward or away from a real or imagined center. It is a kind of circumbulation or movement around, in and through a center. In a Native game, this movement this movement around a center is both real and metaphoric. Such movement has great metaphysical meaning in that mimics the circumbulating movement of celestial bodies in the cosmos.

This circular movement also implies a kind of dynamic balance which is illustrated through the rhythm and flow of a game as players move in relative relationship to each other and the ball striving for the goal. The goal is itself an extension of the symbolic center of the field. As players move around the ball, which metaphorically represents the ever elusive moving center of life, they represent the play of life. They represent the play of the cosmos, and the dynamic nature of the creating a dynamic balance from chaos.

So "finding the center" and creating dynamic balance are achieved through "reverent" play associated with Native games. Playing the game with all one's heart facilitates the players in "finding their heart and finding their face" and while its also brings about an integration of body, mind and spirit. Playing with all one's heart usually requires some level of courage to face all sorts of fears. Ego attachment and the many fears relating to ego are overcome and achieved in such a way that during the players full involvement with the game, they "forget themselves" and thereby become one with themselves, the other players and the dynamic process of the game.

As for the last study's reference to the power of words in creating courage and motivation to face difficulties, it is interesting to note that a native game could be brought to life by praying for it or by singing for it, as well as by fasting for it, dancing for it, celebrating it or actually training for it. The most basic source or purpose for the player came from his personal thought, intention and action. Anything that we intentionally create a place for in our life will tend to come into being. I think this is what the research is telling us if we could see it through our lens. For the Native player, accommodating the extensive training and social requirements for playing a game in one's life and in the life of the community is what really energized the game. Making a place for the playing of a native game is akin to the setting of a sacred goal. Indeed, the setting of such a goal is a metaphor for the larger perspective of striving for the life that is beyond just us. The sacred goal of gaining greater life through participation in the larger game and creative play of the universe is often the underlying theme of the stories told about the origins of Native Games.

Native Games were also used for rights of passage and it may not be a coincidence that those games that were most "frightening" or challenging required the most preparation. And yes, Four Arrows, much of the preparation probably induced trance states for heightened learning. In many cases games as initiation rights for youth were conceived as a metaphoric death and resurrection or spiritual rebirth. The game represented a journey into the face of overwhelming odds.

Four Arrows. Like the *arahipa* run that Tarahumara (Raramuri) Indians do in Copper Canyon that is a right of passage for some youth. It is truly a dangerous and arduous adventure that involves running and kicking a wooden ball for a hundred miles or so through dangerous wilderness up and down an 8,000 foot canyon. There is little to no recognition of personal accomplishment at the end of the race, but rather satisfaction that the world is in better balance as a result of the competition.

Greg. Yes and the key lesson learned is that by striving in service of a higher cause and for a goal higher than those of pure self-interest the athlete realizes himself and comes into control of his own destiny with a renewed sense of integrity and self-esteem. This is the essential life lesson of the warrior hero reflected in the triumphant journey undertaken and accomplished in the face of seemingly overwhelming odds. These themes of trials, tribulations and triumph are metaphorically replayed with each Native game. And the potential for learning these same life lessons is always present for the Native player who participates in this kind of mythic play as symbolically represented in historic and traditional Native games.

Jongmin. I will talk more about this from scientific and maybe even Buddhist view but I wanted to interject here that I agree that courage is based on some-degree of abandonment of one's well-being. I hear you saying this comes from service to a higher cause. How do Indigenous athletes prepare for such Games?

Greg. Since most of the neuroscience studies in Part I confirm that courage can be learned and since I've talked about how Native Games offer such a learning vehicle, I want to share some specific ways Indigenous Peoples train for these games that would therefore be appropriate for the goals of social neuroscience and neuroeconomics, namely learning how to make better choices in life.

First there is visualization. Visualizing is an active form of meditation, a way to focus and concentrate using your mind's eye to influence your emotion and energy. In traditional ways of preparing for Native games, players would seek a place of solitude to visualize their participation in the game to come. This time of meditation and quite before a game helped to focus, center their energy pray and set personal intentions for the game. This practice of imaging success through mediation and prayer enhanced a player's state of mind significantly.

Four Arrows. This idea of imaging is crucial to understanding the nature of fear and the Indigenous ways of making it an ally. I have written much about the connection between fear and hypnotic states. When people are in high stress they become hypersuggestible to the signals of a perceived trusted authority figure. In a spontaneous state of hypnosis, they respond to directives of those who speak with confidence, for better or for worse. Indians, I hypothesize, understand this phenomena as being a part of all creatures and developed ways to assure the individual only turned control over to someone else when intentionally considered. We'll talk more about this in another when we talk about authority research.

Greg. I believe there is also a connection between this idea of trance and the spiritual aspect of this which complements the brain/mind energy equation. Prayer is also a form of mediation, affirmation and petitioning of the spiritual realm using language which may be spoken, sung or thought. In Native thought, prayer is a way to awaken one's own inner spirit and evoke spirits of the natural world to focus them on the task at hand. For Native player it was a way to focus the "talk of the mind" toward the goal of fulfilment of the intention of the game thereby establishing a spiritual context in through which the playing of the game might unfold. This deeper connection to spiritual awareness I am talking about might be better described as "vision" work rather than "visualization" work.

Vision may be said to be a higher order of visualization in that vision is a mental image of what you want to accomplish. Vision becomes a powerful ally, when combined with your motivation, sense of purpose, ideals and ethical thought. Vision combines several inner dimensions which work synergistically to create a visionary context for Native games. These dimensions are focusing, centering, intuition, reflection and relaxation. In the process of focusing, you fine tune your attention and intention on the tasks that need to be accomplished to bring an event into being. It is the systematic zeroing in on the target.

Centering is the larger version of focusing that it encompasses a greater whole and establishes connections to larger goals, ideals, aspirations, cultural and spiritual life ways. In centering you find that place of spiritual and emotional stability, that source of inner strength, rootedness, and tranquillity. It is a place within yourself, which is difficult to describe in words, but rather has to be felt. It is the metaphorical still point in the midst of dynamic action… "the eye of the tiger."

In the application of intuition in Native games you are applying the deeper wisdom of the body, mind and spirit. This might also be called following your instincts or in-born knowledge. This in-born knowledge provides for instantaneous understanding of a situation and how to react to it. While intuition is a basic instinct which all humans possess, in Native games it is the specialized form of knowledge honed through practice and experience. As a matter of fact, the more practice and experience a player may have the greater capacity to use intuition…if they have learned to trust it and act from their sense of center and focused attention. Therein lays the key, learning to trust your inner self, your inner vision and sense of purpose, and at the same time realizing that there are more invisible forces that can work in harmony with you.

Four Arrows. If I may, I would like to share one profound example of visioning and the mysterious connections you are describing. In preparation for a Sun Dance where the temperatures in South Dakota on the Pine Ridge Reservation where I was heading were predicted to be in the 100s, I became seriously worried about going four days without sufficient water as required during the ceremony. I went up on the mountain behind my Idaho home in the Sawtooth Wilderness to cry for a vision. Within an hour a rodent of some sort crossed into my tobacco tie circle and without thinking I reacted by kicking it away. Almost immediately I realized my blunder and knew intuitively that this animal was the answer to my request for help. Then, within a short while, it returned. It came into my circle, turned around and sat facing the same direction I was facing, as if it were a pet dog. I studied its long back legs and tail and wondered what it was. Having no medicine man to guide me on the meaning, I planned on searching the Internet when I returned home the next day before going into the lodge. (Now there is a connection between the material/ energy world and spirituality for you!)

The next day I looked for images of the creature and soon found it. It was a kangaroo rat, the only animal that can go its entire life without drinking water! My fears of dying of thirst disappeared.

Greg. Thanks for sharing this. It is so important to remember our connection to the invisible world we cannot measure. And believing in the possibilities is another form of the kind of biology of belief Lipton studies I think. Our beliefs indeed determine what we become. The first and foremost belief is in ourselves. And this fundamental belief is the basis of our self-esteem. This sense of self worth significantly affects our performance on the game field and in the larger game of life. This belief in our self is also a fundamental component in the complex psychology of "finding face," one of the foundational metaphors of indigenous self knowledge.

Belief also affects mindset in that it facilitates the emergence of motivation, commitment, confidence, courage and concentration (Huang and Lynch, p. 32). The fundamental belief for Native players is that everyone is capable of playing and participation in the context of Native games. It is a fundamental form of self and communal affirmation. Historically, all members of a community were participants in the unfolding of a Native game. For the Native players this belief kept them open and receptive to the creative possibilities for learning within the game play. Ultimately, you learn to play a game by playing it and through the experiences which affords.

At the cultural level, strong belief in why they were playing the game was a strong source of motivation for Native players. Native players in essence lent their vital energy to benefit the greater whole of clan, tribe or community for a particular intention. That intention might have been to resolve a conflict, to bring about healing of the sick, to bring rain, to ensure a good planting or harvest and or any one of a number of personal and communal purposes found on cultural beliefs that might motivate the playing of a game.

Positive thought was always encouraged in Native gaming (and note I am NOT referring to Indian gaming in the casino sense!). To think positively about the game which you are about to play aligns your thought and actions toward success and fulfilling one's intentions for participation. Positive thinking is also first step in a therapeutic process for healing negative attitudes, beliefs and even physical conditions. In many ways the preparations such as prayer, fasting, singing, dancing were all designed to ensure positive thought on the part of all participants before, during and after a game. In the larger context the "game" is always a larger metaphor for life. It was well understood that negative thought created mental and physical weakness which in turn hindered performance of players and made it more difficult if not impossible to realize the essential purpose of playing a game. For the ultimate goal of a Native game was to synchronize with the "vital energies of the world", of the community and within one's self. Given the importance placed on positive thought, players were often reminded by elders, spectators and even other players to think good thoughts, speak good words and behave properly with regard to the game and the opposing team.

Jongmin. I am very interested in what the two of you have been saying. My scientific perspectives, like those in the neuroscience studies presented earlier, and like the Indigenous perspective, tend to see also fear and courage as more or less subject to conscious influence. There may be some different ideas I have but let me start by offering my scientific description of fear. I think fear can be defined as "the anxiety of losing one's well-being or happiness". This specialized psychological response against the risk of existence can be classified by dual major mental mechanisms, reason and affection, alike other psychological behaviours. These subtypes of fear may be described as either emotional fear and reasonable fear.

The reasonable fear is acknowledgement of well-analysed impending risk such as greenhouse effect, earthquake, or collision of comet. The risk may not be only for oneself but for the human community. In this case, we know that we cannot neglect or escape from the risk. Instead, we will get together and become courageous and purposeful and hopefully wise in our efforts to encounter against it. We don't need especially strong courage to encounter this kind of fear as much as we do effective reasoning. Global warming is not the kind of fear that causes a sudden feeling to emerge about some risk against one's well-being.

Four Arrows. Jon, I think the distinction between reasonable fear and emotional fear is useful to a degree but understanding that constant anxiety even without more obvious emotional feelings can be a chronic stress that leads to physical illness.

Jongmin. Of course, I'm just saying that the kind of fear where there is concern for future well-being, but is more vague or less immediate, like global warming is, perhaps unfortunately, for many people, is different in the brain that is designed to respond to fear in the short term. What I am calling "reasonable fear," can be overcome to a significant degree by things like getting together with others to discuss plans, etc. Conditioned fears like being afraid of black cats can be easily overcome with reasonable thinking or re-training. Conditioned fears can be recognized easily and are avoidable.

Four Arrows. This idea of avoiding fear, in my opinion, is built strongly into the Western mindset. This is why we are not doing much to stop global warming to use your own example. Indigenous Peoples ARE afraid about what is happening to Mother Earth. I'm afraid. And, according to Indigenous Wisdom, the goal is to USE the fear respectfully toward finding balance or practicing a virtue as opposed to avoiding fear by avoiding its source.

Jongmin. Perhaps you are right about the tendency in Western culture to avoid fear as opposed to embracing it as an opportunity for growth. However, I think for all cultures avoiding sources of fear can be reasonable; it can be emotional; or it can be both. Knowing the difference may be a sign of emotional and cognitive "intelligence" or conditioning. For example, in our institute in South Korea, one of employee's parking places is located behind forensic medicine building. We could most easily pass though the building to reach our cars. However, most employees go the long way around after sunset. They know very well the fact that no forensic dissection is performed after working time and there is nothing inside the building except corpses within firmly-locked refrigerators. But still they feel vague fear during the evening time. Some have talked about the sudden feeling of posterior neck chillness within the building. This might be an example of conditioned emotional fear with subsequent voluntary avoidance.

Greg. Might it not also be simply a cultural belief relating to ghosts or spirits?

Jongmin. Yes. In fact, in oriental philosophy, we used to think that we are living together with departed souls or ghosts of dead people. The oriental philosophy about passing away is different from the Western style. The lives are circulating and between embodiments of soul all existences, not only human being but also animals, can stay as soul state. This basic philosophy may provoke more emotional fear against ghost or demon. They believe the only solution to overcome this kind of fear is mollifying the souls by praying not fighting against or getting together. This is the reason why religious activity is strong in oriental world. Paradoxically some people used to sublimate the fear against soul to the dependency on guardian soul around them. Subsequently they can overcome the other kinds of emotional fear based on this dependency. All of this tends to confirm the malleable nature of fear response in the brain and nervous system that comes from learned beliefs.

Four Arrow. Jongmin, you have explained fear but what about courage? Is it just a matter of reasonable action as opposed to letting emotions determine behaviour without the balancing force of reason?

Jongmin. What is courage? In my opinion, courage is the positive self-compensatory mental mechanism against fear. A negative compensatory mechanism is a panic attack. The panic attack is freezing the mental and physical function. The person with panic attack cannot overcome the fear, instead he will turn off the switch of his consciousness by fainting. In contrast, the person with courage can boost his mental and physical activity with increased attention on the fear-provoking subject. The panic attack and the courage may be the both extreme of human reaction against fear.

What would be the basic difference between the panic attack and the courage? Keep in mind that although many animal studies have established the importance of the amygdala in the learning and expression of conditioned fear, few human studies have been conducted. We don't know what causes some to panic and some to be courageous except as relates to previous learning. The panic attack stems from extremely strong attachment to one's safety or well-being together with strong worry about losing something. On the other hand, courage reflects a willingness to sacrifice or risk wellbeing for the sake of something more important than safety or well-being.

This is one option it seems. Another is about reflection on experience. Courage can originate from a self-confidence based on detailed knowledge about the source of the fear and the emotion of fear as relates to it. Knowledge gives the power to be courageous in this case. As Four Arrows says, we must become connoisseurs of our fears.

In any case, however courage and fear originate in us, I don't think we were designed for being fear-based, certainly not chronically so as it seems we are. Fear creates stress in the body. It creates a sympathetic stimulation and resultant increase of stress hormones such as cortisol and norepinephrine, blood glucose level, heart rate, blood pressure, respiration rate, body temperature, and muscular tone. Within brain, centers of stress hormones such as pituitary gland and hypothalamus will be activated as well as centers of emotional reaction such as amygdala, hippocampus and prefrontal cortex. These body reactions against fear should be different according to the degree of anxiety provoked by the fear. The well-acknowledged reasonable fear will provoke the least emergent emotional reaction. Whereas, the conditioned emotional fear will provoke strong stress but it will subside quickly after voluntary avoidance. The unexpected sudden emotional fear will provoke the strongest stress reaction of human up to the panic freezing or fainting. By extremely strong anxiety, the autonomic neuromuscular system will work in abnormal way and subsequent hypocirculation of blood into brain occurs with resultant stopping of brain function, fainting. Somehow, the fainting can be regarded as an extreme form of compensatory mental mechanism to block severe psychic trauma, alike the emergent power-off button on radiation equipments. In the absence of fainting, we somehow adapt in ways to continue onward, but the body and health can deteriorate because of the cellular responses to the stress hormones constantly being secreted. Perhaps we should study the brains of people who live in modern times but are able not have constant anxiety. Certainly we can learn much from studying the brains of those who meditate, for example.

Greg. Jongmin, you speak of confidence as a way to build courage to face different fears. Going back to how Native Games were used to build courage, I see that confidence is a by product of having a sense of one's own personal power. It is the result of one's relative balance and strength of inner being. So confidence in one's ability to perform to one's utmost physical, mental and emotional capability is the direct result of inner development. This inner development is the ultimate by product of participation in the holistic context of Native games. Historically, this was the reason that all Native children were encouraged create and or to participate in Native games.

I think much of the stress in modern society comes from not knowing the difference between assertiveness and aggression. Aggression is the negative application of power with equally negative motives and outcomes. On the other hand, assertiveness is the controlled application of your personal power to an activity to accomplish pre-determined goals. In playing a game it is playing to your full physical, mental and spiritual potential. It Native games assertiveness was applied not to dominate the opponent to vitalize the games and apply one's spirit to their dynamic play. The assertive behaviour of Native players was non-judgmental even about the outcome of the game because both teams were playing for the same purpose...seeking life. This expression of assertive behaviour was an expression of detachment. Detachment my be described as not vesting your focus on an outcome or product but rather on the creative and dynamic process of the game itself.

Detachment of your ego from the outcome of the game helps you to remember that the real goal is cultivation of personal power, self-esteem and confidence. Ego is something that we all have and paradoxically can have both positive and negative expressions in our lives. In the mastery of a Native game or any game for that matter, the ego of the player often gets in the way. Ego is our internal psychologically invested image of our selves. We invest our egos with an internal and external sense of who we are. The ego contains our sense of self pride, self worth and external expression. If our ego is inflated meaning that we a greater view of ourselves than we really are – our ego becomes our worst enemy. With an inflated ego, our focus is on defending our sense of greatness and on external recognition and power. Detaching from such needs through a focus on a greater whole leads to selflessness or an abiding interest in the welfare and success of others. This is a major focus for Indigenous ways of thinking.

Four Arrows. Perhaps this relates to the strong emphasis on the significance of others that occurs in most traditional Indigenous child-rearing. Developing confidence and courage in children here is ultimately about attention to the greater good. Children were encouraged to develop strict discipline and a high regard for sharing with a minimum of contradictory messages about more materialistic priorities. I remember a Lakota girl sharing her candy bar award with her classmates when she won the award for missing the fewest days of school. She got in trouble with the teacher for this. In American Indian education, when a girl picked her first berries, her main thought was sharing them with others. When a child carried water for the home, many others in the community would acknowledge the importance of this, especially if courage, patience, and self-sacrifice were associated with the act. Readiness and willingness to take certain risks for the good of the family and community was the primary teaching. Daring to venture into the unknown and being decisive was a product of this teaching.

I think we can now open this dialogue to our readers. I want to close our words by reminding everyone that it is important to remember that our ability to learn about fear and courage from functional MRI machines is very limited. Neuroimaging is only just moving toward multivariate analysis (looking at the activity of many regions simultaneously), so we're still a very long way away from any real understanding of how hundreds or thousands of modules act in parallel and in concert to generate behaviours, or of the continual stream of consciousness that we experience every waking second in the real world. So the emphasis on learning courage and on the cultural influence on fear responses that we have addressed is only part of the story.

I think we can now open this dialogue to our readers. I want to close our words by reminding everyone that it is important to remember that our ability to learn about fear and courage from functional MRI machines is very limited. Neuroimaging is only just moving toward multivariate analysis (looking at the activity of many regions simultaneously), so we're still a very long way away from any real understanding of how hundreds or thousands of modules act in parallel and in concert to generate behaviours, or of the continual stream of consciousness that we experience every waking second in the real world. So the emphasis on learning courage and on the cultural influence on fear responses that we have addressed is only part of the story.

From Indigenous Wisdom we know that it is not just our brains that produce the ability to displace courage and overcome fear. There is a more mysterious dimension, a spiritual reality that we know way before our brains have time to learn. A beautiful illustration of this comes from a *Reader's Digest* story from May 1996 (p. 155–156) that happened in the neonatal intensive care unit at The Medical Center of Central Massachusetts in Worcester. Twin girls, Kyrie, the larger sister at two pounds, three ounces, and her sister Brielel, who weighed only two pounds at birth, were born 12 weeks premature. As per protocol, they were separated at birth and placed in different incubators. Brielle began having serious breathing and heart-rate problems and went into critical condition, gasping for breath and turning blue. Nurse Gayle Kasparian used all protocols to save the baby to no avail. Then Kasparian remembered something she had heard about "double-bedding" preemie twins. She took the risk with the parents permission and Kasparian's nurse manager, Susan Fitzback, was away at a conference, and the arrangement was unorthodox. But Kasparian decided to take the risk. She placed the babies in the same incubator. Immediately Brielle snuggled up to her sister, even placing her arm over her shoulder. Within moments Brielle's vital signs were at the best level they had ever been and the two continued to grow strong. If Indigenous Peoples remind us that "generosity is the greatest expression of fear," then compassion for others, as we learned in Chapter 1, may have something significant to do with fear and courage as well, and may also be a phenomenon that has more spiritual than scientific sources.

I hope our sharing of Indigenous wisdom will be given at least an equal footing when attempting to understand ways to develop courage and not be misguided or frozen by fear.

III. CONTINUING THE DIALOGUE FOR UNDERSTANDING

1. Describe the association between fear and hypnosis. How does brain research relating to hypnotic states connect to the summaries of the five studies reported in this chapter?
2. How would you explain the idea that "generosity is the greatest expression of courage? Go back to Chapter 1 and see if you can make any connections between the studies reported there and those summarized above.

REFERENCES

Carlsson, K., Petersson, K. M., Lundqvist, D., Karlsson, A., Ingvar, M., & Ohman, A. (2004). Fear and the amygdala: Manipulation of awareness generates differential cerebral responses to phobic and fear-relevant (but nonfeared) stimuli. *Emotion, 4*, 340–353.

Cheng, D. T., Knight, D. C., Smith, C. N., Stein, E. A., & Helmstetter, F. J. (2003). Functional MRI of human amygdala activity during Pavlovian fear conditioning: Stimulus processing versus response expression. *Behavioral Neuroscience, 117*, 3–10.

Lewis, P. A., Critchley, H. D., Rotshstein, P., & Dolan, R. J. (2007). Neural correlates of processing valence and arousal in affective words. *Cerebral Cortex, 17*, 742–748.

Norton, P. J., & Weiss, B. J. (2009). The role of courage on behavioral approach in a fear-eliciting situation: A proof-of-concept pilot study. *Journal of Anxiety Disorders, 23*, 212–217.

Spielberger, C. D. (1983). *Manual for the State-Trait Anxiety Inventory (STAI)*. PaloAlto, CA: Consulting Psychologists Press.

Whalen, P. J., Shin, L. M., McInerney, S. C., Fischer, H., Wright, C. I., & Rauch, C. I. (2001). A functional MRI study of human amygdala responses to facial expressions of fear versus anger. *Emotion, 1*(1), 70–83.

CHAPTER 4

HUMOR

Not only do Indians bond and revitalize scapegoat and survive through laughter, but they draw on millennia-old traditions of Trickster gods and holy fools, comic romances and epic boast.

– Kenneth Lincoln (*Indi'n Humor: Bicultural Play in Native America*, 1993, p. 22)

I. NEUROSCIENCE STUDIES OVERVIEW

Laura Rieffel, Suzanne McKann and Doug Lee

Humor is a complicated and multifaceted psychological response that is both, decreased anxiety and depression, higher self esteem, reduced stress, enhanced marital satisfaction, hope, and altruism. The shared appreciation of humor not only reinforces social bonds, it can provide a means to communicate criticism and hostility in a socially acceptable manner that protects social relationships. biological and cultural. Humor appreciation facilitates social interaction and is therefore a basic ingredient for binding social groups. Humor can help individuals cope with daily stressors and may have a positive effect on both the immune system and the central nervous system. Humor appreciation is associated with such pro social behaviours as reduced loneliness. Sex differences in areas of brain activation suggest a greater degree of executive and language based processing in females, possibly implying sex specific differences in the reward response as well as in the integration of cognition and emotion. In adults, problems with humor can be an indicator of impaired social functioning as is evident in disorders such as schizophrenia, autism, Asperger Syndrome, and nonverbal learning disorder.

Humor comprehension and appreciation require complex mental abilities. These abilities include: attention, memory, understanding high-level language, frame shifting, reanalysis and reorganization of previous, novel, and existing information, and new schema development. Whereas humor comprehension is described as the ability to perceive relationships in incongruous ways, humor appreciation refers to the ability to understand and get pleasure from humorous messages. The majority of studies looking at the underlying neurological correlates of humor are based on the incongruity resolution theory (Suls, 1972), which is a two-stage model of processing. First, there is a detection of an incongruous or unexpected element. Next, the incongruous element is connected back to the main elements of the story or joke which resolves the incongruity. Although not all humor processing involves a two stage process (for example, slapstick humor only involves incongruity detection), studies of the development of humor processing in children support a two stage model, indicating that the ability to process slapstick humor (incongruity detection) develops at an earlier age than humor necessitating incongruity resolution. This process parallels children's movement from literal meanings to a higher level pragmatic understanding of non literal language such as sarcasm and irony.

Study 1: "Humor Modulates Mesolimbic Reward Centers"

Summary. Mesolimbic reward activation occurs in response to drugs, monetary reward, beauty, etc. This study is the first to report that humor may also activate the same portions of the brain.

Description. Although studies looking at the cognitive aspects of humor are beginning to surface with more frequency, few studies have approached the question of *why* we laugh from a neurocognitive perspective. A group at Stanford University, headed by Allan Reiss (Mobbs el al, 2003), used *f*MRI technology to look for the "funny bone" in the brain. In the study, participants were shown black and white cartoons from a published series known for its outlandish outlook on contemporary society to explore reward mechanisms of humor. Some of the cartoons were modified so that key elements, which diminished funniness, were removed. Subjects were then asked to categorize the cartoons as either 'funny' or 'not funny'; these categories were used for each subject to determine which brain regions were being activated by the perception of humor. Scans revealed that when funny cartoons were compared to non-funny cartoons, there was activation of a network of cortical structures including the left temporo-occipital junction, inferior frontal gyrus, supplementary motor area. More importantly, the researchers identified a subcortical network which included the ventral striatum, anterior thalamus, ventral tegmentum, hypothalamus, amygdala and nucleus accumbens, a key component of the mesolimbic dopaminergic reward system. Furthermore, individual ratings on the degree of funniness for each of the funny cartoons, revealed a relationship between ratings of funniness and the amount of increased blood flow to these areas, with higher ratings of funniness resulting in greater increases in blood flow.

Their study was notable for being the first to report mesolimbic reward activation, a region of the brain also implicated in the pleasurable response to methamphetamines, cocaine, monetary reward, and attractive faces. While some individuals make extensive use of humor as a stress-reduction mechanism, others do not. The authors hypothesize that, perhaps, people who rely less on humor as a coping mechanism, may find humor less rewarding. Given that one of the central symptoms of depression is the inability to feel a sense of reward from previously pleasurable activities, assessing how the brain's reward center responds to humor may be beneficial in the diagnosis of mood disorders.

Study 2: "The Functional Anatomy of Humor"

Summary. The appreciation of humor involves the juxtaposition of mental sets, a cognitive task, followed by feelings of amusement, the affective component. Different kinds of jokes affect different parts of the brain.

Description. Using *f*MRI, Goel and Dolan (2001) scanned 14 subjects while they listened to jokes in an attempt to isolate these two components of humor. The researchers used 30 semantic jokes (e.g. What do engineers use for birth control?.... Their personalities) and 30 phonological jokes or puns (e.g. Why did the golfer wear two sets of pants?... He got a hole in one), presented to the subjects in random order. Additionally, they set up a baseline condition by presenting the setup lines from the same jokes, but this time the setups were followed merely by descriptive statements.

Although some studies have suggested involvement of the right hemisphere in semantic joke processing, Goel and Dolan's study (2001) suggests that what may actually be captured in these studies is the right temporal lobe's involvement in the integrative process required for coherence, rather than the amusing affective component of the task. Whereas semantic juxtaposition involves the bilateral temporal lobes, puns use a left hemisphere network centered around regions of speech production. It appears that although semantic jokes versus puns involve processing in different areas of the brain, there is common activation of the medial ventral prefrontal cortex's reward system.

Study 3: "Humor comprehension"

Summary. Both hemispheres are involved in humor processing. Studies have suggested that patients with right brain lesions have difficulty with humor comprehension. In contrast, neuroimaging studies suggest that it is the left hemisphere that is involved in both humor detection and comprehension. Previous studies have used verbal jokes or nonverbal cartoons with captions, which may create a bias towards left hemisphere activation. Alternatively, the right hemisphere's role in the processing of higher level language skills, such as comprehension of metaphors or recognizing the moral of a story, may create a bias towards emphasizing the role of the right hemisphere. This contiguity between language and humor processing has made identification of neural networks difficult.

Description. In response to these conflicting results Bartolo, Benuzzi, Nocetti, Baraldi, and Nichelli (2005) used fMRI studies to assess the neural networks involved in the components of humor comprehension and appreciation. Bartolo et al. hypothesized that previously conflicting results may be due to the way humor is researched. For example, verbal material might bias neuroimaging studies for left hemisphere activation and nonverbal cartoons may activate different brain regions based on the comprehension of attributes and intentions.

For this study, the researchers presented each of 21 volunteers, ranging in age from 23 to 36 years, with two cartoons. The storyline began in the first cartoon and ended in the second cartoon in either a funny or neutral way. The cartoons required effort to attribute intention to characters in order to comprehend the story. The funny cartoon pairs showed incongruity from disconfirmation of the intentions initially attributed to the characters in the first cartoon. To resolve the incongruity, participants needed to attribute different intentions for the cartoon characters. Since detection and resolution of incongruity occurred at the same time, during the presentation of the punch line, the researchers proposed that the activated regions involved in the incongruity resolution would be the same for both the funny and not funny cartoons. Any other activated areas would, presumably, be attributable to incongruity detection and amusement. Participants were scanned while presented with funny and neutral stimuli cartoons on monitors above their head in the fMRI and follow-up ratings of the cartoons were administered immediately after subjects were out of the scanner. Temporal resolutions were optimized by focusing on the mesial temporal and part of the frontal lobes at the exclusion of other regions of the brain that may involve humor processing. Results of the experiment showed that subjects' responses to cartoons perceived as funny were faster than to cartoons perceived as not funny. Bartolo et al.'s (2003) analyses revealed that, as expected, both the right and left hemispheres were involved in comprehending and processing humor stimuli, and feelings of amusement. Their findings of fMRI data indicated activation of the right inferior frontal gyrus, left middle temporal gyrus, left superior temporal gyrus, and left cerebellum. Related to feelings of amusement, fMRI data indicated the activation of the left amygdala often identified with the processing of positive emotion.

Study 4: "Right Hemisphere and Joke Comprehension"

Summary. Coulson and Wu (2005) completed two experiments where event-related brain potentials (ERPs) were used to assess neural activity associated with joke comprehension. The research was specifically designed to determine whether semantic activation for joke comprehension affected the right and left hemispheres differently. The authors hypothesized that the *coarse semantic coding* in the right hemisphere aided high-level language tasks such as joke comprehension. Coarse semantic coding is believed to occur when words represented in the RH activate a wide array of semantic fields. Words represented in the left hemisphere (LH) are more related to the immediate context of language activating a narrow range of features and understanding. Stimulating the wide semantic fields in the RH leads to possibilities for increased comprehension through a broader and more diverse interpretation of information. The authors also hypothesized that hemispheric differences in semantic activations would be modulated when the visual fields (VF) were manipulated.

Description. Participants in Experiment 1a and 1b included sixteen adults, aged 18–36, who received monetary payment or university credit for their efforts. Jokes used in the study required frame shifting for their comprehension with the "punch-word" the last word of the sentence. Control sentences had straight endings consistent with the frame or schema evoked by the sentence. For joke sentences, the endings facilitated frame shifting and probe words were related to the humorous inferences in the jokes and unrelated to the themes and content of the straight control sentences. For Experiment, 1a (sentences comprehension trial) each participant read experimental probes where half were preceded by jokes and half by straight endings. In Experiment 1b (word trial) each participant read probes, half preceded by a sentence-final word taken from a joke and half by a sentence-final word taken from a straight control sentence.

In Experiment 1a (comprehension sentence trial), subjects were instructed to read sentences one word at a time and to focus their eyes at all times on a central point just below where the words were presented. After the probe word appeared, they were to read silently without moving their eyes and then say the word aloud when a blue question mark appeared. If they were unable to read the word, they were instructed to say "no." Subjects were asked to press "yes" if the comprehension probe supported the preceding sentences or press "no" if it did not make sense.

In Experiment 1b (word reading), subjects were asked to read two words in a row, reading the second word out loud when the blue question mark appeared, or saying "no" if they had been unable to read it. No comprehension questions were in this part of the experiment as in Experiment 1a. The scalp recorded brain potential (ERPs) amplitudes were measured while subjects read probe words presented after a joke or non funny control sentence.

Experiment 2 included sixteen volunteers who were healthy, monolingual English speakers right-handed, between the ages 18-25 with normal vision acuity and no history of neurological disorders. Experiment 2 using the same sentences and directions for Experiment 1a. In Experiment 2 participants were asked to read the sentences one word at a time; however, the probe words were not presented centrally on the monitor. *Left visual field* (LVF) probe words were placed so the last character in the word was 2 degrees to the left of the of the center of the monitor and the *right visual field* (RVF) probes were presented so the first character was 2 degrees to the right of the center of the monitor. Eye movements were monitored.

Findings for Experiment 1a supported the authors' hypotheses that coarse semantic coding in the RH aided high-level language tasks such as joke comprehension. The priming of joke-related information with sentences rather than one word probes yielded semantic activation in both hemispheres with greater activity in the RH and more narrow activation in the LH in Experiment 1b.

In Experiment 2, the authors' hypothesis that the priming effect was larger when words were presented to the left visual field (LVF) than to the right visual field (RVF) was supported. These results suggested that joke-relevant information was more active in the RH. Larger LVF effects were recorded from both relatively more positive ERPs for related probes and more negative ERPs to unrelated probes.

In conclusion, the authors reported that joke-relevant information triggered more activity in the RH for abstractions, but the LH was important for controlled retrieval in semantic language comprehension. In addition, hemispheric differences in semantic activations were believed to be modulated when visual fields (VF) were manipulated. They suggest that these hemispheric differences reflect right hemisphere coding of thematic information. This is supported by evidence that patients with right hemisphere damage have greater difficulties than those with left hemisphere damage in recalling story themes.

Study 5: "Social Regulation of Humor Response"

Summary. These results suggest that the VMPFC and the hippocampus regions are implicated in the regulation of humor by social norms. The neural responses on *f*MRI results suggested a reciprocal response pattern between the VMPFC and hippocampus regions

Description. The perception of funniness in adult humor typically pushes the boundaries of social norms as a means to create the element of surprise necessary for the experience of humor. However, pushing social boundaries too far leads to the attenuation of the experience of humor. Thus, social norms serve as regulators of the experience of humor. Researchers Goel and Dolan (2007) studied the neural basis of the social regulation of the affective experience of humor when offensive norm violations were presented to adults in cartoons. In this research project, 16 right-handed adults were scanned while observing cartoons that varied in funniness and socially accepted norms. Two groups emerged with one group finding the cartoons less offensive and those finding them more offensive. The group that found the cartoons more offensive showed a negative correlation between funniness and social appropriateness (e.g., the greater the perception of social violation and inappropriateness, the less funny the cartoon was perceived). Neural responses for this group showed an enhanced activation of the right hippocampus along with relative deactivation in the ventral medial prefrontal cortex (VMPFC) on the *f*MRI. In the group that found the jokes less offensive, neural activity on the *f*MRI had an opposite effect for the interaction of funniness by social appropriateness. Results of the *f*MRI for this group showed activation of the ventral medial prefrontal cortex (VMPFC) and relative deactivation in the right hippocampus with implication for the contextual regulation of behaviour and memory.

II. INDIGENOUS PERSPECTIVES DIALOGUE

Greg Cajete, Jongmin Lee and Four Arrows

Four Arrows. I think these studies indicate that humor is a high level, complex phenomenon that requires complementary activity in right and left brain hemispheres, a requirement for all human behaviors that lend themselves to balanced living and, well, happiness or to prevent, as one study indicates, mood disorders. Are these studies enough, however, to bring neurophilosphers to cry for more widespread use of humor in human interactions? In Indigenous stories, ceremonies and daily life was designed to be processed in both hemispheres so as to maximize its benefit for the society at large and not simply to excite a pleasure/ reward center as many of the studies might imply. It would seem that when individuals and their cultures lose their sense of humor in everyday matters, they also lose their sense of being in balance then. Although humor is found in every culture, it seems to me that our dominant, Eurocentric cultural approach to humor tends to compartmentalize it into venues of entertainment or satire and also tends to orient it to more left brain activities that do not always lend to social balance. It is there for entertainment if one chooses. Or if someone ones to buy a satirical publication, that is possible. If its benefit is indeed a way to keep individuals and society in positive, healthy relationships, then the studies do not seem to serve neurophilosophy as full as might a study of a culture or cultures that carefully employed humor in all aspects of life.

Indeed, humor is woven into the fabric of most Indigenous cultures and always has been. The highly respected Lakota scholar, Vine Deloria, Jr., once told me that no Indian movement is possible without it. Any neurophilosophy surrounding these studies might best be grounded in understanding Indigenous cultures where humor has been a more intentionally fundamental part of daily life. For example, in most American Indian ways of being in the world, people find humor in almost all their problems. Most of life's experiences have been articulated in jokes of some form. Teasing is the major approach to child discipline and social control, but it is not a mean-spirited teasing, but rather a way of sharing the awkward imbalance that we all suffer from time to time. In anticipation of such teasing, people joke about themselves to help put behaviors back into balance and for the good of all. Humor is a vital part of all social situations and helps assure equality and group acceptance. In the Navajo culture, the first sacred right in life is the celebration of a baby's first laugh. It is seen as evidence that the soul and body are joined. The person who made the baby laugh takes responsibility for holding a celebration whereby the child gives gifts to the people to help assure the baby will grow up to be generous.

In fact, I do not at all think it is a stretch of logic to suggest that the understanding Indigenous Peoples have regarding the power of humor and the ways most have built it into their existence is largely responsible for our continued existence in the face of remarkable oppression for centuries. Laguna/Sioux poet, Paula Gunn Allen, in her 1986 book, *The Sacred Hoop: Recovering the Feminine in American Indian Traditions,* wrote:

> *Humor is widely used by Indians to deal with life. Indian gatherings are marked by laughter and jokes, many directed at the horrors of history, at the continuing impact of colonization, and at the biting knowledge that living as an exile in one's own land necessitates. . . . Certainly the time frame we presently inhabit has much that is shabby and tricky to offer; and much that needs to be treated with laughter and ironic humor (p. 158).*

If we all could embrace such humor more consistently in the many facets of our personal and collective lives we would be able to better handle the many challenges now facing us all. Consider the power of Will Rogers, a member of the

Cherokee nation, and how it changed the world. In keeping with his learned Indigenous values, his humor contained the courage to challenge everything the conquering United States stood for that was out of balance. Perhaps this is why his twenty one movies have never been released by Fox studies.

Rogers lived from 1879 to 1935. His political humor prompted the kind of reflection we could have used during the Bush administration and still could it seem. "About all I can say for the United States Senate is that it opens with a prayer and closes with an investigation." Why are not more of our public figures engaging such humor more regularly? Here are a few more as examples:

- "Adverstising is the art of convincing people to spend money they don't have for something they don't need."
- Diplomacy is the art of saying "Nice doggie" until you can find a rock.
- Diplomats are just as essential to starting a war as soldiers are for finishing it.
- You take diplomacy out of war, and the thing would fall flat in a week."
- "Do the best you can, and don't take life too serious."
- "Everybody is ignorant, only on different subjects."

That Cherokee traditions and his Cherokee father were responsible for Will Rogers' approach to humor is established in a recent scholarly book that also talks about how he was a major force in helping Americans get through the depression of the 1930s. The book, written by Dr. Larry May of the University of Minnesota, is entitled, *The Big Tomorrow: Hollywood and the Politics of the American Way* and was published by the University of Chicago Press in 2000. May shows how Rogers used his humor and the technology of talking pictures to end isolationist thinking among Americans. May shows that Rogers' Cherokee thinking single-handedly changed much of the Anglo-Saxon values that marginalized women and people of color, following in his father's footsteps. Recounting Clem Rogers' role as a cavalry scout for Confederate forces in the Civil War, May said Will Rogers' father set to recreate a "balance in the universe" that affirmed minorities' rights to land, public education and the right to vote.

An expert on Will Rogers, Joseph Carter, author of *The Quotable Will Rogers* (2006), wrote a book review of Mays' book, Joseph H. Carter noted the Cherokee values that pervaded Rogers' work:

> Although Will Rogers' father would become wealthy, May noted that he was a foremost philanthropist who gave away large sums. Clem Rogers also upheld the Cherokee tradition of women's rights, including suffrage and property ownership...
>
> In talking movies, May said that Will Rogers "did the impossible" by using the popular art to "stimulate instead of thwart" radical reform during the depth of the depression of the 1930s...
>
> May noted that during this dark period, the very rich–or one-tenth of 1 per cent of the population–earned as much as the bottom 42 per cent of American people, a condition that drew some of Will Rogers' sharpest criticism...

> Will Rogers championed a Cherokee belief that "balance must inform all part of life..."
>
> His views, portrayed in twenty-one hit movies, drew controversy, but Will Rogers did not change...
>
> May noted that the Cherokee Nation gave Will Rogers a view of the West as a place where "freedom and community merged" in the place of individualism which were exhibited in many of his movies now owned by Twentieth Century-Fox Corporation...
>
> "Americanism emerging from the bottom rather than the top of the social order" was made clear by the rise of Will Rogers from the urban world of vaudeville and the penny press to become the top male box-office star of the early 1930s...

Thus Rogers used humor in traditional American Indian style to help change beliefs that no longer maintained balanced relationships. It is obvious that his work reflects the trickster characters that inform many American Indian, Alaskan Native and Aboriginal teaching stories. An excellent book that explains in depth the trickster role in learning to live a balanced life is *Living Sideways: Tricksters in American Indian Oral Traditions* by Franchot Ballinger. But Greg, our goal in this dialogue is to merely say enough about Indigenous wisdom to offer neurophilosophy a road map so it will not get lost in the confusions and detours of Western directions. Can you say a few words about how Indigenous ideas about humor relate to these studies our nueropsychologists have summarized for us?

Greg. The basis of traditional Indigenous storying telling is related to four disciplines, and the trickster characters help with all three. These disciplines are attention, creative imagination, flexibility and fluency of thinking. I was thinking of how Will Rogers employed each of these in his humor. Humor recontextualizes ideas and behaviours, sometimes pointing out the absurdities of behaviours that ignore appropriate contexts. When we see ourselves in these stories and can laugh at them and ourselves, we cultivate a humility which in turn prepares us to better understand the discipline of giving attention. Attention in the Indigenous sense has to do with the focus of all these senses. Seeing, listening, feeling, smelling, hearing, and intuiting are important for this, as are all the feelings and emotions in the affective domain.

I think this latter aspect, the affective considerations, stand out as important considerations in the brain research that has been presented. The right frontal lobes were identified as being vital for humor appreciation and for emotional responsiveness. The right brain is also involved in metaphor interpretation. Humor and irony as presenting in Indigenous story telling is an obvious way to assure right brain involvement and thus holistic understanding in the learning context via the disciplines I mentioned.

Of course, celebration is also a very important part of learning to live in balance. Celebrating the joyfulness, even in the contradictions and tragedies we face in life, is a crucial aspect of Indigenous humor and why humorous activities are often a part of Indigenous ceremonies. Oscar Kawagley has said that Yup'ik rituals and ceremonies focus on three things; centering or balancing within oneself and the world; reciprocation to the plants and animals that we must kill in order to live; and the expression of joy and humor. As a third leg of the stool then, perhaps humor fosters mental flexibility and positive emotions in ways that encourage holistic thinking and problem solving. Cultures that understand this along with the value of balance and reciprocity say all there is to say about survival and happiness.

Jongmin. I am thinking about how the last study talked about pushing boundaries of humor into deviating from social norms and effect on brain function in terms of the kind of humor Will Rogers and Indigenous cultures seem to maintain that has not typically done this. This positive humor induces relaxation in brain functions that are balanced in both hemispheres. As an Asian, I can only offer that the Buddha practiced a high level of humor and, like Ghandi, disarmed his opponents often with it. The stories in Buddhism often tell of his enemies winding up laughing at themselves and then joining him in collaboration. Although he taught the facts about human suffering, he taught that a person could not be enlightened without being joyful. Many of the Buddhist dogmas talk about the lighter-heartedness of his followers. Now I know his focus on the ultimate joy being in another world is contrary to Indigenous wisdom. Perhaps for this reason it is not so strong a part of ceremony and story telling, nor such a vital component of Oriental cultures after our Indigenous ways were overtaken.

Four Arrows. It is interesting to speculate as to how humor and its use may have changed as social injustice and oppression and conquering became common place, which they, as mentioned earlier, were not in most pre-contact Indigenous cultures.

Jongmin. No doubt laughter has the ability to release tension. Gandhi offered it as a non-violent outlet for dissent. It may be an escape from life's incongruities. The role of humor in South Korea has an interesting history. In some ways, it does not have the strong role as American Indians have given it. After all, the three influences, Buddhism, Confuciansim and Taoism each in their own ways emphasized self-restraint and serious attention. Perfect virtue, says Confucius, is to always practice gravity, generosity of soul, sincerity, earnestness and kindness. All three teach self-restraint and respect for superiors and acting with propriety in everything one says and does.

On the other hand humor was used to release the stress of wars, invasion, occupation and hierarchy. Especially Taoism, which is more like Indigenous philosophy than Western in its effort to be one with Nature, encouraged a joyful perspective on the relationship between humans and nature in its art especially. So in South Korea, humor is carefully used, certainly not as obviously nor as extensively, but significantly nonetheless, to overcome sadness, to foster optimism and hope, to allow for resistance to oppression, to inform metaphors that remind us of our common humanity.

Four Arrows. I think the use of humor in all these ways to counter negativity is common in all countries it seems. The connection to a more Indigenous relationship to Nature is especially interesting Jongmin, but I'm wondering if the hierarchical structures are ultimately what keeps both Western and Asian humor in a more subtle position than in Indigenous cultures.

I used to give a lecture about Indigenous approaches to conflict resolution. One of them had to do with the good sense of humor that surrounded someone suffering from cognitive dissonance. People would laugh good heartedly, saying, "It is human to be in such contradiction my friend, now let's see what we can do to get it back in balance if we can."

Jongmin. Well, cognitive dissonance creates a discomfort in the brain with regard to holding two ideas at the same time that are not compatible, so if humor can be the thing to release that tension that is good and it is even better if in the release of tension there is a sufficient moral to the joke so that a less contradictory position can be chosen by the person. You know Daniel Wegner wrote a book called *The Illusion of Conscious Will* (2002)where he says it may be that people often or always operate according to more or less unconscious directives. Your Coyote stories seem to be a way to admit that we really don't have so much control of our choices as we may think. Maybe this is also why Zen Buddhism teaches about letting go of the pretense of control and teaches that when one recognizes the illusion of conscious will, then enlightenment comes. So maybe enlightenment is when everything is seen as a great cosmic joke.

Four Arrows. I can't believe you said that. My friend, Dan Millman, author of many spiritual and "new age" books used to tell me that life is a cosmic joke to calm me down about some activism I was doing. I used to disagree with him but I eventually came around to agreeing that he might have it right.

Jongmin. So our clowns, coyotes and comedians can expose this illusion for us perhaps. The humor, like that of Will Rogers's, helps us confront our foolishness and fears and helps us challenge power which we can do better I think when our brain is firing on both sides as a reaction to humor.

Greg. This way to break cognitive dissonance we feel when we recognize our contradiction in a way for us to work toward a more consistent way of being in the world requires compassion and humor, according to Indian wisdom. Conflict resolution in Indigenous cultures always employs humor. Teasing has been the primary vehicle for child discipline and for control of social situations. Tricksters may criticize society's rules, but they do so in behalf of a higher social cohesion.

When our thoughts or actions conflict or contradict the real world, or when our emotions and reasoning do not mesh, then the tricksters dramatize our silliness and make us laugh at it so we can change. We should note that much of the humor in our stories help us move from being overly individualistic to being more concerned with community.

Four Arrows. In his remarkable book, *Living Sideways: Tricksters in American Indian Oral Traditions (*2006), Franchot Ballinger talks a lot about how laughter at egocentricity helps define the nature of our humanity and how amusing tragedies happen to us we when we are too driven by individual desires. I remember one Winnebego trickster story in the book about how the trickster's right and left arms get in an argument while he is skinning a buffalo ending up with his arms being cut. Grasping at social status, tricksters attempt to draw upon resources they do not have, and call the attempt, Power, when in fact it is nothing but warped in self-defeating self-aggrandizement.

Greg. Humor gets to the heart of things. I think the Hopi word for "clowning" is the same word they use for getting an important idea across to someone. In any event, in most tribes that I know of, humor is a vital part of all the most important interactions. In fact, the most serious conversations are often conducted with the most humor. Humor was literally vital. Trickster stories used humor to show how certain ways of acting could be dangerous to the tribe. In order to be fully educated, one had to understand the meaning of the humor in these stories to help assure that rules remained appropriate and when appropriate were followed. Imagine the difference in the Western world if all the people had memorized to heart trickster stories that taught the citizens of nations better and deeper understandings about greed and power and deception and alienation from Nature.

Making stories, especially stories that parody the possible imbalances humans can create in themselves, the vehicle for such deep understanding requires knowing how to mobilize the imagination to interact with the content of a story, to realize their innate awareness of story. Humor can help with this process. The myths we live by define us and if we are alienated from the roots of our primal stories, then our art and images entertain us but do not guide us. If humor connects us to language and understanding as Study 3 indicates, then it can help us live our images. The loss of humor in Western though and philosophy has caused it to become fragmented. Fragmentation arises from strict "objective" analysis and reductionism. Humor offers context. Meaning is context dependent. Indigenous wisdom emphasizes humor in all things because it recognizes that harmony and balance must accommodate change and change inevitably requires addressing the activities of the trickster. Certainly the studies that were presented in this chapter support a return to such an emphasis on humor to contemporary Western society, but without the importance indicated by Indigenous wisdom, the neurophilosophy of Westerners is not likely to underscore this importance.

III. CONTINUING THE DIALOGUE FOR UNDERSTANDING

1. Name two vital benefits of humor to human social interactions that are revealed in the studies and something about the costs to society, specifically, that result from not employing humor to the degree that Indigenous cultures employed it.

2. What can a collaboration between neuroscience and Indigenous wisdom ultimately do for guiding humans toward balance and harmony in their lives as relates to the topic of humor?

REFERENCES

Allen, P. G. (1986). *The sacred hoop: Recovering the feminine in American Indian traditions*. Boston: Beacon Press.

Ballinger, F. (2004). *Living sideways: Tricksters in American indian oral traditions*. Norman, OK: University of Oklahoma Press.

Bartolo, A., Benuzzi, B., Nocetti, L., Baraldi, P., & Nichelli, P. (2006). Humor comprehension and appreciation: An fMRI study. *Journal of Cognitive Science, 18*(2), 1789–1798.

Carter, J. (2001). Book review on Internet. Retrieved April 11, 2009, from http://www.willrogers.com/writers/stories/molded/Molded.html

Carter, J. (2006). *The quotable will rogers*. Latin, Utah: Gibbs Smith Publishers.

Coulson, S., & Wu, Y. C. (2005). Right hemisphere activation of joke-related information: An event-related brain potential. *Journal of Cognitive Neuroscience, 17*, 494–506.

Goel, V., & Dolan, R. J. (2001). The functional anatomy of humor: Segregating cognitive and affective components. *Nature Neuroscience, 4*(3), 237–238.

Goel, V., & Dolan, R. J. (2007). Social regulation of affective experience of humor. *Journal of Cognitive Neuroscience, 19*, 1754–1580.

May, L. (Ed.). (2000). *The big tomorrow: Hollywood and the politics of the american way. Chicago: University of Chicago Press.*

Mobbs, D., Greicius, M. D., Abdel-Azim, E., Menon, V., & Reiss, A. L. (2003). Humor modulates the mesolimbic reward centers. *Neuron, 40*, 1041–1048.

Neuroscience, 18(2), 1789–1798.

Shammi, P., & Stuss, D. T. (1999). Humour appreciation: A role of the right frontal lobe. *Brain, 122*, 657–666.

Suls, J. (1972). A two-stage model for the appreciation of jokes and cartoons. In J. H. Goldstein & P. E. McGhee (Eds.), *The psychology of humor: Theoretical perspective and empirical issues*. New York: Academic Press.

Wegner, D. M. (2002). *The illusion of conscious will*. Cambridge: MIT Press

CHAPTER 5

ART

Art was, and is, a central component of the traditional way of life, of significance in the political domain, in the relationships between clans, and in the relations between men and women. Art was and remains an important component of the system of restricted knowledge, and at a more metaphysical level is the major means of recreating ancestral events, ensuring continuity with the ancestral past, and communicating with the spirit world.

– Howard Morphy (1991) *in Ancestral Connections London: University of Chicago Press*

I. NEUROSCIENCE STUDIES OVERVIEW

Dana Konopka, Virginia A. Hernandez and Margaret Loo

Throughout time, art has been ever-present in all societies and cultures, suggesting that there are shared neuroanatomical structures and cognitive processes that occur within the human brain which allow for the creation of the various forms of art (Zaidel, 2005). There is a growing fascination with the relationship between neuroscience and the arts. Emotion, music, learning, art, beauty, empathy, dance, desire: neuropsychologists have taken a keen interest in all these somewhat loosely-related topics in recent years, revealing new things about the way our brains work, adding credence to the use of the arts in therapy, and adding much to our understanding of what it means to be creative and to be human. Research supports the notion that regardless of the form it takes, (music, drawings, dance, etcetera) art has been identified as a universal way for humans to express themselves (Tramo, 2001). Since art is such a complex form of expression, it is fair to assume that art is produced across multiple regions within the brain (Zaidel, 2005). Instead, art is more of a whole brain production, demonstrating neural networking across hemispheres (Zaidel, 2005).

Study 1: "The Neural Correlates of Beauty"

Summary. The researchers concluded that for a painting to be esthetically judged as ugly or beautiful, the brain must process the picture most strongly in the area specialized for that classification. It appears that a change in the relative activity of the orbito-frontal cortex, an area of the brain involved in feelings of reward, is associated with the judgment of "ugly" or "beautiful."

Description. In attempting to determine whether there are specific brain areas that activate when people perceive a painting as beautiful or ugly, Kawabata and Zeki (2004) at University College of London showed hundreds of paintings to 10 right-handed, healthy young adult students, 5 men and 5 women, with no special art or art history experience. The four categories of paintings - abstracts, still lifes, portraits, and landscapes - appeared on computer monitors and were first scored by each subject as either "ugly," (score 1–4), "neutral," (score 5–6) or "beautiful" (score 7–10). Paintings classified by some as "beautiful" were classified by others as "ugly" and vice versa, so for each subject a unique presentation was designed based on these preliminary exercises. Then, subjects were each presented with the paintings that they had classified, in a controlled quasi-random order, and they pressed buttons to indicate whether each painting was ugly, neutral, or beautiful while an fMRI scanner monitored brain activity. Results showed that viewing different categories of paintings produced different strengths of activity in various areas of the visual brain. Painting deemed "beautiful," when appearing amongst paintings deemed "ugly," activated the medial orbito-frontal cortex alone, and when contrasted with neutral painting, they also activated the anterior cingulate gyrus and the left parietal cortex. Ugly paintings, when appearing amongst beautiful paintings, also bilaterally activated the motor cortex, but produced little activity when contrasted with neutral paintings. The activation of the motor cortex in response to aversive stimuli is not a new finding; previous studies found that bilateral activation of the motor cortex also occurred during the viewing of ugly or fearful faces or other emotionally salient stimuli such as anger (Armory & Dolan 2002; Dougherty et al., 1999, in Kawabata & Zeki, 2004). It is possible that unpleasant stimuli activate the motor cortex more than pleasant stimuli do because it is more important for the brain to prepare to move away from, or to defend against, a source of potential danger than to move toward pleasant stimuli (Kawabata & Zeki, 2004).

Study 2: "Music and Emotion Connection"

Summary. Music stimulates a variety of emotions. This study reveals the possibility that musical training and understanding of tone and pitch may determine emotional response. They provide the explanation that the songs they used were better known at the time of the previous studies than at the time of their study, which supports the cognitivist position that reactions to music are learned.

Description. Thompson, Schellengerg and Husain (2004) found that seven-year-old children who studied piano and drama were capable of making more accurate emotional judgments about the prosody of spoken utterances than children who did not take such lessons. They also found that the benefits of music lessons did not apply to children who took singing lessons. They attributed this disparity to singing's emphasis of non-prosodic uses of the voice and particularly for the imprecise pitch levels and intervals of children's voices. However, alternate factors such as method of teaching and amount of practice could have accounted for their lower performance (Thompson, Schellengerg, & Husain). If the process of detecting emotion in speech prosody is the same as in music, then Thompson, Schellengerg, and Husain's proposal that music training benefits the ability to decode emotion in speech prosody makes sense.

Rather than present only this study to make the connections between music and emotion, we would like to cite a number of related studies in order to better summarize the latest research on this topic. Numerous studies have built support for the emotivist position that music elicits emotions. Many of these studies have evaluated emotional responses to music by recording physiological measures such as skin conductance, heart rate, respiration, blood pressure, and electroencephalograph (Sloboda & Juslin, 2007). When people are emotionally aroused, there is measurable activation of the sympathetic nervous system: heart rate, respiration, and blood pressure increase, and skin temperature decreases, in preparation for fight or flight action. Such physiological arousal has also been associated with emotional responses to music (Rickard, 2004). Tempo, vividness, and pitch in music have been found to be key factors in this phenomenon (Nielzen & Cesarec, 1982). For instance, tempo is directly related to evoking various emotions changing the arousal level of the listener (Rickard). Fast tempo is associated with excitement, happiness, surprise, anger, fear, and an overall increase in arousal level; slow tempo is associated with calmness, solemnity, tenderness, sadness, and an overall decrease in arousal level (Bruner, 1990; Thompson & Robataille, 1992). Schubert (2007) found that the higher an arousal level that a musical piece creates, the more listeners prefer it over a piece that creates lower arousal. The intense emotional arousal that a piece of music produces increases physical changes in the listener in contrast to less emotionally arousing music (Rickard, 2004). Sloboda (1991) found that physical reactions to music, such as chills and goose bumps, were associated with new harmonies, sudden dynamic changes, and textural changes.

It is difficult to separate whether it is the novelty of the change in sound that elicits these reactions or whether the recognition of change in the music is cognitively developed. A study by Grewe, Nagel, Kopiez and Altenmuller (2007) sought to determine the capacity of entire musical pieces to alter physiological change, motor activation, and subjective feelings and to identify distinct musical events that induce significant change. They found less evidence of music evoking reactions such as chills, goose bumps, and shivers down the spine than in previous studies, and they could not find musical events that produced affective events. They provide the explanation that the songs they used were better known at the time of the previous studies than at the time of their study, which supports the cognitivist position that reactions to music are learned.

Study 3: "Music syntax as a Language Structure"

Summary. Maess, Koelsch, Grunter, and Friederick (2001) purported that music is structured with syntax similar to language. Their results strengthen the hypothesis that detection of musical syntax, like language, is an implicit ability.

Description. They investigated how cognitive processing of music is influenced by the context of the preceding musical tones. For instance, in Western music, harmonic progressions and melodies in music can seem to make sense because of its correspondence to speech tones such as in the tonal progression IV to I corresponding to the "amen" at the end of a hymn illustrating the preferences for certain harmonic intervals in music. Another example is the feeling of closure at the end of a song such as the harmonic progression from the V chord to the I chord which simulates the descending vocal prosody at the end of a sentence. The investigators conducted event-related brain potential (ERP) experiments to study the cognitive processing of the buildup of expected tonal context and the brain processing of tonal violations of "non-musicians." They found that expected in-key chord progressions elicited similar ERPs as words in a complete sentence.

Koelsch, Gunter, Friederici, and Schröger (2000) also investigated whether "non-musicians," defined as individuals who never learned to play a musical instrument or never had music and/or singing lessons, are affected by musical syntax. They found that unexpected dissonant chords, introduced instead of chord progressions following Western theory of classical music, elicited neural processes detected by event-related brain potential (ERP) effects which were similar in amplitude to ERPs elicited by words following the course of a sentence. By using "nonmusicians," the investigators ensured that the results would have broader generalization. Their results strengthen the hypothesis that detection of musical syntax, like language, is an implicit ability.

Study 4: "Music Recruits Domain-General Attention and Working Memory Circuits"

Summary. Music is a whole-brain production, and they have strong implications toward the influence of artistic training upon the learning process and ultimately upon the structure of the brain. Training within the arts promotes various forms of learning; furthermore, these studies demonstrate that changes to brain structures may occur with early exposure to such training.

Description. As defined by Janata, Tillmann, & Bharucha (2002) polyphonic music can be viewed as a synthesis of multiple streams, where the whole is appreciated but individual parts can also be analyzed. Although previous studies have focused upon selective attention to one of two streams of stimuli, little research has focused upon selective attention with more than two streams of stimuli. Thus, the current experiment was conducted in order to determine which areas of the brain are utilized during attentive listening, and which other areas are recruited during selective listening when listeners are presented with simultaneously occurring streams of auditory stimuli.

Research conducted by the authors involved two experiments designed to identify which brain areas were being utilized during attentive versus selective listening of musical excerpts (Janata, Tillmann, & Bharucha, 2002). Comparisons made between listening conditions with single instruments versus attending to multiple instruments demonstrated considerable differences depending upon the demands of the specific tasks required. Overall, Janata et al (2002) found that attentive listening to music utilizes areas of the brain that serve general functions as opposed to music-specific ones. According to the authors, results indicate that attentive listening enlists neural circuits associated with the following: attention, motor imagery, semantic processing, target detection, and working memory.

Study 5: "Emotion and Embodiment: Mirror Neurons in Dance Therapy"

Summary. This study reinforces the close connection between body and mind and between body posture and emotional considerations. It concludes that these connections can support the importance of dance therapy for issues such as anger.

Description. Winters (2008) cites recent research in social psychology and neuroscience to support the concept of *embodiment*, or the idea that thoughts, emotions, and attitudes are grounded in the body (Koch, 2006; Niedenthal et al., 2005; Barsalou et al., 2003, in Winters). This new view represents a shift in psychology away from the dualistic view of cognition, the long-held belief that body and mind are separate entities that ought to be treated as such. Several studies conducted over the last twenty-five years have shown that the bodily states that one experiences can produce similar bodily states and affective experiences in observers. Bodily posture has been shown to be even more important than facial expression in discerning emotion; in situations in which facial expressions and bodily postures are in conflict, people tend to pay more attention to the emotions expressed by the body than to facial expressions (Meeren, Van Heijnsbergen, & de Gelder, 2005, in Winters).

In Winters's latest study, the researchers sought to explore the differences between observing another's bodily posture and actually assuming the posture oneself. Participants were asked to categorize people in a variety of postures and to answer in an open-ended format to allow for a wide range of responses. There were two conditions in this study; in one condition, participants observed a model embodying the various postures from the DANVA-POS (Diagnostic Analysis of Nonverbal Accuracy Test of Posture), and in the other, participants viewed photographs of the postures and embodied each one themselves. Responses were coded for basic emotions: sad, happy, fearful, angry, embarrassed/ashamed, and surprised. The 41 voluntary participants, 4 men and 37 women, were master's students of creative arts therapy or bachelor-level students of psychology, and they were each randomly assigned to one of the two conditions. The results showed no significant difference between responses in the posture-embodying condition and the posture-observing condition. The one notable exception was that participants were more likely to identify an emotion as anger in the embodiment condition. The researchers attributed this result to the idea that anger is a more primitive, unconscious, and culturally-suppressed emotion that originates in the limbic system and directly stimulates physical behavior in response to threats and physiological needs. The strong, primitive connection between anger and behavior could explain why embodying certain bodily postures, especially those involving crossed arms, forward-leaning, or fists, unconsciously triggers feelings of anger (Winters, 2008).

Dance/movement therapists are trained to perceive emotions in patients' bodily postures and to mirror those emotions in order to achieve an empathic connection. The Winters (2008) study reinforces the importance of dance/movement therapy, particularly in dealing with feelings of anger, and it also reinforces the connection between body and emotions and between neuroscience and the arts.

II. INDIGENOUS PERSPECTIVES DIALOGUE

Greg Cajete, Jongmin Lee and Four Arrows

Four Arrows. From these studies I conclude that art and music are a form of language to the brain that, depending upon historical associations, produce emotional reactions by processing via the whole brain. Jongmin, is this an accurate, albeit simplistic perhaps, summary?

Jongmin. I would only add that music and art seem to either evoke a positive or a negative response. For example, a Japanese study in 2008 by Kawaba and Zeki found that people asked to describe various arts as desirable or not activated different regions of the brain depending on their preferences. I think they also showed regions activated when there was indifference. But like you indicated, they also found that art responses involved regions in both hemispheres, such as the orbito-frontal cortex.

Four Arrows. Yes, I'm happy you added this because it does seem that in all of the studies there is some reference to a reaction to art as opposed to the creation of art and this for me is where Indigenous wisdom seems to make an important contribution to neurophilosophy, especially as relates to whole brain involvement.

In Indigenous ways of thinking, to speak a word, to sing, to paint, to dance, etc., is to initiate a process of vibrational energy that enters into relationships that ultimately connect us back to Nature. All vibrational creations, from painting to music, are ultimately sacred ways to understand and connect empathetically to Nature and of course to ourselves. Indigenous languages themselves are often more poetic and rhythmical than Indo-European ones because the former intends to reveal a closeness to the invisible or spirit world that helps inform the experience in the visible world. Art, and I am including music when I say art, to Indigenous cultures is not a form of entertainment, amusement or escape as it often is in dominant cultures. Art represents creations that define place and lead to transformations. It enables experiences of mutual support and empathy that go beyond ordinary communicative language. The goal of Indigenous art is thus to reconnect with the source of life, to express the connection of the natural world with the spiritual world. Rather than seeing brain activity as relates to art as being about beauty or unattractiveness, I think the wisdom expressed above would be more useful in drawing a philosophy of art and would lead neuroscientists toward more ecopsychology studies that show the importance of our engagement with Nature.

I want to add also something Robert Lawlor said in his 1991 text on Aboriginal Peoples of Australia. He says that Aboriginal art symbols are ambiguous because they conjoin many meanings and levels at once. "The positive ambiguity of ht image or sound allows it to capture the spirit of invisible transformative powers (p. 291)." This sense of a sort of universal but ambiguous creation seems to me very different from the understandings likely to emerge from the empirical studies in neuroscience alone. If we see music and art and the skills and devotion to the raw materials for both as a vital form of creative communication intended to honor and understand of university connections, then we see why all Indigenous Peoples are artists, musicians, singers. In Western culture I would venture to say that most people would claim to be none of these things yet will pay money to go and be entertained by some artist.

Jongmin. I think that Oriental art comes closer to what you are talking about Four Arrows. Asian artists are interested in interpreting the spiritual dimension more than a photographic representation of reality and seems always to integrate humanity and Nature. I think in the West it is the contrast between humans and Nature that is expressed in much art. The Eastern view of art seems to contain the mystery of the, as you say, "invisible" world and is not about analyzing or mastering anything in Nature or communicating some specific idea to an "audience."

Four Arrows. This makes me thing about images and songs of the owl in Indigenous cultures. It seems that in every culture I have studied, people see the owl as a mysterious messenger for disruption. Some tribes have become somewhat superstitious about it in a negative way, worrying about an owl that shows up being evidence that someone is going to die, but this is because we are losing are deeper understandings we once had. The elders still remember that death can be the death of something that transforms in positive ways. My point is that there is some vibrational phenomenon that comes from the owl image we understand at some deep level of our psyche, an understanding that will likely never be verified through empirical research or brain scanning. Rather, the arts, whether dance, drama, story, fine arts, music, etc., are more likely the vehicle for understanding. This is why much of my book, *The Authentic Dissertation: Alternative ways of knowing, research and representation* (2008), has so many examples of arts-based research.

Jongmin. This idea you share about vibrations might be thought of also as rhythms. Music and dance and other art forms create activity in the brain that lead to what we can call trance-like activity. I know we have a chapter later that focuses on hypnotic phenomenon, but it has application here too I think. One theory about the role of rhythm is that it creates trance. Although there is no empirical evidence in brain science for saying that there is a relationship between trance state and tuning in to the connections we have with the invisible world, it is interesting to consider.

Four Arrows. Perhaps. In any event, Native art is not about a collection of objects in Nature but a dynamic, flowing, creative, changing process that may require both normal and altered states of consciousness for participation.

Greg. From the Indigenous perspective, whether art is a manifestation of or requires trance state or not, there is no doubt it is considered magical. In the magic of creation, the artist becomes immersed within the art media as part of the fabric of creative energy itself. To honor this intimate relationship, the artist must understand and master his or her own creative center and have a clarity of purpose for art is conceived as bringing forth of bringing something into being. In each process of the art creation, there is an initiation, a purification, a death and a rebirth. There is no doubt that art is connected therefore to all of Creation, and thus to Nature.

Every tribe incorporated into their traditional art forms a sense of the sacredness of Nature. Some art forms reflected important relationships between animals and humans. Many petroglyphs incorporate and communicate relationships between the hunter and the animals hunted. They represent the forces that combine to bring completeness to the sacred relationships. For example, in whatever habitat the deer was found, it was venerated for its spiritual qualities as an important food source. The tracking of animals by both hunters and gatherers is in itself an amazing example of the magical understanding of each animal's magical qualities.

Jongmin. Such mastery and experience must mean that there were special artists in Indigenous cultures as there are in Eastern and Western ones, no? How does this fit with what Four Arrows said about total participation of all individuals?

Greg. It is true that all Tribal People participated in the creation of art. Young and old, men and women, each in their own way and with their own degree of experience, created art. People recognized mastery that came from experience of course. Whether songs, ceremonies, dances, pottery, baskets, dwellings, boats or bows, Indigenous People were all engaged in creating the utilities for their live and each was also a work of art. Thus art was an integral expression of life, not something separate as seems to be the assumption operating in the neuroscience studies and the emphasis on positive or negative reactions to art. Everyone was an artist and things had functional use and inherent symbolic meaning. This meaning was intentionally instilled in the creation. Art was thus also a way of expressing one's self in relationship with the tribe and with the spiritual essences that informed the artist's world. Therefore, it was functional and meaningful at the same time. It was also a way to evoke and focus the re-creative healing power of the foundational guiding myths and traditional knowledge of a tribe.

I think one of the problems with looking at what happens in the brain when looking at an art product in terms of Indigenous wisdom is that art is more about process than it is product. Art is a reforming of both artist and the viewer of art. It is thus about a process of life-enhancing relationships. The product is only a symbolic documentation of the creative and spiritual process that gives it form. For brain research to shed any useful light in this field it would do better to measure brain activity of an Indian artist during the ceremony of art. The art object should be studied when it is used in ceremony by someone as well. Then perhaps we could learn that art is doing something in the brain that is about curing and reharmonizing.

Four Arrows. I remember reading once that Carl Jung painted mandalas when he was stressed. I think he wrote a book on this actually, saying that the process of creating a mandala triggered some reorganising principle in the brain that helped sort out chaos and restore balance. It seems you are saying this as well. He saw the art of a mandala as a representation of the unconscious self.

Greg. Yes, the concept of the mandala is useful in understanding how art relates to transformation. Mandalas embody a therapeutic ritual that honors our impulse toward wholeness through striving toward centering, healing, and growth. Creating a mandala is a process that recognizes the relatedness of elements in a specific context to a person, place or group. Mandalas show the relationships of elements to problems that are being addressed and the also mirror the nature of self-relatedness to the creator or to participants (not viewers) in the art. I think the creation of art by Indigenous artists is ultimately a creation of a mandala, where typically the artist begins with purification through prayer, fasting or meditation, followed by very ritualistic steps that lead to the completion of the art.

Jongmin. Mandalas are commonly used by tantric Buddhists as an aid to meditation. A Buddhist mandala is considered to be a sacred space. Even though many consider it to be a place where enlightened spirits reside, participation with the mandala as creator or co-creator in viewing it, one learns to understand that enlightenment is within oneself. The presences of a mandala remind the viewer of one's full potential in Buddhist thinking. The purpose of the mandala is to help people gain a correct view of reality. It is a way to discover the divine within each of us. I think, from a neuroscientific perspective, it might be interesting to consider the possibility that neurons work best when they are organized in mandala like modules within the cerebral cortex.

Greg. It indeed is interesting to consider that our neurons organize themselves according to patterns that are reflections of our relationships and our awareness of our connection to Nature. Certainly the making of art in Indigenous societies provided a pathway to wholeness for both the artist and for those who utilized the artist's creation. Art is a way of seeing, of being, of becoming. The ceremony of art touches the deepest realms of the psyche and the sacred dimension of the artistic creative process. This way of relating to art makes the process of art much more important than the product. Until neuroscientists grasp this, I'm afraid their research into art and brain responses will be on the wrong path. Until Western neurophilosophers truly understand this, the conclusions drawn from contemporary studies like those presented earlier will be misleading.

Four Arrows. I agree. Art in all of its forms plays a vital role in social maintenance. It contributes to authentic reflection that is based on a subjective brain experience that expresses limitless possibilities. The artist gives meaning to that which calls for such reflection. At this moment in time, it seems that human existence cries for such meaning as may only still exist large scale among Indigenous Peoples.

I suggest that understanding art as we have offered rather than as the studies tend to suggest is important, perhaps the creative mind can help us regain our balance. What may be considered as "beautiful" or as "ugly" will then return to a relatively valid perspective about how well the object or process in question leads to a sense of harmony and spiritual awareness that reminds how deeply we are all related.

III. CONTINUING THE DIALOGUE FOR UNDERSTANDING

1. Compare the study that implies that thoughts and emotions are grounded in the physical body with the Indigenous view as relates to vibrational energy is associated with creative expression.
2. Talk about the problems that might lead neuroscientists down the wrong road if the Western perspective of art as product is assumed (as opposed to the Indigenous emphasis on process.)
3. Describe the relationship between art and animals in Indigenous cultures and contrast/compare this with art in Western culture.

REFERENCES

Bruner II, G. (1990). Music, mood, and marketing. *Journal of Marketing, 54*, 94–104.

Grewe, O., Nagel, F., Kopiez, R., & Altenmüller, E. (2007). Emotions over time: Synchronicity and development of subjective, physiological, and facial affective reactions to music. *Emotion, 7*, 774–788.

Kastner, M., & Crowder, R. (1990). Perception of the major/minor distinction: Emotional connotation in young children. *Music Perception, 8*, 189–202.

Rickard, N. (2004). Intense emotional responses to music: A test of the physiological arousal hypothesis. *Psychology of Music, 32*, 371–388.

Schubert, E. (2007). The influence of music, locus of emotion and familiarity upon preference in music. *Psychology of Music, 35*, 499–515.

Sloboda, J. (1991). Musical structure and emotional response: Some empirical findings. *Psychology of Music, 19*, 110–120.

Thompson, W., & Robataille, B. (1992). Can composers express emotions through music? *Empirical Studies of the Arts, 10*, 79–89.

CHAPTER 6

NATURE

The American Indian is of the soil, whether it be the region of forests, plains, pueblos, or mesas. He fits into the landscape, for the hand that fashioned the continent also fashioned the man for his surroundings. He once grew as naturally as the tree...Kinship with all creatures of the earth, sky and water was a real and active principle.

– Luther Standing Bear (*Oglala Lakota*) (1911, p. 193)

I. NEUROSCIENCE STUDIES OVERVIEW

Brian Hanson, Joo Yeon Ri and Baruch Wohlender

This chapter reviews a number of studies that have investigated the effect of natural environments and nature scenes on cognitive functioning. Previous research has demonstrated the positive psychological, physiological, and cognitive benefits from exposure to natural environments. Both Stress-Reduction Theory (Ulrich, 1983) and Attention Restoration Theory (Kaplan & Kaplan, 1989) have been proposed in an attempt to provide a theoretical grounding for the restorative effects of natural environments. While the literature is somewhat robust in anecdotal evidence and qualitative research, methodological and theoretical issues continue to confound any potential coherent quantitative research design. The paucity of quantitative studies reveals the inherent difficulties researchers face when attempting to examine the positive psychological and cognitive effects of natural environments.

Nonetheless, research has demonstrated that people experience a broad range of emotional and physiological responses to nature, and that there are positive physical (Moore, 1981; Ulrich, 1984), cognitive (Cimprich, 1990; Hartig et al., 1991), and psychological (Kaplan & Talbot, 1988; Kaplan & Kaplan, 1989) benefits from having contact with nature. These benefits are most likely the result of a combination of psychological/emotional and physiological changes relating to the psychological (Kaplan, 1973; Kaplan & Kaplan, 1989; Kaplan & Talbot, 1988), physical (Moore, 1981; Ulrich, 1984), and cognitive aspects (Cimprich, 1990; Hartig et al., 1991) of nature exposure. According to Ulrich (1983), experiencing nature is physiologically healthy and has biological value for people. Wilson (1984) posited that humans have a genetic predisposition for forming a close affinity with nature. Mayer & Frantz (2004) provided further empirical evidence that a connection to nature is associated with subjective well being.

Study 1: "Cognitive Benefits of Interacting with Nature"

Berman, Jonides & Kaplan (2008) proposed that nature could improve cognitive functioning through the restoration of directed attention as delineated in Attention Restoration Theory. By comparing the restorative effects on cognitive functioning of interactions with natural versus urban environments, their studies extended previous research that has demonstrated interactions with nature can improve attention and memory (Berto, 2005; Faber-Taylor, Kuo, & Sullivan, 2002; Ottosson & Grahn, 2005).

Experiment 1 explored how interactions with nature or urban areas would affect cognitive performance as measured with a backward digit span test amongst 38 participants. The participants initially had their mood assessed using the Positive and Negative Affect Schedule (PANAS) and then were administered the backwards digit-span task. Their directed attention was fatigued even more through a directed-forgetting task that consisted of 144 trials and lasted for 35 minutes. The participants were then randomly assigned to take a 50 to 55 minute walk in either a nearby park (tree-lined and secluded) or downtown area (traffic and buildings could). Afterwards, the participants again performed the backwards digit-span task, the PANAS, and questions assessing their walk. The procedure was repeated one week later with participants walking in their complementary locations.

Berman et al. (2005) found that performance on the backwards digit-span task significantly improved when the participants took the nature walk but not the downtown walk. Statistical analyses confirmed that the results were not a consequence of changes in mood or different weather conditions. Post-walk ratings of "how refreshing to nature walk was" (p.1209) correlated reliably with post-walk backward digit span scores. The authors concluded, "interactions with nature improved directed attention abilities as assessed with the backwards digit span test" (p. 1209).

Experiment 2 was designed to test Attention Restoration Theory by using the Attention Network Test (ANT; Fan et al.) in order to identify three different attentional functions: alerting, orienting, and executive attention. The authors believed that interactions with nature would improve only executive functions, as it requires more cognitive control, which is quite similar to directed attention. Twelve participants were first administered the PANAS, the backwards digit span task and were then given the ANT. Afterwards, they viewed 50 images of either nature scenes or urban settings, which the participants rated on a scale of 1 to 3 regarding how much they liked each image. Following the image viewing the participants again performed the PANAS, the backwards digit span task, and the ANT. The procedure was repeated one week later with participants viewing complementary images.

Berman et al. (2005) confirmed their hypothesis and found participants improved only on the executive portions of the ANT and only after viewing images of nature as opposed to urban settings. Statistical analyses confirmed that the results were not a consequence of changes in mood. Moreover, the results of the Experiment 1 were replicated as participants reliably improved their backwards digit span only when viewing images of nature. The authors concluded that

Experiment 2 extended the results of Experiment 1 by "confirming that improvements achieved through interacting with nature were selective to directed attention (p. 1210).

The results from both experiments demonstrate the positive effect of nature interventions on cognitive functioning as brief exposure to natural settings increases the individual's ability to elicit cognitive control. The authors emphasize that this is especially important in light of the difficulties facing researchers attempting to discover various methods of improving cognitive performance and remind us that "considering the availability of nature as merely an amenity fails to recognize the vital importance of nature in effective cognitive functioning" (p. 1211).

Study 2: "Nature as a Stress Reducer"

Chang, Lin, & Chou (2006) attempted to expand the work of other researchers who have determined that natural landscapes promote both mental and physical well-being by investigating "the relationships among the natural environment, the viewer's experiences, and the benefits of the psychophysiological indicators" (p. 139). They hypothesized that through viewing different nature-based landscapes, participants would experience significant psychological and psychophysiological benefits and their experiences would correlate accordingly.

For the purpose of this study, 60 participants viewed films consisting of six types of natural environments (a mountainous area, a stream, a seashore, a cultural landscape - that is a heritage of an aboriginal tribe, a rural farm, and an urban farm). Thirteen questions from the Psychological Outcomes of Recreational Experiences were utilized in order to assess participants' satisfaction in each landscape site. Psychological benefits were measured using the State-Trait Anxiety Inventory, which ascertained how the participants felt when viewing each natural landscape. Psychophysiological benefits were calculated through EEG (a-b) and EMG measurements.

The researchers found that participants scored the seashore and the urban farm lowest in satisfaction while the stream setting had the highest. State-anxiety results varied while viewing different nature scenes while the culture landscape and rural farm were associated with higher scores. Psychophysiological measurements determined significant differences in left hemisphere brainwave activity (EEG-a) as the participants viewed the various landscape scenes. The rural farm scene elicited the highest level of left-brain activity followed by the stream environment. Right-brain activity was highest when participants viewed the urban farm scene followed by the stream environment as well. Both left and right brain activity were at their lowest levels during the culture landscape scene. In general, participants' satisfaction was significantly correlated with their state- anxiety although satisfaction was not strongly correlated with psychophysiological responses except for the cultural landscape.

The authors believed that the marked difference in participants' experiential satisfaction between the stream environment and urban farm scene might be related to the fact that the stream depicts an entirely natural scene while the urban farm contains a number of human manufactured elements. It was speculated that the lower brain wave activity elicited in response to the culture landscape was caused by the participants' knowledge of inter-tribal warfare at the site as well as exhibited weaponry. In addition, results demonstrated the rural landscapes provided a more relaxed environment for the participants, and consistent with the EEG-b measurements, the greatest benefits were conferred by the rural farm landscape experience.

Study 3: " Nature's Role in Activating Reward Receptors"

Beiderman and Vessel (2006) proposed that human beings are "infovores" who are innately driven towards the attainment of new information due to the pleasure the process elicits within the brain. They claimed the process is dependent upon an opioid-based reward network in the parahippocampal cortex that encourages the acquisition of new information such as simply viewing a natural landscape. The hunger for new information "begins with a simple preference for certain types of stimuli, then proceeds to more sophisticated levels of perception and cognition that draw on associations the brain makes with previous experiences" (p. 247). This process can only occur when the other goal-oriented behaviors are not occurring (e.g. hunger driven, harm avoidance) and is designed to enhance the speed by which people acquire new information thereby increasing their perceived intelligence.

The authors asserted that the parahippocampal cortex, which is involved in the later stages of recognition, is essential to this reward system as the greatest densities of opioid receptors are found there. Stored information (i.e. semantic and episodic memories) in the parahippocampal cortex is activated when the brain tries to interpret visual or auditory information. When the information is perceived as interesting or novel, opioid receptors are stimulated thus providing an evolutionary-based "reward" to people who strive to learn about their environment. Beiderman and Vessel (2006) presented two groups of subjects (non-fMRI and fMRI) with a series of images depicting real-world scenes. The non-fMRI group was presented with the pictures several times and was asked to rate their preference for each picture after every viewing. The fMRI group was shown the same images without voicing their preferences. Each scene was first presented for one second and then revisited again after the subject viewed an average of an additional 15 scenes. This process was repeated five times and potential confounding effects were reduced by including "buffer" images throughout each sequence as well as changing the order in which the images were presented.

The researchers found that the most highly rated scenes elicited the most fMRI activity in the parahippocampal cortex (especially the posterior portion). They claim that this result was not indicative of a simple "feed forward" mechanism, because the lateral occipital area (a region involved in early visual information processing) was activated the most when subjects viewed scenes of low preference. Scenes involving natural settings were typically preferred to manufactured environments and generally involved expansive landscape views, a hidden vantage point, and an element of mystery (something was happening or could happen).

The authors contend that while the underlying mechanisms of perceptual preference are imbedded in "the connections the brain makes with stored information" (p. 253), the results of their study are consistent with evolutionary and anthropological explanations of perceptual preference. The authors explain that the higher rated natural scenes may indicate "a primitive need to find the best location for camp or a village" (p.253).

Study 4: "Nature versus Cocaine, Alcohol and Sex"

Garavan et al. (2000) reported that despite the fact that it has been hypothesized that cocaine related cues induce a craving response that perpetuates drug addiction, the underlying specific neuroanatomical mechanisms have thus far eluded the understanding of researchers. They attempted to determine if "a neuroanatomical response observed in cocaine users when exposed to cocaine related stimuli would be unique to cocaine users(i.e., not present in cocaine-naive comparison subjects) and unique to cocaine stimuli (i.e., not present for neutral stimuli) but perhaps shared by nondrug evocative stimuli"(p. 1790).

Twenty-four experienced cocaine users and 18 comparison subjects were each given an fMRI analysis while they were shown three different films (a cocaine film that depicted two African-American men engaged in drug specific dialogue while smoking crack cocaine and drinking alcohol, a sex film that contained explicit group heterosexual activity, and a nature film that depicted scenic outdoor images). After each film, participants were given a working memory task that served as both a distracter and a means of determining the effects craving on cognitive performance in brain activation. Subsequently, participants completed an 11 question self-report measure that evaluated their response to the film viewed.

The results suggested that participants gained the most enjoyment from viewing the nature film, and they wanted to see the nature film more than the other two films. However, despite the subjective enjoyment reported, fMRI data illustrated "few regions were significantly activated in either the cocaine users or the comparison subjects when viewing the nature film" (p. 1794). In direct contrast, "the majority of regions identified as craving site exhibited similar reactions to the sexually explicit material, thus implicating common circuits in drug and nondrug reactivity" (p.1797). The data seems to indicate that the pleasure obtained from viewing nature scenes may be quite neuroanatomically distinct from the pleasure derived from sexual activity or drug use.

II. INDIGENOUS PERSPECTIVES DIALOGUE

Greg Cajete, Jongmin Lee and Four Arrows

Four Arrows. Colleagues, and I'm now referring to the contributors of the neuroscience overviews, before Greg, Jongmin and I begin our dialogue, I wanted to ask you to talk more in-depth on this topic from your own perspectives as doctoral students who did this initial research. I know I'm departing from our book's structure somewhat, but this is such a vital chapter for us. I'm especially interested in how the research describes the benefits to humans from contact with Nature and how this differs from the "pleasure" related to sex and drugs.

Brian, Joo-Yeon, and Baruch. As we said in our introduction, there really is a paucity of solid research in this arena. Most studies do note that there are specific benefits to an individual's mental health from having some type of relationship with nature (Taylor et al., 2001). Contact with nature through a window has been found to foster recovery from general mental fatigue as office workers who had a view of trees and bushes from their office experienced significantly less frustration than those lacking such a view (Kaplan & Kaplan, 1989). In addition, viewing nature has been shown to be effective in relieving stress and improving overall wellbeing (Kaplan, 1992; Leather, Pyrgas, Beale, & Lawrence, 1998, Lewis, 1996). Ulrich (1982; cited in Rohde & Kendle, 1994) has demonstrated that when people view natural scenes, particularly natural scenes including water, positive psychological and health benefits are experienced. Ulrich (1983, p. 103) commented that viewing nature scenes effectively lowers stress and "when stress is lessened, levels of stress hormones, such as norepinephrine, are often are lowered as well. The reduction is stress hormones may also in turn alleviate the experienced intensity of pain."

Ulrich (1999) suggests that having a view of a natural environment as opposed to an urban scene is more effective in restoration from stress. When patients cannot be provided with an actual view of nature or direct contact with nature, representing nature in photographic images and other artwork has also been shown to be beneficial—though the results are not quite as dramatic. Nature photographs and artwork of natural scenes are common in the more progressive hospitals today. Expanding on this concept is the Sky Ceiling, an illuminated ceiling system that provides an illusion of an attractive sky scene that helps people relax. (Ulrich, 1983, p. 201)

Indeed, laboratory, and clinical investigations have found that viewing nature settings can produce significant restoration within less than five minutes as indicated by positive changes in blood pressure, heart activity, muscle tension, and brain electrical activity (Cackowski & Nasar, 2003; Ulrich, 1981; Ulrich et al., 1991). In addition, Tsuchiya et al. (2003) found that playing nature sounds to patients undergoing general anesthesia had a positive impact on blood pressure and heart rate that also corresponded with reduced stress in patients. Cackowski & Nasar (2003) offer support for the stress-reduction theory perspective taken by Ulrich and colleagues (Ulrich, Dimberg, & Driver, 1991) suggesting, "nature reduces stress for evolutionary reasons" (Cackowski & Nasar, 2003, p. 747).

This type of evolutionary perspective concerning the power of nature to impact human well-being at its most basic level is supported by research that determined experiences in nature can help support the activities of the right hemisphere of the brain as well as restore harmony to the functions of the brain as a whole (Furnass, 1979). In addition, it has been discovered that by simply contemplating nature, the individual's brain and nervous system activity is reduced (Yogendraji, 2007).

Schiffer (1998) commented that, "a healthy left and right mind with a respectful, cooperative relationship between them can lead to a life of greater meaning, creativity, productivity, and fulfillment and only when the relationships within yourself are in harmony are you best able to sustain a healthy relationship with another person" (p. 15).

In fact, Rossi (2007) suggests that when one experiences "equal nasal dominance" the brain enters a balanced state, such that both body and mind attain equilibrium, thus allowing the individual to behave in ways that are more healthful. This is an essential part of the Swara yoga belief that "nostrils are the windows to the state of our body and mind" (Chowdhard, 2007, p. 39). Research shows that our two nostrils have slightly complementary functions and that most people without deviated septums alternate between the two at different times. A number of studies (see, for example, Pratap's, ***"Diurnal pattern of nostril breathing"*** (*Yoga Mimamsa*, Vol. XIV : 3 &. 4;1–18; 1972) show an increase in electrical activity in brain regions in the hemisphere opposite the right or left nostril.

Support for the idea that there might be a relationship between a balanced state of being an equal nostril dominance is established in a literature review performed by Wernts et al. (1981) who found that during the deepest states of consciousness; nostril breathing is equal, indicating a balance between both sides of the brain. Empirical research conducted by Ri (2008) established that when subjects watched a nature film depicting various sights and sounds of nature, they experienced equal nasal dominance and entered a state in which their brain was completely calm as measured by fMRI brain scans. This research indicated that there was an active communication through the corpus callosum between the right and left hemispheres, and that the sights and sounds of nature film put the participants' brains into a balanced state. Ri's (2008) research seems to support Schiffer's (1998) theory that "a healthy left and right mind with a respectful, cooperative relationship between them can lead to a life of greater meaning, creativity, productivity, and fulfilment" (p. 15). As Rossi and Lippincott (1992) commented: "An extensive matching of the clinical-experimental data of chronobiology and psychology suggests that what the biologist calls the *"entrainment of ultradian and circadian rhythms by psychosocial stimuli"* is the psychobiological bases of what psychotherapists call *"hypnotic suggestion to facilitate mind-body healing."*

Alexander et al. (1977) noted that "In some way, which is hard to express, people are able to be more whole in the presence of nature, are able to go deeper into themselves, and are somehow able to draw sustaining energy from the life of plants and trees and water" (p. 806). Kellert (2005) argued that an affinity for nature is learned and is something that is fostered in humans from an early age, for example "children's emotional, intellectual, and evaluative development depends on varied ongoing experiences of natural process and diversity" (p. 88).

Ulrich (1983) suggested that the positive benefits are largely due to evolutionary causes because as "humans evolved over a long period in natural environments, we are to some extent biologically adapted to natural as opposed to build content. A theme common to this perspective is that individuals are innately predisposed to respond positively to many natural settings" (p.116).

The concept of restoration is a fundamental element of research examining the positive effects of nature on mental health. Ulrich (1983) and Kaplan & Kaplan (1989) have both contributed to a body of research that underlies a theory of restoration in which natural environments elicit restorative benefits for individuals. Ulrich (1983) has offered a Stress-Reduction Theory by which he asserts people becoming increasingly stressed as they respond to their environment in an effective manner. Due to a lack of information processing, the individual is exposed to various inherent and involuntary emotional responses to demanding situations and stimuli that serve to constantly increase stress levels. At some point, restoration must occur through a reduction of arousal. Ulrich (1983) claims that nature has a restorative effect on the individual, because it is a non-taxing stimulus that elicits positively toned emotional states and blocks negatively toned feelings accompanied by a reduction in neurophysiological arousal and a continued interest in the stimulus. These responses are thought to occur because natural settings continued to be associated with more positive affect through predispositions to respond positively to surroundings conducive to well-being or survival (Hartig, Mang, & Evans, 1991, p.6–7).

In direct contrast with Ulrich (1983), Kaplan & Kaplan (1989) believe that regaining the ability to focus attention is a central component to the restoration of the individual. According to Attention Restoration Theory (Kaplan & Kaplan, 1989), normal everyday activities in modern society necessitate directed attention such that individuals must exert sustained effort in order to prevent competing thoughts or stimuli from impinging upon attentional processes. Over time, this sustained effort breaks down and inhibitory control is lost, which creates a situation in which the individual's capacity for directed attention becomes fatigued causing decline in mental functioning and frustration tolerance. Kaplan & Kaplan (1989) posit that attention restoration can occur only through a process of engaging a person's involuntary attention by utilizing four separate components: fascination, a sense of being away, extent, and compatibility.

For most people, natural environments provide fascination through beautiful scenery; a sense of being away due to modern society's urban character; extent as a function of being connected with and part of a larger whole; and compatibility via the many different outdoor activities available to individuals. Attention Restoration Theory (Kaplan & Kaplan, 1989) provides an integrative framework for current research that focuses on the cognitive benefits of natural environments.

Four Arrows. Thanks Brian, Joo-Yeon and Baruch for this additional material. I remain concerned about what I see as an interpretive theme emerging from all of this analysis. It seems that Nature is seen as a restoration opportunity, scenery, escape and a pleasure source according to the research grammar. Instead of a necessary spiritual and physical requirement, like breathing, the research makes me think that we are looking at Nature as a vacation offering. I hope I'm not being too cynical but I think that an important contribution from Indigenous wisdom is simply that we need to avoid this sense of using nature as only a counter-point to "normal" environments. As long as we see nature as escape, pleasure, scenery, as a way to *temporarily* remember we are part of a larger whole, or merely as a way to enjoy "outdoor activities," we will remain in trouble ecologically and spiritually. I propose that it would be better that we see our "normal" lives as an interruption to a more natural way of relating to the world. This does not mean we all have to move into the woods, but it means that we begin to take the Nature perspective and sensibilities we have and apply them everywhere, all the time, and do our best to be mindful of them, even while at the computer. I think the concept of being in balance goes beyond, though it certainly should include, the idea of pleasure or feeling good. Neuroscience will not help us regain our ecological balance or even survival if we cannot understand how we must use this mindfulness in every activity to try and be in harmony with the natural world.

Greg. Yes, Four Arrows, balance is a more complex and more important word to describe the Indigenous reasons for its wisdom about the relationship between humans and nature than pleasure. If someone learned from all this research that they would get pleasure from nature (with the little "n") many people in the dominant cultures would choose another path to it, perhaps T.V., air-conditioning, money or even drugs, rather than truly immerse themselves into nature if pleasure were all that was at stake.

Relationships to the natural world formed the basis for all traditional education. A direct and abiding understanding of the special significance of Nature's cycles-life, death, struggle, and survival-was integral to the survival of Indian people and to their spiritual understanding of interconnectedness with all. Guided by this metaphysical principle, Indian people acknowledge that all living and non-living entities of Nature have important inherent meaning within the context of human life. Based on this understanding, American Indians symbolically recognized the balance between plants, animals, stones, trees, mountains, rivers, lakes, and a host of other living entities.

Jongmin. Although I see Buddhism as different from Indigenous wisdom in that Buddhism gave humans a superior positioning in the world through the triple refuge of the Buddha, Dhamma and Sangha, the reverence for Nature by the Indigenous Peoples that came before Buddha nonetheless remained. Buddhism tends to be mostly about ending human suffering so there is not much in Buddhist writings specifically about nature, although animals are to be respected equally as humans. I believe nature is thought of as everything not organized or constructed by man. So from a position as a scientist and an inhabitant in Buddhist area, I think the research presented earlier fits well with Buddhist philosophy. Buddhist non-aggressive attitude toward nature and its anti-greed views and its desire for human contentment are supported by the brain research it seems.

Four Arrows. Interesting in that Buddhism as a philosophy would not be an enemy to Nature, but it would not embrace Nature with the equality or depth of Indigenous views. Balance might be achieved through both approaches, but I wonder. Greg, please say more about the sacred reality that Nature is in Indigenous Wisdom and maybe we can see if such wisdom tells us more about the potential for true balanced life than either science or religions per se. On the other hand, Peter Gold wrote a book in 1994 entitled, *Navajo and Tibetan Sacred Wisdom: The Circle of the Spirit* that did reveal some very interesting parallels between Buddhism and Indigenous spiritual symbolism. At the least both philosophies of life focus on the fundamental goodness of the human heart and on non-duality concepts. Still, if balance is what brain science is revealing, Indigenous wisdom may enhance the narrower view about reward and pleasure and enlighten interpretations about balance, in the brain hemisphere activity and in life in general.

Greg. I think, whether talking about Buddhism or any other religious principles, it is important for us to help one another understand the cultural principles that all our knowledge systems operate from. A lot of the misunderstanding on the part of native people is the feeling that Western science is totally antithetical to native philosophy and maybe at certain levels it is. What is vital is for us to develop an ecological reverence, philosophy and consciousness that can guide all of us. I know that people are looking to non-Western spiritual traditions like Buddhism to find such a way of relating to Nature. In any case, referring back to our neuroscience studies, I think it is necessary to remember there has to be a kind of consciousness that guides science rather than the other way around as it has been in the past. I think our looking at Indigenous wisdom as we are in this dialogue can help us work in ways that benefit both humans, as per Buddha's main goal, and all other life on Earth.

Four Arrows. As I think about what both you and Jongmin are saying, and I consider our original reasons for writing this book, it strikes me that neuroscience itself is just another way to develop this consciousness you are describing. Neurophilosophy may become another religion and when Indigenous wisdom challenges the conclusions being drawn from it, I hope people will remember that our understandings are in fact based on a much larger body of scientific observations than that of the relatively new neuroscience.

Greg. In the face of the rapid transformation of the Earth by Western science and technology and the ecological crises that is unfolding at the same time, leading thinkers in every field and walk of life in many cultures are searching for models that may sustain Nature rather than destroy it. And yes, as you pointed out in the Introduction, many of these thinkers have found that Indian cosmologies offer profound insights for cultivating a sustainable relationship to place and a spiritually integrated perception of Nature that may be needed to address our global crises.

Four Arrows. There is a risk that neuroscience may continue rather than than realizing the mistake in the Western paradigm that has been more about conquering Nature than engaging an authentic relationship with it.

Greg. Through the denial of the Western ego of its relationship with Nature, the natural world was objectified so it might be controlled and subsequently exploited for economic gain or glory. The use of brain research as a way to enhance marketing is an example. I think the advantage of looking at the neuroscience relating to the specific concepts we address in this book offer neurophilosophers a chance to re-engage Nature at a relationship level I refer to as "ensoulment." By this I mean that human participation in Nature reflects a map of one's soul. The Earth itself becomes a living soul. The word "Indigenous" is derived from the Latin root inuu that is related to the Greek word, enina, meaning "entrails." Indigenous means being so completely identified with place that you reflect its very entrails, its soul. Maybe it is not possible for a population that is so separated from place and Nature to ever replicate the American Indian sense of place and the importance of being in harmony with it, but if anything can come from the studies about Nature being nurturing to human health and happiness, I hope that we can re-educate ourselves accordingly to make this happen. Such an ensoulment can give us all back our sacred covenant with the land so that we can reclaim our heritage of living in a harmonious and sustainable relationship with Nature.

Jongmin. In South Korea there is still some wilderness areas and we love our Nature settings and try to preserve them, but most of life is lived in cities. Can such ensoulment occur when fewer and fewer people have the opportunity in the world to engage the land, its plants and animals, the way our ancestors did?

Greg. I think Western society must become Nature centered if it is to make the life-serving and ecologically sustainable transformations required in the next decade. Certainly America, a central player on the world's stage in this arena, is an extension of our collective Tribal minds. Just like South Korea and many other countries tend to follow the American customs, from building MacDonald's hamburger joints to wearing clothing and driving bigger cars, if the world could instead "import" the powerful collective memory of the many First Nations whose sense of place in this unique land, then maybe we can re-member our soulful connection to the land. Indigenous wisdom and the neuroscience studies both point to the important of ending our sense of separation from Nature. If Indigenous wisdom can tell us that it is not just about a more pleasurable experience but something much greater, maybe this deeper ensoulment can help us understand life energy in the world so we can maintain our right relationship to it.

Four Arrows. I want to make sure our readers know that when you are speaking of Nature and ensoulment, this is not just about landscape which seems to be emphasized in the research studies, but also about the animals, birds, fish and insects. I worry that people think of only the images of mountains and streams and don't "see" the animals hidden in them. I mean I'm sure none of the studies in neuroscience about Nature used wild creatures as part of the representation of Nature either.

Greg. In every place where hunting occurred among human populations, and it occurred everywhere, it brought the individual and community in direct contact with the magical reality of animals and with the life of the natural environment surrounding animals. As we saw in the research about generosity, animals appear to have the same ability to express virtues as do human. In fact, Indian People's see the animals as teachers of such virtues as patience, courage, fortitude, humility, honesty, etc. When hunters came into direct contact with the life and death of fellow creatures, right relationships was a matter of survival. All teaching based on hunting was predicated on the principle of abiding respect and relationship with the animals hunted. Individuals learned that we have within us an animal spirit and understanding that spirit was and is an important lesson in self-knowledge. The concepts of sharing, connecting, and relating one's life to animals formed a basic premise of Indigenous education. Of course, the animal world was not the only focus of reverence. Plants, stars and the celestial bodies of the cosmos provided an equal opportunity for establishing and understanding our place in the world.

Four Arrows. I have a sense of urgency about the importance of our understanding this innate relationship again. Every life system is in decline and I do not believe technology, including brain research technologies, will get us out of the mess we face without the Indigenous perspectives that can help us remember who we are.

Greg. Collectively we must begin to address ways for revitalizing our innate relationships in the world if we are to survive.

Four Arrows. Indigenous wisdom belongs to all of us. This does not mean that the holders of it who are alive today throughout the world may not have a special role in serving as our teachers, or that we should continue to ignore and oppress the cultures that still remember the old ways, but that we must gather all our resources for the challenges ahead, including collaboration about what we can learn about our brains from neuroscience. I am still excited about the possibilities surrounding Ri's study about what happens in the brain when watching the simple sounds and sites of Nature.

Jongmin. This was indeed an unexpectedly interesting experiment that you and your doctoral student, Joo-Yeon Ri did for her dissertation in 2008. As the technical consultant, I expected only that the sounds and sights of nature film would provoke centers of human happiness or satisfaction in ways similar to a stimulation by opium or other drugs. However, we could not find any strong activations of anything in the brain, in spite of the beautiful images of peaceful nature. Instead, the only significant activation was in the central area of corpus callosum. Although the number of subjects was not enough to conclude concretely, we conceived that the nature film evoked deep relaxation while opening up communication between bilateral hemispheres.

Of course, it is true that many people see mostly risks in the natural world. Beautiful scenery, landscapes, birds, and rabbits are nice, but being caught in a downpour, lost in the woods, or facing ferocious animals are to be avoided. In fact, many people avoid going into nature for fear of bugs or snakes or simply for lack of modern conveniences. For the many humans who possess this desire to avoid real nature, perhaps the instincts for balance and survival have atrophied. This is, it seems to me, unnatural if being in nature creates an absence of stress hormones and a balance between right and left hemispheres.

This unfortunate alienation from Nature might have something to do with how humans have produced so many other ways beyond engaging the natural world to stimulate enjoyment, including consumerism, competitions, drugs of all sorts, movies and television, alcohol, parties, pornography, musical concerts, etc. However, as the research has shown, remember that being in nature activates different brain structures. Somehow, pleasure is not the same as balance and contentment. It is more like a mother's breast. It seems to combine a more holistic sense of well being than drugs or entertainment can provide.

Therefore we should respect and love nature as we love our mothers. In Buddhist temples, there are three percussion objects for a ceremony during sunset. These are a big drum, a wooden fish, and a bird-carved bronze plate. Every evening, a monk plays them to console lives in land, water, and sky, respectively. The consolation is for well-being of all lives in nature and for inevitably killed lives by basic human survival actions. This ceremony recalls the wisdom of the Indigenous and reminds us that respecting Nature also means remember that we are a component OF Nature.

Four Arrows. Jongmin, I really appreciate your talking about loving Nature. I think the sense of oneness and the appreciation for Nature that is so engrained in Indigenous thinking has helped prevent them from losing their sense of unconditional love for the beauty in all things. In my book, *Primal Awareness*, I say that "primal awareness of Nature puts us back in touch with the origins of love (Jacobs 1998, p. 230)." We are naturally attracted to the sights, sounds, aromas and sensations in Nature. We spontaneously love the colors, the energy and the beauty that fills our senses. Our senses are made whole in Nature, but our dominant culture has rationalized our separation from Nature and has presented Nature as a dangerous place (except for distant landscapes it seems). I love the poem of D.H. Lawrence and how expresses the connection between Nature and love. I quoted it in the above referenced book (p. 231) and would like to share it again here:

> Oh, what a catstrophe, what a maiming of love when it was made personal, merely personal feeling. This is what is the matter with us: we are bleeding at the roots because we are cut off from the earth and sun and stars. Love has become a grinning mockery because, poor blossom, we plucked it from its stem on the Tree of Life and expected it to keep on blooming in our civilized vase on the table.

III. CONTINUING THE DIALOGUE FOR UNDERSTANDING

1. The studies presented imply the following:
   - Nature is important for healthy cognitive functioning.
   - Being in Nature or viewing it can reduce stress.

  - Learning about Nature is an activity that triggers reward responses in the brain.
  - Relating to Nature triggers pleasure centers in different ways than drugs or sex.
2. Do these conclusions lead you to believe that a radically different way of relating to Nature would be better than your current way? Why or why not? What would a different way, more in harmony with these possibilities, look like? Do they support a more serious look at Indigenous understanding about Nature? Why or why not?

REFERENCES

Alexander, C., Ishikawa, S., & Silverstein, M. (1977). *A pattern language*. New York: Oxford University Press.

Berto, R. (2005). Exposure to restorative environments helps restore attentional capacity. *Journal of Environmental Psychology, 25*, 249–259.

Cackowski, J. M., & Nasar, J. L. (2003). The restorative effects of roadside vegetation: Implications for automobile driver anger and frustration. *Environment and Behavior, 35*, 736–751.

Chief Luther Standing Bear. (1911). *Land of the spotted eagle*. Boston: Houghton Mifflin.

De Vries, S., Verheij, R. A., & Groenewegen, P. P. (2003). Natural environments-healthy environments? An exploratory analysis of the relationship between green space and health. *Environment and Planning, 35*, 1717–1731.

Evans, G. W. (2001). Environmental stress and health. In A. Baum, T. A. Revenson, J. E. Singer (Eds.), *Handbook of health psychology* (pp. 111–137). Mahwah, NJ: Lawrence Erlbaum.

Faber-Taylor, A. F., Kuo, F. E., & Sullivan, W. C. (2002). Views of nature and self-discipline: Evidence from inner city children. *Journal of Environmental Psychology, 22*, 49–63.

Fan, J., McCandliss, B. D., Fossella, J., Flombaum, J. I., & Posner, M. I. (2005). The activation of attentional networks. *NeuroImage, 26*, 471–479.

Furnass, B. (1979). *Health values*. In J. Messer & J. G. Mosley (Eds.), *The Value of national parks to the community: Values and ways of improving the contribution of Australian national parks to the community* (pp. 60–69). University of Sydney: Australian Conservation Foundation.

Hartig, T. H., Mang, M., & Evans, G. (1991). Restorative effects of natural environment experiences. *Environment and Behavior, 23*, 3–26.

Kaplan, R. (1992). The psychological benefits of nearby nature. In D. Relf (Ed.), *Role of horticulture in human well-being and social development: A national symposium* (pp. 125–133). Arlington, VA: Timber Press.

Kaplan, R., & Kaplan, S. (1989). *The experience of nature: A psychological perspective*. Cambridge: Cambridge University Press.

Kaplan, R., & Talbot, J. F. (1988). Ethnicity and preference for natural settings: A review and recent findings. *Landscape and Urban Planning, 15*, 107–117.

Kellert, S. R. (2005). *Building for life: Designing and understanding the human-nature connection*. Washington, DC: Island Press.

Korpela, K. M., & Ylen, M. (2007). Perceived health is associated with visiting natural favorite places in the vicinity. *Health & Place, 13*, 138–151.

Korpela, K. M., Hartig, T., Kaiser, F., & Fuhrer, U. (2001). Restorative experience and self-regulation in favorite places. *Environment and Behavior, 33*, 572–589.

Lewis, C. A. (1996). *Green nature/human nature: The meaning of plants in our lives*. Urbana, IL and Chicago: University of Illinois Press.

Lloyd, D., & Rossi, E. (Eds.). (1992). *Ultradian rhythms in life processes: An inquiry into fundamental principles of chronobiology and psychobiology*. New York: Springer-Verlag.

Ottosson, J., & Grahn, P. (2005). A comparison of leisure time spent in a garden with leisure time spent indoors: On measures of restoration in residence in geriatric care. *Landscape Research, 30*, 23–55.

Pennebaker, J. R., & Lightner, J. M. (1980). Competition of internal and external information in an exercise setting. *Journal of Personality and Social Psychology, 39*, 165–174.
Rohde, C. L. E., & Kendle, A. D. (1994). *Report to English nature—Human well-being, natural landscapes and wildlife in urban areas: A review*. Department of Horticulture and Landscape and the Research Institute for the Care of the Elderly, University of Reading, Bath.
Schiffer, F. (1998). *Of two minds: The revolutionary science of dual-brain psychology*. New York: The Free Press.
Takano, T., Nakamura, K., & Watanabe, M. (2002). Urban residential environments and senior citizens longevity in mega-city areas: The importance of walkable green spaces. *Journal of Epidemiology and Community Health, 56*, 913–918.
Taylor, A. F., Kuo, F. E., & Sullivan, W. C. (2001). Coping with ADD: The surprising connection to green play settings. *Environment and Behavior, 33*(1), 54–77.
Thayer, R. E., Newman, J. R., & McClain, T. M. (1994). Self-regulation of mood: Strategies for changing a bad mood, raising energy, and reducing tension. *Journal of Personality and Social Psychology, 67*, 910–925.
Ulrich, R. S. (1981). Natural versus urban scenes: Some psychophysiological effects. *Environment and Behavior, 13*(5), 523–556.
Ulrich, R. S. (1983). Aesthetic and affective response to natural environment. In I. Altman & J. Wohlwill (Eds.), *Human behavior and environment* (pp. 85–125). New York: Plenum.
Ulrich, R. S. (1984). View through a window may influence recovery from surgery. *Science, 224*, 420–421.
Ulrich, R. S. (1999). Effects of gardens on health outcomes: Theory and research. In C. Cooper-Marcus & M. Barnes (Eds.), *Healing gardens: Therapeutic benefits and design recommendations* (pp. 27–86). New York: John Wiley.
Ulrich, R. S., Dimberg, U., & Driver, B. L. (1991). Psychophysiological indicators of leisure benefits. In B. L. Driver, L. R. Brown, & G. L. Peterson (Eds.), *Benefits of leisure* (pp. 73–89). State College, PA: Venture Publishing.
Werntz, D., et al. (1981). JB Earle cerebral laterality and meditation: A review of literature. *The Journal of Transpersonal Psychology, 13*(2), 155–173.
Yogendraji, S. (2007). *Hatha Yoga simplified* (22nd ed.). Santa Cruz-Mumbai: The Yoga Institute.

CHAPTER 7

BALANCE

The Indian priority is about balance and following the rules for keeping balance.

Glenn Moore, Sr., Yurok Tribe

We are at a crossroads - either return to balance or face global disaster.
Arvol Looking Horse, Keeper of the Original Lakota Sacred Pipe

I. NEUROSCIENCE STUDIES OVERVIEW

Susie Spicer, Carol Swann and Henry Soper

The brain is divided into two hemispheres. When neuroscientists refer to a function like language being lateralized in the left brain, they are referring to the location where most control of the function occurs. Generally speaking, the left brain is considered analytic in approach, while the right is described as holistic and global. Left brain activity, for example, will focus on the details of a story, rather than understand the gist of the story, a function primarily reserved for the right brain. Hemispheric differentiation, however, is not as simple as "this side does this and the other side does such and such." It is more accurate to think of how different areas process information or stimuli.

Although the two brains can and do operate relatively independently when they do not communicate with one another via the information processing back and forth along the corpus callosum, it appears the two hemispheres operate mostly in a complementary way. In 1989, Zeier wrote in the *International Journal of Neuroscience* (July, pp 175) about how remarkable it is that neuroscience now describes complementary functions of the two brain hemispheres with the same kind of language that was previously reported in philosophical and psychological literature. For centuries philosophers wrote about the implications for individuals and societies that relate to engagement of apparent dichotomies, such as rational thought and emotional feelings, before knowing that control of each resides in different sides of the brain and that a seeming goal of the brain is to enhance cooperation between the two seemingly opposing constructs.

Contemporary studies in lateralization continue to discuss and contemplate the advantages and disadvantages of the complementary functions of both brains in an effort to better understand the concept of living a "balanced" life. We offer the following studies to begin a more in-depth dialogue about this concept of balance.

Study 1: "The Lateralization of Language Functions"

Summary. Theil et al (2006) examined the manner in which the brain compensates for loss of left hemisphere language function by developing left hemispheric language functions in the right hemisphere. The authors studied right-handed patients with left hemisphere brain tumors as a model of continuously progressive brain damage to the left hemisphere language areas. They found that only patients with slowly progressing brain lesions recovered right-sided language function as detected by transcranial magnetic stimulation (TMS). In patients with rapidly progressive lesions, no right-sided language function was found.

Description. It has been widely accepted in the field of neuropsychology that language production in right-handed subjects is mainly a function of the left brain hemisphere. This was first discovered in the 1800s when Paul Broca described compromised language production in his patients having left hemisphere brain lesions (Broca, 1861). In right-handed patients with left-sided focal brain lesions, development of language in the right hemisphere has been frequently described (Heiss, Lessler, Thiel, Ghaemi, & Karbe, 1999; Ohyama et al., 1996). Right side activation of language has been reported in patients with aphasia after stroke (Karbe et al., 1998) and in patients with brain tumors (Holodny, Schulder, Ybasco, & Liu, 2002; Thiel et al., 2001). Within the profession of neuropsychology, there is some debate as to the functional relevance of this contralateral activity and the authors of this study have hypothesized that disease duration may be a crucial factor determining whether the activated areas in the right hemisphere can successfully be integrated into the language network.

This study examined 8 male volunteers without previous history of neurological or psychiatric disease and 17 patients (7 female and 10 male) with known or suspected gliomas. In 7 patients the tumors were diagnosed for the first time. All other patients had a recurrence of a known brain tumor. All tumors were restricted to the left hemisphere and none of the patients had a tumor which crossed the midline.

The authors performed PET scans and TMS (transcranial magnetic stimulation) to determine there was indeed essential language function of the right hemisphere in these right-handed patients with brain tumors of the left hemisphere. The shift of language function to the right hemisphere was correlated with disease duration and language performance. Therefore, it can be concluded that in the case of slowly progressive brain damage and long disease duration, the right hemisphere can be integrated in the language network and compensate for the loss of left hemisphere language function.

Study 2: "Ambidexterity and Magical Ideation"

Summary. Barnet and Corballis (2002) designed this study to examine the relationship between handedness and magical thinking. The authors indicate that those who are ambidextrous and lack consistent lateralization may be more than usually prone to what has been termed *magical ideation,* or the belief that events have a causal relation with each other when, according to the concepts of a particular culture or the laws of nature, they do not have such a relationship. The authors cited an earlier study by Chapman and Chapman (1987) that showed there was a higher proportion of mixed-handers, but not left-handers, among those with high scores on a scale they also used, the Magical Ideation Scale, than among normal controls. Barnet and Corballis are demonstrating in their study that magical ideation is related in an orderly fashion to variations in handedness.

Description. The subjects in this study were 250 healthy undergraduate psychology students, 70 men and 180 women, whose ages ranged from 18 to 59 years, with a mean of 23.8 years. All subjects completed two questionnaires. The first was the Magical Ideation Scale. This was a 30-item true and false scale that assesses the presence of hallucination-like experiences and paranormal beliefs. The second measure was the Edinburgh Handedness Inventory which asked subjects to state which hand they preferred for activities, which eye is their dominant eye, and which foot they use to kick a ball.

The results of this study showed that "magical thinking" is associated with the lack of consistent handedness, and shows further that the relation is an orderly one; that is, the greater the degree of absolute handedness, the lower the score on the Magical Ideation Scale" (Barnet & Corballis, 2002, pg 79). Thus, right and left mixing is associated with an increased risk of "hemispheric indecision" and magical ideation. It is also associated in some cases with schizophrenia or psychopathy.

Price (2009) explains this by saying that the brain is more likely to encounter faulty neuronal connections when the information it is processing has to shuttle back and forth between hemispheres. These authors (Barnett & Corballis, 2002) are expressing the same concept. When information crosses the corpus Callosum, there is an increased opportunity for error. Magical ideation, schizophrenia, and lower IQ scores may be a result of these faulty neuronal connections, according to these authors.

The authors referenced Jaynes (1976) who proposed that cerebral lateralization may have arisen in response to natural disasters, leading to the emergence of self-consciousness and individual responsibility for action, mediated by the left hemisphere. Jaynes believed that prior to this, the unlateralized "bicameral mind" was guided by hallucinations or disembodied voices that instructed people what to do. Jaynes believed that the critical events leading to lateralization occurred in the second millennium BC. This hypothesis is largely rejected but has some interesting ideas to consider.

Study 3: "Advantages and Disadvantages of Cerebral Lateralization"

Summary. Vallortigara and Rogers examined lateral brain biases exhibited in naturalistic settings. They indicate there are obvious disadvantages in having directional asymmetries in wild animals because relevant stimuli (food or predators) may be located to the animal's right or left at random. However, the authors argue that lateralization of function may enhance cognitive capacity and efficiency in the brain, and therefore might counteract the ecological disadvantages of lateral biases in behavior. The authors indicated that until recently, most research on cerebral lateralization had been conducted in the laboratories of experimental psychologists and neuropsychologists and was largely focused on humans. In the past few years however, research has examined lateral biases in the natural environment in a number of species. They believe this new focus on lateralization in animals in the natural setting may bridge a gap between neuropsychology and evolutionary biology. One main point the authors are stressing is that the alignment of the direction of lateral biases in most individuals in a population may have evolved as an evolutionarily stable strategy and "under social pressures occurring when individually asymmetrical organisms must coordinate their behaviour with the behaviour of other asymmetrical organisms of the same of different species" (Vallortigara & Rogers, 2005, pg 575).

Description. The authors indicate that a crucial advantage that lateralization may offer is to increase neural capacity, because specializing one hemisphere for a particular function leaves the other hemisphere free to perform other additional functions. The authors indicate this would produce brain evolution that would avoid useless duplication of functions in the two hemispheres, and would thus save on neural circuitry.

Similarly, there would appear to be, according to the authors, obvious disadvantages to possessing a perceptual system that is asymmetrical. The physical world is indifferent to left and right, and any lateralized deficit might leave an animal vulnerable to attack on one side or unable to attack prey appearing on one side.

The authors discussed lateral brain biases in various animals including rats, toad, fruit flies, and chicks. The authors indicated that toads, for example, are more likely to react when a simulated predator is introduced into their left monocular field than when it is introduced to their right (Lippolis et al., 2002). The same result was found in dunnarts (Lippolis et al., 2005). These finding suggest that predator-escape and associated fear responses are controlled by the right side of the brain. This would appear to have disadvantages to the animals. However, the authors argue that a prey species might avoid predation if it can predict the strategy of its predator and under these circumstances, population-level lateralized behaviour of a predator would be advantageous for the prey though not for the predator itself. In this manner, the alignment of the direction of lateral biases may have evolved as an evolutionarily stable strategy.

In a response to this article written by Vallortigara and Rogers, Michael Corballis argued that one possibility is that the fundamental distinction and argument should not be between left and right dominance, but rather between asymmetry and symmetry. We should be searching for a directional bias or the absence of any such bias rather than focusing on left and right dominance.

Study 4: "Suppression of Magical Thinking"

Summary. Bell et al (2007) studied brain lateralization as relates to the tendency to perceive meaning in noise (apophenia) that is linked to "magical thinking," a distinctive form of thinking associated with a range of normal and abnormal cognitive styles. Magical thinking gives meaning or causality to events that might otherwise be considered coincidental or illogical. It describes a process by which meaningful connections are made between apparently unrelated things. This study used single-pulse transcranial magnetic stimulation (TMS) to stimulate either the left or right lateral temporal areas. Inhibition of the left lateral temporal area produced significant reduced tendency to report meaningful information, suggesting that left lateral temporal activation may be more important in 'magical thinking' and therefore producing and supporting anomalous beliefs and experiences. The effect cannot simply be explained by TMS induced cognitive slowing as reaction times were not affected. It may be possible to reduce levels of magical thinking by targeting the areas identified in the left brain, whereas previous studies have implied that this phenomenon is a right brain function.

Description. 12 healthy participants, balanced for similar levels of magical thinking and delusional ideation were stimulated with TMS at either the left or right lateral temporal areas. They were asked to indicate if they had "detected" pictures claimed to be present by the experimenters in visual noise. The researchers expected that the right hemisphere would be preferentially involved and increase chances of participants detecting information, but instead the reverse happened. This findings show that the TMS stimulation reduced non-existent meaningful images in visual nose by inhibiting localised areas of the left lateral temporal cortex. The tendency to perceive meaning in noise, a component of magical thinking, is thought to be a process that leads to psychosis. However, it also is seen in normal individuals, as when seeing images in clouds. It past research it appeared that a bias for right hemisphere processing might facilitate the emergence of uncommon associations in both healthy participants and patients. This conclusion, however, is at odds with the possibilities of left hemisphere bias as being responsible.

II. INDIGENOUS PERSPECTIVES DIALOGUE

Greg Cajete, Jongmin Lee and Four Arrows

Four Arrows. I find it interesting that Vallortigara and Rogers are proposing that there are possible disadvantages for wild animals living in the wild, even though they do admit that *maybe* there are aspects that counteract the disadvantages. Aside from the fact that the literature about animal brain specialization and lateralization is weak, the idea that Western science is considering that animals, seen in Indigenous cultures as "teachers" about life, might be structurally disadvantaged seems to be an example of our anthropocentric nature. If there are disadvantages in lateralization phenomenon in the brain, it is far more likely that humans have somehow created disadvantageous circuitry. Perhaps the contradictory conclusions about "magical thinking" are a place we can start to understand such possible disadvantages. Relatively normal humans seem more inclined to delusional thinking than other normal creatures. In any case, it is interesting to see Julian

Jaynes's work mentioned as a possible explanation of how human cognition may have come to a disadvantaged state. Although most scientists reject his claims. I think he is closer than many want to admit.

Jaynes's hypothesis is that prior to around 2000 BC, humans did not have a self-directed, internalised consciousness that directed behaviour. Rather, we were directed from some external phenomenon. He suggests that the gods gave us commands. He proposes that a series of unprecedented environmental stresses in the second millennium B.C. forced the two halves of the brain to merge into unicamerality, claiming this was a cultural, not a biological, transformation. In an Internet article entitled, "Julian Jaynes's Software Archeology," Dennet says there may indeed have been a revolution in the organization of our information processing system that came after language. He says in the article that even though Jaynes is probably wrong with his details, his story offers us an important place to start looking for what really might have happened.

Perhaps Jaynes was referring to the loss of Indigenous ways of knowing that were forcibly and deceptively oppressed and replaced with authoritarian heirachies of power. I think that humans did have automatic behaviours for survival similar to the remarkable activities and abilities other creatures display. Like all creatures, we had a brain function that allowed for hypnotic phenomenon to make us hypersuggestible to the instructions from perceived authority figures, whether a dominant herd leader or "god." Humans had an especially viable brain circuitry for the hypnotic phenomenon and when some individuals who assumed dominant power roles realized this, they replicated the original higher source of authority and took it over. As a result, our brain circuitry, which did not physically change all that much, became more organized around the replacement language now in the hands, not of some Natural force, but of other humans. Indigenous wisdom may stem from this realization of possibly losing our connection to Nature's authority. We understood the hypnotic or trance state phenomenon and thus used it with responsible intentionality, aware of the risks of allowing others to utilizes have control of it. So, I propose that our ceremonies, stories, reflective practices, songs, art, etc., are all designed with an understanding of how transformation relates to states of concentration or focus the medical literature now calls "hypnosis". With dominant culture, we have the same knowledge but are unaware largely of our ability to recapture it and, worse, are constantly susceptible to those who do know how to use it to their advantage.

I am starting our dialogue about the concept of balance with these ideas about the phenomenon of hypnosis because I feel strongly that brain mechanisms in humans and other animals are designed to be receptive to hypnotic signals that create special or unusual behaviours that affect our perceptions of reality in ways that can enhance or disrupt balance. I also believe Indigenous wisdom helps prevent us from relinquishing our natural complementary brain processes to an out of balance state based on inappropriate hypnotic scripts. It is as if Indigenous People's understood the power of trance phenomenon, which is largely a right-brain activity. There have been a number of studies that indicate that American Indians are more right-brained than non-Indians, although the studies have also been challenged. For example, Hynd and Scott (1980) published the remarkable finding that in Navajo children a pattern was observed that was, exactly opposite to that seen in whites: the left ear showed superior performance. However, Mckeever and Hunt (1984) conducted another study with Navajo children and found that Navajo children showed a pattern that was identical to that of Whites: superior right ear performance. Another study (McShane, Risse and Rubens, 1984) found that in Indians the two brain halves were more similar to each other in size than in average white right-handers who had larger posterior parts of the brain on the right and larger anterior parts on the left. Other studies regarding learning styles, etc., point to a more balanced brain in traditionally raised Indigenous children. In any case, my point is that Indigenous wisdom created cultures that were not as likely to fall pray to unintentional hypnosis as have been Euro-centric cultures. As a result, dominant cultures are out of control and out of balance and if we can learn anything about right-left brain balance, it is that we need to regain our ability to regain both.

Greg. Well, you warned us that your theory would be radical Four Arrows. I'll have to ponder what you have said. I agree about the priority of maintaining balance that exists in Native cultures of course. There is an organic balance between cultivating individuality or personal power with realizing the close connection we have to one another and that our physical and biological survival is intimately interwoven with the communities that we create and that create us? Perhaps our ability to find balance within chaos is that we are indeed aware of how to manage or avoid external hypnosis so that we do not forget the higher wisdom our cultures maintain. For us, the idea of "truth" is not a fixed point, so we would by this idea alone be less inclined to following another persons suggestion for a particular way to be. For Indigenous Peoples, truth is not a fixed point, but rather an ever-evolving point of balance, perpetually created and perpetually new. Also, and this may support your idea somewhat, the Native American metaphorical mind and its right brain orientation allows the individual to perceive and process multiple layers of changing reality in order to find balance in chaos. Such a mind would not likely get stuck so easily in one "post-hypnotic suggestion".

Four Arrows. You write in your books that these multiple layers involve the understanding of energies and the relations of energies to each other and to all beings on a multi-dimensional level. I think that Julian Jaynes might say if he were alive that we are in touch with the original "gods" he says stopped talking to Western humanity five thousand years ago. Instead, we have allowed ourselves to listen to human authorities and we are literally hypnotized by their mandates to live our illogical, contradictory lives of imbalance!

Greg. Each individual is obligated to consider how differing energies, including those created as an aspect of her actions, impact the existence of other beings within the community of all her relations. To have this perspective one has to be aware of the invisible as well as the visible energies. This also creates a habit of critical reflection on the merits of all activities and their impact on the community.

Unless one is open to metaphoric thinking, Indigenous natural philosophy will remain mysterious because it has evolved from multi-level and multi-layered symbols that came to us long ago when we could talk to the animals and hear the gods or God more easily perhaps, to return to your hypothesis regarding Jaynes's ideas. The mediators for the transference of this knowledge and the re-establishment of these basic foundations of balance, were primarily the healers or medicine people. These included specialists in plants and herbs, in physical anatomy, in animal symbolism, etc. The most pronounced role was the shaman who embodied the integration of relationships between humans and the more invisible entities around them. These teachers provided a centering point for a teaching process that was all about establishing and maintaining balance between individuals and communities and the forces that acted upon them to disrupt this balance. Perhaps, Four Arrows, the shaman was the ultimate hypnotherapist, but the hypnosis was always oriented toward the healing of relationships. In the philosophy of Indigenous systems of healing, illness and disease were often caused by improper relationship to the natural world, to the spiritual world, to the community, and/or to one's own spirit. Thus, illness is an environmental imbalance.

Jongmin. In his book, *The Illusion of Conscious Will* (2002), Wegner describes a circle of influence where cultures create expectations of themselves and on another until what he calls a "suggested society" emerges (p. 314). Perhaps all of our cultures are in this way created and those where more illness exists are those who have fostered unnatural relationships.

Four Arrows. I think this is partially true and I also think that the language stem of European languages allows for a greater susceptibility to categorical assumptions. These languages which drive the dominant cultures of the world are much more noun oriented than process oriented. In Indigenous languages it is more difficult to pin down a large-scale or social hypnotic image. Context is more important. Categories are complicated or do not exist. Time is not a steam moving from past to present to future. Everything is in the process of becoming and the language is oriented toward this manifestation or transformation. The language and hence the culture is continually unfolding and enfolding as constant movement, whereas English, for example, it is much easier to picture being something or acting in a particular, static way. So, I think you are right about how the hegemony of a society builds upon its hypnotic scripts and that Indigenous cultures through their observations of Nature had more balanced scripts, I also think Indigenous Peoples' languages prevented people rising to power who could use the language of hypnosis to direct and control people, as did the kings and queens in Jayne's hypothesis.

Jongmin. In Asia, I think that Buddhism, meditative practice and yoga are all "languages" like the Indigenous languages in that balance is expected to come from keeping things in motion, in process, not getting stuck or categorized as you are saying Four Arrows. Balance is what these practices or belief systems are all about. Balance in the world and inner harmony even in the absence of temporary imbalance. In Buddhism, balance is about peace and oneness and a union of yin and yang principles. So it seems these traditions, like Indigenous ones, somehow realized the importance of right and left- brain hemisphere complementary functioning. I also think that in yoga, which ultimately aims at a union between the person and with Supreme Reality, a trance state helps mediate the balance between yin and yang. The trance state in yoga is "samadhi." Breathing and postures, with practice, lead to autonomic changes that may give rise to balanced living and the health that follows. It leads to inner harmony, which in this tradition is most important.

Four Arrows. Although all of the yoga traditions seek this balance, svara yoga seems most directly associated with left and right brain balance because of the focus on dominant nostril breathing, nostrils correlating with the opposite hemisphere side. It correlates breathe with the sun, the moon, the elements and uses an understanding of what the right and left brain's primary control functions are.

Jongmin. Yes, and you recall in Ri's study, the participants moved into balanced nostril breathing that correlated with high activity along the corpus callosum and low stress in both hemispheres.

Four Arrows. I would like to see neuroscientists do more studies of this nature. The popular applications of lateralization have emphasized right or left functions too much and it seems there has not been enough about balance and complementarity coming from neurphilosophy. Although there is significant diversity among the Indigenous peoples of North America, most have a concept of balance as integral to well-being. The Medicine Wheel illustrates the importance of balance for wellness.

Greg. I would add that the Medicine Wheel is divided into four quadrants. The health of a person or group depends on a balance with all four functions, moving to that point of balance within the four directions. The connection of the four directions to the central point of harmony and balance can achieved with a variety of images. Thus, Native science works with many symbols, images and stories. There is no single interpretation or fundamental premise. Understanding comes from real experience that dances between and among the various levels of meaning. This relates to Borhr's idea about complementarity. A traditional Indigenous story can be viewed from a variety of context, each context presenting a different but connected perspective.

Four Arrows. I think this has an important neurophilosophical relationship to the early study on "magical ideation" where the researchers conclud "magical ideation, schizophrenia, and lower IQ scores may be a result of these faulty neuronal connections." I think it is another example of how Western science is missing the boat when it comes to understanding the nature of balance, complementarity and

Indigenous ways of knowing. So called "magical thinking" describes a process were meaningful connections are made between seemingly unrelated ideas. Why characterize this as a result of faulty neurons when this process may be exactly the kind of creative, multi-dimensional, interconnected thinking that Indigenous wisdom would say we need to get out of the imbalanced state our world is currently experiencing!

Jongmin. I see uncommon associations in both healthy and unhealthy people. Some clinical literature does show that psychotic disorders relating to magical thinking correlate with left hemisphere hyperactivity, but strictly hemispheric correlations lack precision as to what neural systems are involved in magical thinking. I think the scientists are just trying to understand certain pathologies relating to delusional thinking.

Greg. Jongmin, I think this is a challenge for Western science in that pathology seems to guide it more than health potential. The observation that there is something else besides just brain activity is a major point for neurophilosophers to get from our efforts to bring Indigenous wisdom to bear on neuroscience. The notion of spirit or soul or something outside our physical brain per se is missing from Western science. Indigenous science acknowledges interactions between individuals and Nature that have sources of influence beyond or external to gray matter alone.

In fact, I think this Western way of thinking reflects an illusion in itself. The tendency for Western education to divide myth and poetry from music, dance relationship to Nature, community, spirituality, history and politics exemplifies this fragmented way of thinking. Nothing in Western thinking allows for engaging people as deeply and multidimensionally as Indigenous mythopoetic traditions. I think the Homeric poems came close and Jaynes refers to how music and poetry are instruments for trance state learning. Music and poetry evoke right hemisphere "cooperative" activities for interpreting and understanding ideas and their context.

Within Tribal cultures, the evolution of a cultural/social mythology parallels the evolution of an individual's mythology. The evolution of human consciousness has generally been marked by transformations of the guiding myths that a society holds. The re-emphasis on a mythologically instructed community should be a neurophilosophical goal as relates to the study of laterality. If this happens, then I also suggest that the wisdom embedded in many Indigenous cultural myths be also reconsidered as to their appropriateness for contemporary Indians and non-Indians alike. Joseph Campbell wrote, "Whenever men have looked for something solid on which to found their lives, they have chosen not the facts in which the world abounds, but the myths of an immemorial imagination (1989, p. 2)."

Four Arrows. Greg, I am happy you brought the importance of cultural myths and how they can guide individuals and societies into this conversation about brain laterality and balance in our lives. I have a good friend, Dr. Howard Teich, who is well known for his work in what he calls the "Psychology of Light," has written extensively about a particular myth that speaks both to this influence on the individual and collective psyche and to the functions and complementary potential of right and left brain hemispheres. Rather than me trying to explain this very relevant material, I've asked Howard to briefly share with us some things about "twin hero" myths.

Howard. I appreciate being able to join in this dialogue. To be brief about some of the concepts I want to share will be difficult but I'll give it a try. First of all, I agree entirely with Dr. Cajete about his ideas on "mythologically constructed communities." In fact, the fields of epigenetics and epigenomics are now allowing Western scientists to support the intuitive and observational wisdom of Indigenous Peoples in many ways. Although epigenetics was first defined by a developmental biologists named Conrad Waddington back in the 1940s as relating to how genes and the environment interact to possibly modify DNA structures, relatively recent studies are showing how language and thought, thus by inference mythology its influence on both conscious and unconscious perceptions, can program or change DNA phenotypes. Genetic scientists like Marcus Pembrey and Wolf Reik are telling us that environmental manipulations turn genes on or off and the results cannot only affect an individual transformation but such changes can be handed down to future generations. The collective unconscious, which I believe exists, and the psychic life of our ancestors, both which are informed by cultural myths, can be the kinds of environmental triggers that can do this switching on and off of behavioural mechanisms. In 2003, German writers, Grazyna Fosar and Franz Bludorf, published a book Vernetzte Intelligenz, meaning Networked Intelligence," in which they argue that the DNA of all sentient beings, including plants, is linked in an intelligence network that allows for a hypercommunication of information. I think what Four Arrows was talking about earlier in terms of hypnosis relates to such hypercommunication as does perhaps the intuitive and unconscious processing of archetypes that emerge from our cultural mythologies. In fact, if you don't mind me saying so, this all may be more significant in many ways that what is happening with regard to brain activity and neuroscience, although they may be related of course.

Four Arrows. Rupert Sheldrake is another scientists talking about this hypercommunication through what he calls a morphogenetic field. He talks about this in his book, *A New Science of Life*, published by Tarcher. Morphogenetic fields, according to his theory, can carry this hyperinformation. Thus the DNA in the genes of an animal or plant can retune the DNA. It is like what happens to an ant colony when the queen ant dies. She was sending instructions via this field to direct the ants, but when she dies the ants all stop working.

Howard. Of course I don't know if our mythologies come to us through such a hypercommunication field or if they are in our DNA or somewhere in our brains or conscious or unconscious minds. It does seem though that beliefs can act epigenetically to influence every kind of genetic expression. Maybe when we lost our "Queen Ant," whatever that might mean, we stopped working also.

In any event, I'm not a genetic scientists, but my understanding is that a number of studies show that gene regulation by RNA molecules is not determined by genetics but by a complementarity between the RNA and its targeted gene. What is interesting is that the degree of complementarity that exists (and I understand that plants normally have more perfect complementarity than animals for reasons I do not understand) is an important factor in how epigenetic mechanisms can promote DNA changes. In any event, all this brings us back to the concept of balance, brain laterality and cultural myths you asked me to discuss.

Staying with the idea of a collective consciousness, every ideal emerges in pairs. Sometimes the relationships between the members of the pairs are configured as harmonious, sometimes neutral and at other times oppositional. The theme of twin brothers seems to be a basic structure in the mythology of tribes and cultures starting from before 2000 BCE. The nature of the relationship between the twins in whatever tribal story describes it tends to mirror the nature of the culture out of which twins were born. What is interesting in terms of contrasting Indigenous wisdom with Western science (with the goal in mind I think you have of finding complementarity) is that in the Indigenous myths the twins ARE complements to one another. In the Western myths, one twin kills or subjugates to a lessor position the other. Think about this in terms of social balance.

Most Indigenous cultures, in one way or the other, have multiple gods or creative sources for life. Western culture is marked by monotheism. Since monotheism follows the premise that a single god is better than several, it should not be surprising that whenever conceptual twins appear the dominant culture's religions a dominant twin emerges. For example, in the Bible, whether it is Isaac and Ishmael or Cain and Able, one is called good or god-like and the other evil or the enemy of god. While Cain is described as the murderous brother, for example Abel is portrayed as an innocent victim; Jacob betrays Esau. Christ is the loyal son whereas Satan is a rebellious angel. It is likely these stories stem from earlier Greek and Roman twin stories. Take Castor and Pollux, for example, where one of whom was a god and the other immortal. There is also Romulus who killed his twin brother Remus surrounding an argument about which should be king.

Contrast this with the twin hero myths of Indigenous Peoples who tend to work cooperatively. One of the most famous is the Navajo story, "Where the Two Come to the Father." This is a classic example of showing how living a good life and fighting the "monsters" that are always trying to put us out of balance requires collaboration between or minds and hearts. Child Born of the Water is the heart brother. He is more passive and reflective like the moon. Monster Slayer is the mind brother. He is more aggressive and direct. They do not kill one another but listen and cooperative. When Monster Slayer wants to shoot an arrow into the monster with the long arms, Child Born of the Water begs him instead to sing a song to the monster. They do and are successful in bypassing this particular obstacle to positive movement.

I refer to the affect of such myths on our psyche as "solar-lunar" consciousness and refer to therapy I do as being a "psychology of light," though I find most respond better when I just talk about balance or I refer to "complementary psychology."

Obviously the Solar dynamics are those that are often assigned to the left hemisphere of the brain and the Lunar dynamics those described as primary functions of the right hemisphere.

The psychology of light is based on the symbolic significance of the two natural sources of light that illuminate life on earth. Usually when we think about light in Western culture, most of us focus on the sun. Yet equally crucial to our consciousness is the fact that as part of daily life on earth, we experience two kinds of illumination: sunlight and moonlight. This is more likely how Indigenous cultures think of light and why for thousands of years the Sun and Moon served as symbols for different but complementary modes of awareness. In working with executives and leaders of corporations, I who them that by restoring a balance between solar and lunar consciousness in their individual psyches as well as in other functional dimensions of their organization, that can increase the organizations ability to operate "in balance." I am quite sure this same dynamic is operating in society at large and am confident that bringing Indigenous wisdom to help people reflect on and reconsider their myths might be a significant contribution to neurophilosophy.

Four Arrows. Thanks so much Howard. I agree that there are forces beyond the balanced activity in right and left brain hemispheres that determine how humans and other creatures maintain or achieve balance and harmony in response to changing environments, stress, etc., and think that as you and Greg point out our myths may be one of these forces. I invited Howard to share his research with us to underscore what Greg says about the myths that inform our psyches, but before turning the dialogue over to our readers, I want to bring the idea of balance back more directly to brain lateralization and neuroscience per se.

In know it is a little cliché to say, but Western culture is out of balance and it seems to be out of balance with regard to an overemphasis of left hemispheric emphasis. (I don't think Howard mentioned it but it is important to note that it is usually the twin with the solar traits that kills or obscures the twin with the lunar traits in Western mythology.) Referring back to the noted neuroscientists, Dr. Damasio, he says in his book, *Descarte's Error,* "Intriguingly, the representation of extrapersonal space, as well as the processes of emotion, involve a right-hemisphere dominance (p. 67)." I think that Indigenous languages are much less susceptible to deceptive ways of thinking and behaving because it they evoke a balance between left and right brain hemispheres in ways that allow the brain to work as it was intended, without all the effort that deception requires. Indigenous ways of seeing the world beyond just the languages invoke significant right-brain involvement and collaboration! Indigenous learning traditionally is about discovery, symbols, metaphors, even dreams. It was fully holistic, which is largely a right brain way of seeing the world. Many tribes used only symbols, for example, to record history. All of these things, from discovery learning to dreams, are right-brain oriented. Since the right brain does not think in words, and words are intimately related to the concept of deception, this gives pause. Also American Indian elders teach young people to think twice before speaking or acting on anything. This gives time for the right hemisphere to collaborate with the left, especially as relates to emotional processes.

We have seen how story telling tended to cause learning in primarily the right brain for learning was most likely to occur during alpha brain waves. Alpha waves occur during light trance states and Indigenous peoples understood that in such a state of awareness, whether induced by stories or ceremonies or perhaps peyote, this is the state where most transformative learning takes place. Since simple logic is more a function of the left hemisphere, the right brain is also emphasized in Indigenous learning because the languages are more inclined to focus on results than on causes. Furthermore, lexical categories in Indigenous languages emphasize place and spatiality, which is a right brain function. Indigenous languages are non-linear and this also is a function of the right hemisphere. And finally, ceremonies that utilize dance, artistic symbols and music, which like holistic views of the world, also activate right brain activity.

I know I sometimes sound like a broken record when I refer to the concept of trance and hypnosis, especially spontaneous hypnosis, as being the most important phenomenon for brain science to study, but I want to say again that I think we have allowed a cultural worldview, including our myths, to couple with an ignorance about spontaneous hypnosis, to put us out of control. We have thus replaced values like respect and compassion with more materialistic and ego-centric ones that have led us further away from the Indigenous wisdom we all once had. Or to quote Umberto Eco, "A democratic civilization will save itself only if it makes the language of the image into a stimulus for reflection, and not an invitation to hypnosis." I hope this chapter on balance will lead neurophilosophers and neuroscientists to more seriously consider how this form of "hypercommunication" may be the most important target for neuroscience research.

Howard. If I can say one more thing I feel I should have mentioned?

Four Arrows. Of course.

Howard. I think the demise and oppression of Indigenous cultures around the world is partially a by-product of gendering the archetypal symbols such as the sun and the moon and the twin hero stories we have been discussing. By misunderstanding the concept of solar and relegating it to being only a representation of the masculine, the male dominated Western world has through this corruption lost site of the balance in Nature afforded by the Sun and the Moon.

Four Arrows. Thanks Howard. This is important especially in light of how most Indigenous cultures honor the balance between men and women. For example, in Lakota cultures men could decide to go to war but unless the women agreed to make new moccasins the warriors would stay at home. In a chapter called "Where Are Your Women?" in my book, *Unlearning the Language of Conquest*, Barbara Mann writes about how even the Academe has largely misrepresented the vital role of women in Indigenous societies, many of which were matrilineal to boot.

In any event, I want to close our chapter on balance with an appeal for a reconnecting between Western and Indigenous sciences, much of which I borrow from my text, *Primal Awareness*. The Hopi have an ancient legend that tells about a red and white brother with solar and lunar traits. The white brother goes far away to make discoveries that can help everyone, but his ego becomes so large that he does not return to share his knowledge. As a result, the world loses its harmony. Similarly, The Kogis of South American also see that light and dark skinned people must work together to keep the Earth in balance. They believe the white race, whom they refer to as Younger Brother is causing the world to end. Their wise elders, called Mamas, say Younger Brother must stop desecrating the planet and work together with the Older Brother to put the world back in harmony.

If the Western world is going to continue to raise neuroscience to such a place of importance as it seems to be, it is up to the neurophilosophers who interpret and apply it in such a way that incorporates Indigenous wisdom.

III. CONTINUED DIALOGUE FOR UNDERSTANDING

1. Describe the connection between hypnotic phenomenon and balance as relates to both laterality and Indigenous wisdom. Be sure to include epigenetics as part of your description.

REFERENCES

Allen, H. A., Humphreys, G. W., & Matthews, P. M. (2008). A neural marker of content-specific active ignoring. *Journal of Experimental Psychology: Human Perception and Performance, 34*(2), 286–297.

Awipi, T., & Davachi, L. (2008). Content-specific source encoding in the human medial temporal lobe. *Journal of Experimental Psychology: Learning, Memory, and Cognition, 34*(4), 769–779.

Barnet, K., & Corballis, M. (2002). Ambidexterity and magical ideation. *Laterality, 7*(1), 75–84.

Carey, B. (2008, December 4). H.M., an unforgettable amnesiac, dies at 82. *The New York Times.* Retrieved December 20, 2008, from http://www.nytimes.com/2008/12/05/us/05hm.html?_r=2

Campbell, J. (1989). Primitive mythology, quoted in Sam keen and Anne Valley-ox. *Your Mythic Journey*, p. 2.

Chapman, J., & Chapman, L. (1987). Handedness of hypothetically psychosis-prone subjects. *Journal of Abnormal Psychology, 96*, 89–93.

Corballis, M., Hattie, J., & Fletcher, R. (2008). Handedness and intellectual achievement: An even-handed look. *Neuropsychologia, 46*(1), 374–378.

Cunliffe, L. (2005). The problematic relationship between knowing how and knowing that in secondary art education. *Oxford Review of Education, 31*(4), 547–556.

Diana, R. A., Yonelinas, A. P., & Ranganath, C. (2008). The effects of unitization on familiarity based source memory: Testing a behavioral prediction derived from neuroimaging data. *Journal of Experimental Psychology: Learning, Memory, and Cognition, 34*(4), 730–740.

Christensen, A. (1975). *Luria's neuropsychological investigations.* New York: Spectrum.

Francks, C., Maegawa, S., Lauren, J., Abrahams, B., Velayos-Baeza, A., Medland, S., et al. (2007). LRRTM1 on chromosome 2p12 is a maternally suppressed gene that is associated paternally with handedness and schizophrenia. *Molecular Psychiatry, 12*, 1129–1139.

Four Arrows. (2006). *Unlearning the language of conquest.* Austin, TX: University of Texas Press.

Goldstein, K. (1942). *After effects of brain injury in war.* New York: Grune & Stratton.

Josse, G., & Tzourio-Mazoyer, N. (2003). Review: Hemispheric specialization for language. *Brain Research Reviews, 44*, 1–12.

Jacobs, D. T. (1998). *Primal awareness: A true story of survival, awakening and transformation with the raramuri shamans of mexico.* Rochester, VT: Inner Traditions International.

Jaynes. (1976). *The origins of consciousness in the breakdown of the bicameral mind.* Boston: Houghton Mifflin.

Heiss, W., Kessler, J., Thiel, A., Ghaemi, M., & Karge, H. (1999). Differential capacity of left and right hemisphere areas for compensation of poststroke aphasia. *Annals of Neurology, 45*, 430–438.

Holodny, A., Schuler, M., Ybasco, A., & Liu, W. (2002). Translocation of Broca's area to the contralateral hemisphere as the result of the growth of a left inferior frontal glioma. *Journal of Computer Assisted Tomography, 26*, 941–943.

Kaplan, E. (1983). Process and achievement revisited. In S. Wapner & B. Kaplan (Eds.), *Toward a holistic developmental psychology* (p. 144). Hillsdale, NJ: Lawrence Erlbaum Associates.

Karbe, H., Thiel, A., Weber-Luxenburger, G., Herholz, K., Kessler, J., & Heiss, W. (1998).

Lippolis, G., Bisazza, A., Rogers, L., & Vallartigara, G. (2002). Lateralization of predator avoidance responses in three species of toads. *Laterality, 7*, 163–183.

Lippolis, G., Westerman, W., McAllan, B., & Rogers, L. (2005). Lateralization of escape. Responses in the striped-face dunnart, *Sminthopsis macroaura* (Dasyuridae: Marsupialia). *Laterality, 10*, 457–470.

Luria, A. R. (1980). *Higher cortical functions in man* (2nd ed.). New York: Oxford University Press.

Ohyama, M., Senda, M., Kitamura, S., Ishii, K., Mishina, M., & Terashi, A. (1996). Role of the nondominant hemisphere and undamaged area during word repetition in poststroke aphasics. A PET activation study. *Stroke, 27*, 897–903.

Price, M. (2009). The left brain knows what the right hand is doing. New research explores how brain lateralization influences our lives. *Monitor on Psychology, 40*(1).

Poreh, A. (2000). The quantified process approach: An emerging methodology to neuropsychological assessment. *The Clinical Neuropsychologist, 14*(2), 212–222.

Thiel, A., Habedank, B., Herholz, K., Kessler, J., Winhuisen, L., Haupt, W., et al. (2006). From the left to the right: How the brain compensates progressive loss of language function. *Brain and Language, 98*(1), 57–65. IBID, pp. 212–222.

Thiel, A., Herholz, K., Koyuncu, A., Ghaemi, M., Kracht, L., Habedank, B., et al. (2001). Plasticity of language networks in patients with brain tumors: A positron emission tomography activation study. *Annals of Neurology, 50*, 620–629.

Vallortigara, G., & Rogers, L. (2005). Survival with an asymmetrical brain: Advantages and disadvantages of cerebral lateralization. *Behavior and Brain Sciences, 28*, 575–633.

Werner, H. (1956). Microgenesis and aphasia. *Journal of Abnormal and Social Psychology, 52*, 347–353.

CHAPTER 8

SPIRITUALITY

The ultimate goal of Indigenous spirituality is the same as in all approaches to learning about life. At its innermost core, spirituality evolves from exploring and coming to know and experience the nature of the living energy moving in us, through us and around us.

– Greg Cajete *in Look to the Mountain* (1994), p. 42.

The experience of visionary transformation is fundamental to Native American spirituality. Although it is ultimately personal and begun in isolation, the quest for it is fundamentally conversational and social. Power comes from a person's conversation with the supernatural. It comes from an encounter with sentient beings with whom humans share the breath of life. It comes to a person when he or she is humble and pitiable…It comes to people who listen carefully to the storied world around them. It comes when the story of a person's life becomes that of life as a whole.

–Robin Ridington *in "Voice, Representation and Dialogue" in Native American Spirituality, Edited by* Lee Irvin (2000), p. 101.

I. NEUROSCIENCE STUDIES OVERVIEW

Ann Gelsheimer, Kari Lannon and Laura Luna

In our exploration of studies in neuroscience that relate to the concept of spirituality, including related concepts studied in the neurophilosophical arenas referred to as "neurotheology" or "spiritual neuroscience," such as alternative consciousness or oneness with the universe feelings, we found four studies that seem to reflect current neuroscientific assumptions.. To stay updated on this controversial field of inquiry, we suggest checking in at Andrew Newberg's website at *www.andrewnewberg.com*. Dr. Newberg is in the Department of Radiology at the University of Pennsylvania and author of *Why God Won't Go Away: Brain Science and the Biology of Belief*. Newberg, a neuroscientist at the University of Pennsylvania, has focused on the tendency of people from different religious traditions to report similar mystical experiences, which typically relate to a sense of transcendence. He uses a modified Positron-Emission Tomography machine that images neural activity right after the participant claims to be entering a different consciousness during prayer or meditation.

Since meditation or meditation-like experience seems to be a significant factor in most of the studies, we start out with two studies are summarized that present the spiritual practice of meditation as a form of mental training or "cortical remodeling process" by which significant changes in mental functioning are produced that continue beyond the meditation period, as well as changes to specific cortical structures depending on the type of meditation practiced. A third study is summarized that suggests mystical experiences produce patterns of neural activation that are distinct from other socio-emotional experiences and are mediated by several brain regions and systems. Finally, a fourth study using neuropsychological measures to examine the relationship between self-reported spirituality and neuropsychological abilities associated with specific cerebral regions in persons with traumatic brain injuries found that changes in the activity of specific parts of the brain were related to reports of increased intensity of spiritual experience.

Study 1: "Meditation Practice Improves Cognitive and Affective Functioning"

Summary. Lutz et al (2004) concluded that the mental training involved in meditation relies on mechanisms in the brain that are involved in the global coordination (also known as "neural synchrony") of brain activity and may induce both short-term and long-term changes in the brain. The research focused on gamma-band synchrony, which is usually associated with higher cognitive and affective processes, and the authors note that, to their knowledge, the high amplitude gamma-band activity found in the experienced meditation practitioners was some of the highest reported in the literature in a non-pathological context. This well-developed gamma-band synchrony is consistent with the idea that attention and affective processes are flexible skills that can be trained and suggest that the further study of experts in mental training may reveal more about higher cognitive and affective processes.

Description. Davidson and Lutz explain that meditation or mental training is understood by practitioners "to be a process of familiarization with one's own mental life leading to long-lasting changes in cognition and emotion" (Brunette, 2004), however little is known about this process and its impact on the brain. In order to better understand the brain processes underlying mental training, they decided to focus on neural synchrony, which is a "mechanism by which groups of neurons, oscillating at different frequencies, fire in phase. The transient coordination of these neural circuits across the brain is comparable to the coordination of jazz musicians who are playing and improvising together." (Brunette, 2004) In particular, the researchers focused on a range of fast frequency oscillations known as the gamma-band rhythms, which have been associated with higher mental activities such as attention, perception, consciousness, learning, and affective processes.

The subjects of the study included eight Tibetan Buddhist monks between the ages of 34 and 64 years of age and with 10,000 to 50,000 hours spent in mental training over a span of 15 to 40 years. The control subjects were healthy university students between approximately 19 and 22 years of age with an interest in meditation but no prior experience. The control group was given 1 week of training during which they were asked to practice 1 hour per day to develop a state of unconditional loving-kindness and compassion defined as "unrestricted readiness and availability to help all living beings". They were instructed to first extend the practice to those they love and then to all living beings without thinking of anyone in particular, at which point the meditation has no particular object, memory, or image. During the neutral periods, all the subjects were asked to be in a non-meditative, relaxed state.

The researchers collected electroencephalogram (EEG) data from all subjects during a baseline/neutral period, then during a meditation session, and again after the meditation session. Each meditation session included a 30 second block of resting activity and a 60 second block of meditation after allowing 20 seconds of meditation before beginning the EEG data collection for the meditation block, and this was repeated four times sequentially. EEG signals showing eye movements or muscular artifacts were manually removed from the study and other technical precautions were taken to minimize the chance that gamma-band measurements obtained were mere artifacts from other sources.

From their analysis of the EEG data, the researchers discovered that the long-term meditators and the control subjects had significantly different baseline brainwave patterns prior to beginning meditation—a difference that was enhanced during meditation and persisted into the post-meditative resting period. The Buddhist monks demonstrated a higher ratio of fast gamma-band rhythms to slower, complimentary oscillatory rhythms as compared to the control group. Although the age difference between the subjects and controls did not sufficiently account for this difference, the total hours of practice did significantly predict relative gamma activity during the baseline period.

During the meditation period, the amplitude of gamma oscillation activity increased slightly for the control group but the increase was considerably greater among the experienced meditators (greater than 30-fold as compared with controls). The amplitude of gamma activity was greater among the monks than the researchers had ever seen reported for a healthy person. Additionally, long distance neural synchrony, which is thought to reflect large-scale brain coordination, was greater in size for experienced meditators than for controls. In summary, not only did the researchers find much greater activation of fast moving and unusually powerful gamma waves in the brains of the experienced meditators, they also found that the movement of the waves through the monks' brains was far better organized and coordinated than in the students.

The findings reported here suggest that long-term meditation practice changes the baseline of the brain. Given the association between gamma-band EEG synchronization and higher-order cognitive and affective processes, these results are consistent with the idea that attention and affective processes are flexible skills that can be trained and that the study of experts in mental training may offer a unique research strategy for the further investigation of high-order cognitive and affective processes.

Study 2: "Meditation and a Cortical Remodeling Process"

Summary. Lazar et al (2005) found that the regular practice of Insight meditation, defined as sustained, nonjudgmental attention to the moment to moment experience of internal and external stimuli, is associated with increased thickness in a subset of cortical regions related to somatosensory, auditory, visual and interoceptive processing. Additionally, regular meditation practice may slow age-related thinning of the frontal cortex. Other forms of meditation and yoga would likely have a similar impact on cortical structure, but the pattern of cortical thickening would vary based on the specific mental exercises employed. The practice of meditation may be conceptualized as a *cortical remodeling process* through the focus of attention on behaviorally relevant stimuli over repeated practice sessions while in a relaxed state.

Description. Referring to the changes in mental state and resting EEG patterns that endure beyond the meditation period found by Lutz et al., these researchers hypothesized that regular mediation practice should also result in significant changes to cortical structures engaged during specific mental trainings. To test this hypothesis, they recruited twenty subjects from the community who had extensive training in a form of Buddhist meditation practice known as Insight meditation. This form of mental training involves the cultivation of sustained, nonjudgmental attention or "mindfulness" of moment to moment internal and external stimuli. The participants were not monks, but rather typical Western practitioners who incorporate their regular meditation practice into daily routines along with family, friends, professions, and other interests. The participants had an average of 9.1 years of meditation experience (ranging from 2 to 16 years) and practiced weekly for an average of 6.2 hours (range 2.2 to 10.2 hours). Fifteen control subjects with no meditation experience were also recruited and were matched for gender, race, and years of education. All subjects were screened for good physical and psychological health.

The researchers hypothesized that there would be between-group and experience-dependent differences in cortical thickness found in brain regions involved in attention and sensory processing. To find this evidence of cortical plasticity, they used magnetic resonance imaging to visualize the differences in cortical thickness. They found that the mean thickness across the entire cortex did not differ between the groups for either hemisphere, but there were significant differences in the distribution of thickness between groups across both hemispheres and within each hemisphere separately, with the meditation subjects demonstrating significantly thicker cortical areas as predicted. The increased thickness of the cortex was not due to the growth of new neurons, according to Dr. Lazar, but rather it is the result of wider blood vessels, more supporting structures such as glia and astrocytes, and increased branching and connections (Motluk, 2005). To test for the cumulative effects of meditation experience on brain structure, the researchers performed a correlation between cortical thickness and the measure of respiration rate during meditation, which is known to drop significantly among experienced meditators.

Both years of practice and change in respiration rate were correlated with cortical thickness in two regions, the inferior occipitotemporal visual cortex and right anterior insula. A partial correlation between cortical thickness and years of meditation experience remained significant when age and individual right-hemisphere average thickness were controlled.

Most of the regional differences in cortical thickness were found in the right hemisphere, which is essential for the task of sustaining attention that is a central aspect of the practice of Insight meditation. A large between group difference was found in the right anterior insula, which has been associated with tasks related to bodily attention and increased visceral awareness. This cortical difference is consistent with the expected increased capacity for awareness of internal states, particularly breathing sensations, by practitioners of Insight meditation and is in line with studies showing that accomplished musicians, athletes and linguists all have thickening in relevant areas of the cortex.

Another large difference was found in Brodmann areas 9 and 10 in the right frontal lobe, which has been shown to be involved in the integration of emotion and cognition. Additional analysis of the right frontal Brodmann 9/10 area revealed expected age-related decreases in cortical thickness among the control group, but this finding was not significant among the meditation group. It has been hypothesized that meditators become increasingly more aware during formal practice, and that this self-awareness is applied to stressful situations that occur outside of the meditation session, allowing for more beneficial choices. The researchers note that this eastern theory of emotion is compatible with Damasio's theory that connections between sensory cortices and emotion cortices play a crucial role in processing emotionally meaningful material and in making good decisions.

Although many factors such as age, sex, genetics, neuropathology and psychopathology confound the researchers' ability to detect changes in cortical thickness specifically occurring due to meditation practice, they conclude that these initial results provide support for the occurrence of cortical plasticity in adults through the practice of meditation in areas important for cognitive, sensory, and emotional processing, and that meditation may impact age-related declines in cortical structure. From these findings, they suggest that the practice of meditation may be conceptualized as a *cortical remodeling process* through the sustained focus of attention on behaviorally relevant stimuli over repeated practice sessions while in a relaxed state.

Study 3: "Looking for a neural Correlate for Mystical Experience"

Summary. Beauregard et al (2006) used functional magnetic resonance imaging (fMRI) to identify the neural correlates of a mystical experience, and more specifically, to test the hypothesis that there is a "God module" in the temporal lobes as some researchers have suggested. The results of this study indicate that mystical experiences are mediated by several brain regions and systems and produce patterns of brain activation that are distinct from other kinds of social-emotional experiences.

Description. In this study of the neural correlates of mystical experience, it is assumed that the brain mediates all religious/spiritual/mystical experiences (RSMEs) as it does all other forms of human experience. However, Beauregard and Paquette preface their article by stating clearly that identifying the neural substrates of RSMEs does not diminish their value or meaning, nor does it confirm or disconfirm the external reality of God. For the purposes of this study, mystical experience was understood in the Christian sense as characterized by a sense of union with God and as possibly including other elements such as feelings of joy, peace, having touched the ultimate ground of reality, union with all of humanity and the universe, and experiences of timelessness and spacelessness. The subjects of this experiment were fifteen Carmelite nuns between the ages of 23 and 64 (mean age 49.93 years) with an average 19.27 years of affiliation with the Carmelite order (between 2 & 37 years), all of whom reported at least one prior mystical experience. They were physically healthy women with no diagnosed psychological or neurological disorders.

Using functional magnetic resonance imaging (fMRI), blood oxygen level dependent signal changes were measured during three conditions: a baseline or restful state; a Control condition when the nuns were asked to remember and relive (with eyes closed) the most intense state of union with another human ever felt in her life while affiliated to the Carmelite Order; and the Mystical condition in which they were asked to remember and relive (with eyes closed) the most intense mystical experience ever felt in their lives as a member of the Carmelite Order.

The nuns were asked to practice the control memory and the mystical memory in the week preceding the experiment. On the day of the experiment, the subjects wore earplugs and earpad foam cushions to significantly reduce the noise generated by the fMRI scanner. A block-design paradigm was used: rest for 30 seconds, Control condition for 5 minutes, rest for 1 minute, Control condition for 5 minutes, rest for 1 minute, Mystical condition for 5 minutes, rest for 1 minute, and Mystical condition for 5 minutes. At the end of the scan, each subject was asked to rate the subjective intensity of the experience during the Control and Mystical conditions lived during the experiment, not the memories recalled to self-induce the Control and Mystical states. The phenomenology of the Mystical condition was assessed using 15 items of the Mysticism scale most compatible with Christian mysticism and qualitative interviews were conducted regarding the nature of subjective experiences during the Control and Mystical conditions.

The results of the study suggest that several brain regions and systems mediate the various aspects of mystical experiences. The researchers explain that this corresponds to the complexity and multidimensionality of these experiences, in that they involve changes in perception (such as visual mental imagery), cognitions (representations of the self), and emotion (i.e. feelings of peace, joy, and unconditional love). Their results also suggest that the Mystical condition activated specific brain regions relative to the Control condition. The relatively different regional patterns of brain activation between the socio-emotional memories of the Control and of the Mystical conditions is surprising, as one might have expected that the neural systems supporting the recall and re-experiencing of a state of union with a "divine" other would be largely the same as the neural systems supporting the recall and re-experiencing of a state of union with another human being.

From this difference, Beauregard concludes that the Mystical state is something other than an emotional state. It appears that several brain regions and systems mediate the various aspects of mystical experiences. The researchers explain that this corresponds to the complexity and multidimensionality of these experiences, in that they involve changes in perception (such as visual mental imagery), cognitions (representations of the self), and emotion (i.e. feelings of peace, joy, and unconditional love.

Drawing on prior research linking RSMEs and temporal lobe epilepsy, particularly religious conversion and ictal experiences as well as interictal intensification of spiritual and mystical feelings, Beauregard and Paquette hypothesize that the right temporal activation found during the Mystical condition was related to the subjective sense of contacting a spiritual reality. Feelings of joy and unconditional love may be related to activation of the caudate nucleus, whereas the bodily changes associated with those feelings may have caused the activation found in the brainstem. The processing of these emotions, bringing them to conscious awareness, and experiencing them as subjectively pleasant would account for the activation of other parts of the brain as observed in the study. Additionally, parts of the brain known to be involved in the spatial perception of self were activated, suggesting an alteration of the body schema during the Mystical condition that might reflect the feeling of something greater than themselves absorbing them. Finally, parts of the brain associated with visual mental imagery were activated and were likely related to the visual mental imagery reported by the subjects during the Mystical experience.

In his discussion of this study in his book, The Spiritual Brain, Beauregard asserts that their study demonstrates there is no single "God spot" in the brain located in the temporal lobes as was suggested by earlier researchers. His research with Paquette has shown that RSMEs are complex and multidimensional experiences that are mediated by many brain regions including those normally implicated in perception, cognition, emotion, body representation, and self-consciousness. Additionally, he concludes that the difference in the pattern of brain regions activated between the Mystical and Control conditions suggest that the mystical experience is something other than an emotional state.

Study 4: "Spiritual Experience as Concentration and Archetype Influence"

Summary. Johnstone and Glass et al (2008), using neuropsychological measures to evaluate 26 adults with traumatic brain injury, assessed the relationship between self-reported spirituality and neuropsychological abilities in the frontal and temporal lobes and in the right parietal lobe. and the proposed neurophysiologic model of spiritual experience proposed by Newberg, d'Aquili, and their colleagues. The results of their study suggest that certain aspects of spirituality (such as transcendence) are related to decreased activity of the right parietal lobe (normally associated with visual-spatial perception), and that other aspects of spirituality such as the experience of religious archetypes are related to increased left temporal lobe functioning (associated with auditory memory). In light of both the previous research and this current study, the authors conclude that such brain-spirituality relationships exist for people in both nonclinical samples (i.e. meditators) and clinical samples (persons with epilepsy, traumatic brain injury), and in terms of both neurophysiologic and neuropsychological functioning.

Description. After reviewing a number of neurophysiologic studies, Johnstone and Glass explain that certain parts of the brain are differentially activated or inhibited during meditation, prayer, and religious experience, but the specific pattern of interaction is not clear. Unfortunately, there are many variations across the studies that may be related to the discrepancies between results reported including the variety of neuroradiological procedures and the different types of meditation employed across the studies, the different cognitive processes used during the different meditative practices, and the different times when individuals were scanned in relation to the act of meditating or praying (i.e. before, during, after). Additionally, the preliminary research into the neurophysiologic basis of spiritual experience has been conducted largely with nonclinical populations such as those engaged in meditation and prayer.

Given that the field of neuropsychology developed an understanding of the "behavioral geography" of the brain by comparing the neuropsychological test performance of individuals with known brain damage to the performance of those without brain damage, Johnstone and Glass chose to further map the "spiritual geography" of the brain by considering how spiritual phenomena is affected when specific parts of the brain are injured. In particular, they designed their study to assess whether a general measure of spirituality would be associated with specific neuropsychological abilities, and specific cerebral structures by implication, for a group of 26 individuals with traumatic brain injuries. These individuals were being seen as outpatients on average 42.6 months after the occurrence of their injuries. The average age was 34.3 years (range 18-53 years) and average years of education was 13. Most of the subjects were male (69%) and 96% were Caucasian, 4% Hispanic. All participants received comprehensive neuropsychological evaluations including assessment of intelligence, memory, language, visual-spatial skills, and divided attention. Intrinsic spirituality and core beliefs was measured using the INSPIRIT self-report questionnaire.

Drawing on previous research, Johnstone and Glass hypothesized that spirituality would be negatively correlated with neuropsychological indices of right parietal functioning (associated with visual-spatial perception), and positively correlated with both neuropsychological indices of frontal lobe functioning (associated with such abilities as finding words and dividing attention between two tasks) and left temporal lobe functioning (associated with memory for what is heard). What they discovered was a significant negative correlation between right parietal lobe functioning and greater intensity of spiritual experience as self-reported on the INSPIRIT questionnaire. However, they found no significant correlation between frontal lobe functioning and intensity of spiritual experience and a non-significant positive correlation between left temporal lobe functioning and spiritual experience. Right temporal lobe functioning (associated with memory for what we see) was non-significantly negatively correlated with intensity of spiritual experience.

Based on their findings, Johnstone and Glass propose "a neuropsychological model of spiritual experience that suggests that spirituality is a multifaceted construct related to the interaction of different cerebral structures that involve different neuropsychological processes." (p. 871) They suggest that minimizing right parietal functions, either through the conscious effort of meditation or through reduced ability due to brain injury, may give rise to the feeling of transcendence including a sense of universal unity and decreased sense of self. They further hypothesize that increased activity in the left temporal lobe may lead to the normal and common experience of religious and cultural archetypes, which is then interpreted by individuals according to their specific cultural experiences. Johnstone and Glass note that the left temporal lobe is connected to the limbic system, where experiences are provided with their emotional valence. These religious archetypes assist us in defining our theological, moral, and ethical constructs and help to provide existential meaning. Individuals with temporal lobe epilepsy and certain types of psychopathology often report intense religious experiences without the associated decreased sense of self and feelings of bliss and unity that advanced meditators report, which the authors suggest may be due to experiencing the normal religious archetypes in an abnormal way due to neurological injury or psychiatric dysfunction. Johnstone and Glass also suggest that the frontal lobe activity seen in various other studies may be due to the intense concentration that is associated with deep spiritual states, which was not assessed within their own study. Finally, they suggest that while their neuropsychological model of spirituality presents individuals of all cultures as experiencing the same neurophysiological/neuropsycholigical functions during spiritual experiences, it also offers a rational for how these similar brain activities (nature) are interpreted differently based on how religious archetypes are culturally defined (nurture).

II. INDIGENOUS PERSPECTIVES DIALOGUE

Greg Cajete, Jongmin Lee and Four Arrows

Four Arrows. I wish to begin this final chapter with my best effort at explaining to the reader some concerns and sensitivities surrounding any discussion of Indigenous spirituality. As I mentioned in the Introduction, there is a risk in presenting material that claims to describe Indigenous spiritual practices. The risk is not so much about offending my brothers and sisters who may feel the information is too sacred or private to be shared with "outsiders." I have long ago made peace with my decision to share Indigenous wisdom with as many people as possible in an effort to make the world a better place for my grandchildren and all other sentient creatures on this remarkable planet. It is both sad and humorous for me to think about the division in Indian country about this issue. I remember one day when my wife and I were playing piano and banjo for a group of parents, mostly Navajo, at a charter school in Arizona for which I sat on the Board of Directors. We were teaching them some old American standards, like "Heart of My Heart" and everyone was having fun. At the close, I sang a Lakota thank-you song, a ceremonial song used in the purification lodge and Inipi ceremony. Within five minutes I a respected Navajo spiritual leader approached me and reprimanded me. "You should know better than to bring this song out of the circle," he scolded. I thanked him, suggested my disagreement, and went on my way. Five minutes later, another respected spiritual leader, one perhaps a little older and wiser, also came to me. He said, "Thanks, thanks much Four Arrows, for bringing this traditional Lakota song out of the circle to share with all of us Navajos and non-Indians. As your Lakota friends say in their famous prayer, "We are all related."

Although I've come to terms with my decision to spread the word as best I can about Indigenous ways of knowing, this does not mean there is still not a serious risk in contributing somehow to the appropriation of Indigenous wisdom in ways that not only does not honor reciprocity, i.e., giving back to the Peoples themselves. There is also a risk in misrepresenting ideas of different tribes with the pan-Indian approach we take in trying to identify common denominators among the various First Nations. Rather than speak to these particular risks and how Greg and I over the years have engaged them, for now I just want to appeal to the reader's sensitivities enough that you will consider them. For example, reading Vine Deloria, Jr.'s book, God is Red would be a start. Another good text with several chapters covering these topics is Lee Irwin's edited volume, Native American Spirituality: A Critical Reader, published by the University of Nebraska Press.

Jongmin, before Greg and I address these studies from an Indigenous perspective, since most of them relate to the concept of meditation and meditation is perhaps most famously practiced in your part of the world, would you begin our dialogue today?

Jongmin. I would be honored to do so. I want to start by just sharing my own ideas and then offer some from Buddhism per se that will hopefully clarify or enhance some of the findings from the four studies presented for this chapter.

I think of spirituality as believing in the existence of spirit and trying to know more about the spirit. Both of these are required. In fact, when I read Greg's opening quote I was interested to see how close it comes to my own definition. I also think that spirituality is the highest level of human mental function because it is not engaging a process that relates to somatic responses but to something that goes beyond normal bodily survival or maintenance functions. In fact, paradoxically it seems that spiritual activities, such as meditation or praying, require diminished physical activity. Perhaps this is because our brains may not be able to gain information about the spirit in this real world.

Four Arrows. I think what you are saying is very interesting but I'm not sure that people who practice yoga as a spiritual exercise would agree that spiritual practices always are about diminished physical activity. Also, from an Indigenous perspective

I think that the physical environment and activities in relationship to it are very much a part of spirituality. Perhaps this is an example of how your Western scientific lens shapes your ideas in the same way that most of these studies seem to imply that hours of quite meditation and focus increase the brain's ability to think at higher levels. In other words, it seems that what you are saying thus far is a kind of compartmentalization of inner and outer worlds or between everyday physical being in the world and a more subtle mental function relating to something different. Such compartmentalization is a common problem with Western science.

Greg. I would have to agree. Engagement with wind or with hunting activities, for example, are "higher order" sacred activities that engage being in the world activities, even those relating to survival, with as much spiritual or sacred relevance as in Eastern meditation practices.

Jongmin. I appreciate your challenges to my ideas. I think Tibetan healing practices are based on subtle bodies that correspond to our physical selves. However, …

Greg. Yes, to the Native healer, physical matter and subtle energies of the spirit world interact to make meaning or to help assure what I refer to as "thinking the highest thought." Song for example is spirit, but song is also being. It is physical. And song is one of the most important forms of Indigenous spiritual meditation.

Jongmin. OK, but as I started to say, it seems that even the Tibetan recognition of the subtle essences that correspond to our physical beings might come from the kinds of meditation practices that were examined in the neuroscience studies presented earlier. Maybe the reduced respiration rate during the meditation can be explained as by decreased basal metabolic rate. The meditator's body requires less oxygen and energy resources than the body of normally-acting subject. During the meditation, eyes are usually closed. That means visual stimulation is blocked in contrast to well-functioning the other sensory organs. In this case, the visual cortex will be activated in different way from normal visual stimulation. The visual cortex may need more energy to figure out the thinking contents. Or during the meditation, the visual cortex may be stimulated continuously by deep vision-based conception. For this reason, the stimulated cortex may have higher metabolic rate that leads to Greg's idea of "thinking the highest thought" which is inferred in the conclusions of most of these studies what show increased thickness of the cortex and "higher-order cognitive and affective processes," to quote one of the studies.

I would thus speculate that such introspective meditation somehow reinforces the superego, the aspect of personality that holds all of our internalized moral standards and ideals that we acquire from both parents and society that overrides the more basic needs for simply seeking pleasure or avoiding pain. The disciplines of a Buddhist monk academy nearby used to have a winter meditation course. During the whole winter season, they only meditate without talking any sentence. There are no topics for speculation. Only silent meditation about any topics.

During this meditation, they will speculate about Buddhist dogma, philosophy, or even themselves. In Buddhist philosophy, talk is compared to the vehicle for transferring one's thinking. By closing mouth, the discipline can speculate more and will not conclude his thinking too early. By the meditation, the superego can be enhanced and spiritual understanding as relates to living the good life or walking the right path will also be enhanced. Subsequently the religious conviction will be fortified based on this process.

Greg. You explain this very well Jongmin. There are many paths to the Center and infinite ways to get to it. I think what you are describing is one of the ways.

Four Arrows. Is it not true, Jongmin, that in Buddhism the fourth noble truth is that meditation as you have described it is the way to end the cause of suffering by abandoning expectations about the way things should be and just gaining an awareness about them? Could not there be other ways of becoming mindful and aware, like the singing of songs, the telling of or listening to stories, the vision quests or sweat lodge practices of many tribes, or even the hunting rituals?

Jongmin. Of course, Buddhism allows for any religion although it calls any religion false or unsatisfactory if it believes in omniscience or is based only on logic or on speculation. It also does not believe in making a God of a religious teacher, though it does feel that the wisdom of the Buddha is supreme.

Four Arrows. Hmmm, is there a difference? And isn't the conclusion about higher cognitive thinking that the studies describe and your talking about the superego in terms of higher moral decisions sort of relying on reasoning?

Jongmin. Not necessarily. These studies or at least the neurophilosophy about such studies tend to define spiritual experience as being about distortions of time or dissolution of fear and self-consciousness a sense of oneness with the universe. Keep in mind that the studies show that meditation increases gamma ray potential. Enhanced gamma band activity increases our capacity to process and respond behaviourally to multiple incoming stimuli, including memory, learning and attention. So it is not just about logical reasoning.

According to Buddhist dogma, every living-form in this world consists of two existences. One is physical existence in this world and the other is spirit. The spirit is constant in contrast to everything else in life that is impermanent. The spirituality in Buddhism is realizing the existence of the unchangeable spirit and the impermanence of physical realities.

Four Arrows. In Buddhism the first noble truth is that life is frustrating and full of suffering. Ultimately, the suffering relates to attachment or attachment to desiring things. I think Indigenous spirituality, although it recognizes that suffering is a significant part of life and that materialist attachments or dogma are not appropriate, places more of an emphasis on the beauty in life.

Greg. In my book *Look to the Mountain* I talk about seven connected rings of Indigenous visioning. The seventh ring is bout being joyous, thankful, reflective of the gifts of life. Such a vision is important in terms of states of mind or consciousness because this sense of joy or beauty about the gifts relating to the physical realities that surround us on Mother Earth open us to the illumination of the place where our soul and spirit reside, "the place that the Indians talk about."

Since all the studies we have seen in this book, especially perhaps the ones on self-deception, generosity, art and this one, the Western scientists seem to constantly interpret with dualities in mind and with an emphasis on reward and punishment as the primary constructs the brain gives its attention to. I don't see in most religions, including Buddhism which I think more of as a philosophy than a religion, this emphasis on the beauty of life as a gift.

I agree that worldly knowledge alone does not lead to a life with good heart, harmony, etc., without a deep understanding of those spiritual things that teach us how interconnected everything is. We knew for thousands of years that without the sense of spirituality the kinds of horrors relating to power and greed that we see today with Western materialism in self-centered thinking. We knew that we were not all that different from and certainly not better than the animals. We...

Jongmin. In Buddhism in contrast to Christianism, spirits of animals are acknowledged. This philosophy would be the background reason why no human discrimination has existed in Buddhist society. In Shamanism in Far-East Asia, the spirits of trees and even non-live forms such as mountains, rocks, and rivers are also acknowledged.

Greg. I know and I like how this contrasts with most Western religions. Although I think that Buddhism, while acknowledging consciousness in all sentient beings, sees consciousness exists at different levels with humans at a higher rung, and this would likely be different in Indigenous views and again relates to my point about seeing what the Navajo call the Beauty Path or the Beauty Way that sees a primary motive for spiritual practices is about recognizing the beauty of life, not the frustrations. I mean Nirvana, although I'm sure a complicated concept, is ultimately about extinguishing the cycle of physical existence. Celebration is more of a defining quality of Indigenous spirituality. The Navajo Sing embodies such a celebration of life. It exemplifies the identification of the Indigenous individual with their community educational process, their family, clan, tribe and the entire natural universe. It incorporates art, ritual and communion with internal AND external forces to restore the beauty and harmony between an individual and the rest of the world. In the Sing the ritual creation of a sandpainting provides an expression and a context for Indigenous wholeness. Through the Sing, a person who is out of balance re-establishes a harmonious relationship to his or her community as related by the mythic story behind the particular ceremony. The Sing exemplifies the fact that communities are organic. They are vehicles for human wholeness.

Four Arrows. Seeking life, not avoiding it is key here, it seems. I want to relate this to the studies but also to Buddhism. Taoism is the Indigenous tradition of China, stemming from Shamanism. Jongmin, isn't Taoism connected to Buddhism?

Jongmin. Well, in South Korea we are largely influenced by Confucianism, Buddhism and Taoism, but in history these three philosophies conflict. Still, people have borrowed from each in daily life.

Four Arrows. Well, I've thought about the differences between the Taoist meditation and the Buddhist meditation, though I'm sure our neuroscientific studies are based mostly on the Buddhist tradition, even when Christian people prayed silently. In any event, Taoist meditation is more practical and does not seem to reflect the duality of Western science and that is implied in Jongmin's opening remarks. There is much more of an emphasis on promoting not only morality and thinking at the highest level but also it has a very physical aspect. In an article entitled, "Taoist Tradition of Meditation: History, Transformation, and Comparison," by Liu Xiaogan, presented in an International Symposium hosted by the Camaldolese Institute in 2000, Liu writes:

> The physical aspect as the orientation of Taoist meditation is more remarkable, perhaps unique feature. It indicates eliminating ailments and diseases, improving physical health, promoting vitality, prolonging life, and even pursuing physical immortality in early age and spiritual after the medieval period. Thus, Taoist meditation is more practical, and easy to be incorporated into modern life. (http://www.bedegriffiths.com/dialogue/ciew_xiaogan.htm)

So I think that there is something in Indigenous wisdom that is different from most Eastern and Western traditions that relates to this separation of physical and spiritual. Robert Lawler refers to this difference in his book, Voices of the First Day:

> The world monotheistic religions, in combination with materialistic philosophy and rationalistic science, have created a devastating conceptual and linguistic separation between the realms of the spirit and mind and between the levels of mind and body. Our survival as a race may depend on the marriage of Psyche and Soma, or what some mythologies call the Divine Marriage. The psychic, psychological and physical processes of consciousness must be reintegrated (p. 346)

Lawlor goes on to say that over 100,000 years ago the Aboriginal worldview had already achieved this integrated goal. His book is about how every aspect of Aboriginal daily life expressed a sense of fusion between all levels of consciousness. He describes how their psychic and magical practices are based on the integration of mind and matter. Like most Indigenous Peoples, the Aborigines see all causation as a combination of physical and spiritual forces acting in harmony with energetic emanations of the Earth. Lawlor again:

> Scientific methodologies reflect a misunderstanding of the universal nature and influence of language. Rational empirical scientism is banal in its attempts at utter concreteness. Its methods of investigating and structuring reality make little use of metaphor or symbol, of analogy or simile; it compartmentalizes, isolates, and fragments reality (p. 33)

Jongmin. I understand this criticism of Western science. I find it interesting that I am an Asian Christian with proclivities toward Buddhism who is trained as a Western scientists and lives in South Korea, where you and Greg are Indigenous individuals practicing Indigenous ways while working in Western educational institutions, one in old Mexico and one living in New Mexico. It may be difficult for any of us to complete escape Western empiricism. But I don't think we want to escape the miracle like accomplishments of this kind of science. We all know the many benefits of Western science and medicine.

Four Arrows. Well, if I may interrupt, you know that you and I have strong disagreements about Western medicine's purported accomplishments, especially in the treatment of cancer.

Jongmin. But let me stay with my flow as relates to the neuroscience of spirituality, our topic. If recent findings, like those in the studies presented at the beginning of this chapter, hold up with repeated studies, as they have, then we cannot deny that, although there MAY be other ways, certainly quiet intrapersonal meditations that reduce physical engagement with the external world do things to our brains to help them work optimally. Gamma waves operate faster. Our cerebral cortex gets thicker. You yourself, Four Arrows, say that trance-states are a vital aspect of transformation even with Indigenous cultures, and both of these effects are related to what happens in trance-states. So I'm not sure we are really saying different things.

Four Arrows. Maybe, maybe not, Jongmin, but I think we are in this sense saying different things. I agree that the trance-like focus that occurs in prayer and meditation is making these changes in the brain that empirical appear associated with enhanced cognitive processes and a realization of "oneness" that, depending on one's religious beliefs, is either an escape from current reality or an integration with it. But trance or hypnotic phenomenon is not an isolated event in Indigenous cultures. For example, in my book *Primal Awareness*, I speak of the CAT-FAWN Connection. CAT (Concentration Activated Transformation) refers to this hypnotic or trance phenomenon. FAWN represents the four major influences that move the possibilities for transformation. How one understands and engages the concepts of Fear, Authority, Words and Nature determines the outcome and benefits of the trance. Indigenous Peoples use all sorts of opportunities to induce the trance state. Songs, stories, ceremonies, art, tracking, hunting, gathering, making crafts, preparing food, and sitting and staring at a canyon for eight hours, are all equally powerful ways to do what the study participants where doing, keeping in mind that in Study 4, 96 were Caucasian and most were male. It think it is also worth mentioning that I contrast how Indigenous wisdom reveals how these four forces are best understood. For example, fear is an opportunity to practice a virtue; authority only comes from a reflection on personal experience in light of knowing we are all related; words are sacred vibrations that demand integrity; and Nature is a teacher and a source of all that brings harmony.

Greg. This dovetails with what I mean by seeking life and becoming complete as being a theology of Nature.

Four Arrows. And is not this process also about human thinking in ways that promote the ideal of a good life?

Greg. The Indigenous ideal of living a good life in Indian traditions is sometimes referred to as striving to "always think the highest thoughts." This metaphor refers to the framework of a sophisticated epistemology of community based ecological education. Thinking the highest thought means thinking of one's self, one's community, and one's environment richly. This thinking in the highest, most respectful and compassionate way systematically influences the actions of both individuals and the community. It is a way to perpetuate the spiritual life and becomes a context for learning how to live ecologically. This is what I see missing in simply learning that concentrating on something for a long time increases a certain brain wave frequency or strengthens a part of the brain we THINK has something to do with thinking. The subjective and cultural orientation to ecology and to the spirits that surround and inform us is missing in these studies and I can' see how they can help us with our current ecological crises!

In the eyes of Tribal people, Nature and spirit are essentially the same. This is why Indigenous tracking is so intimately involved in coming to the source of spirit. I would love to see an MRI scan of a traditional, trained tracker's brain while he was tracking an animal. The trance phenomenon Four Arrows describes occur during some relationship with Nature as one of the four influences on trance outcomes. In the process of tracking, actions and relationships are reflected in the patterns that reoccur in all of Nature. Tracking connects people to their own spirits, the spirits of the land, the animals, plants and other entities. Four Arrows, I don't know if you know it but in your mnemonic the use of the word, "FAWN," has special connotation in Navajo mythology. Fawn gives advice to First Hunter about how to respect the spirit of the deer. Fawn also refers to Talking God as the holy being who decides when and how the Deer People will give their life to sustain humans.

Anyway, none of us do much tracking any more, but teaching spiritual ecology remains vital. While our relationships with animals have undergone significant transformations since earlier times, they are still there in spirit if not in reality. The crises of our times beckons us to retrace the tracks of our ancestors and the animals they knew. We must understand the meaning of our lives in relationship with the natural world. We ARE spiritual beings and we must reclaim this. There are many ways for us to get to know the animals today. Focusing on what happens in our brains is not one of them, although if we learn to understand animal behaviors through neuroscience in ways that does not harm the animal or its spirit, maybe there is a connection.

Four Arrows. So to sort of recap all of this I want to briefly note some of the findings from the studies. In Study 1: Buddhist monks demonstrated a higher ratio of fast gamma-band rhythms to slower, complimentary oscillatory rhythms as compared to the control group and amplitude of gamma activity was greater among the monks than the researchers had ever seen reported, even for normally healthy persons. In Study 2, typical Western meditators also were able to increase capacity for awareness of internal states and also thickened relevant areas of the cortex., inferring that "good decisions" are more likely. In Study 3, we learn that the mystical feelings of oneness that occur during meditation activated numerous places in the brain but seem to be different from other kinds of social and emotional experiences. Parts of the brain associated with visual imagery were, however, activated. In Study 4, we again see a multifaceted involvement of cerebral structures and different processes associated with prayer and meditation that the authors infer may relate to how their experiences are culturally understood.

I submit that the Indigenous wisdom offers that all of this is evidence that any muscle gets strong from use and it is good to make the parts of the brain strong from practicing how to focus and concentrate and learn how to be still and quiet, etc. However, without the subject, cultural beliefs that ALSO activate parts of the brain associated with visual imagery, and without being open to participating authentically in the real beauty and mystery and challenges of actual living; without a deep belief that we are truly related to everything on Earth; without being open to the external communication of the spirit world; and without having an ecological perspective that includes an intimate relationship with plants and animals, any study of spirituality is unlikely to offer a real solution to the crises humanity is facing in 2010. I would like to close by offering a list of assumptions that typify Indigenous Wisdom to close this chapter and our book and implore all neurophilosophers to incorporate them into interpretations and analysis of neuroscience now and in the future in order to help bring forth practical solutions to the challenges and acknowledgement of the gifts residing in our world today. I assume all responsibility for this list and its language, though it is gathered from many years of interacting with Indigenous people of wisdom. Some might be found in many spiritual traditions, but this is up to the reader to determine.

- The natural world is ultimately more about cooperation than it is about competition.
- The concept of reciprocity can guide living systems toward balance.
- Human decisions are best made from the heart as well as the mind.
- Humans are entwined in and with Nature and the idea of "conquering" or "being in charge" of it rather than honouring the relationship more authentically is considered an aberration.
- Children are scared and possess inherent value.

- A Great Mysterious Spirit or Energy is within all its creations.
- Material possessions are less important than generosity
- Generosity is the highest expression of courage
- Diversity gives strength and balance to the world.
- Deception and self-deception are an aberration not an evolutionary survival mechanism.
- Resolution of conflict is about restoring harmony rather than enacting punishment.
- Cognitive dissonance is best met with humor followed by corrective resolution.
- Women are naturally wise and powerful and are inclined to bring forth social harmony if we encourage their solar and lunar balance and if men can become more right-brained.
- Prayer and ceremony hep us connect to the invisible world and thus have value in maintaining harmony.
- Fear is an opportunity for practicing virtues.
- Words are forces that shape images and affect energy. They are to be treated with great respect.
- Altruism exists because we are truly all related not because it is a vehicle for self advantage.
- Art in all of its expressions is both an expression and a vehicle for receiving truth and beauty and understanding.
- Balance and health are ultimately about genuine respect for self and other that honors walking a path that balances intuition, reason, experience, learning and prayer.
- Animals, birds, insects, fish and reptiles and the elements of wind, earth, water and fire, as well as the cycles of Nature, are our ultimate teachers.

I don't mean to create any orthodoxy or "rules" with this list, but to reveal the general understandings of most Indigenous cultures that are ultimately "spiritual" aspects of life, according to our view. I ask the reader to contemplate on congruencies and differences that might exist when comparing and contrasting these ideas to Western religion. At this point in my life, I find myself more and more unable to rationalize a tolerance for any religious fundamentalism that claims being "the only way" and hope that our presentation here in conjunction with social neuroscience might allow for people to recognize the difference between the deep and authentic resonance they may have for a particular religion and any hypnosis from habit, fear, or false authority that does not also resonate with intuition, reason, research. Enough horrors have historically occurred owing partially or largely to the blind belief in one religious orthodoxy or another. We are at a time in human civilization where many crossroads face us and our decisions about which path to take may determine our very survival.

III CONTINUED DIALOGUE FOR UNDERSTANDING

1. Why do you think meditation is the focus for many of the studies selected for neuroscience research related to the concept, "spirituality?"

2. List several options for scientifically explaining spontaneous "mystical insights" and discuss them.
3. Do some research about mental health and affiliation with religious fundamentalism. What does it reveal? Why do you think this is?
4. Briefly contrast what you believe Indigenous spirituality is all about with several religious precepts in Western traditions.

REFERENCES

Antoine, L., Greischar, L., Rawlings, N. B., Ricard, M., & Davidson, D. (2004, November 16). Long-term meditators self-induce high-amplitude gamma synchrony during mental practice. *Proceedings from the National Academy of Sciences of the USA, 101*(46), 16369–16373; doi:10.1073/pnas.0407401101.

Beauregard, M., & O'Leary, D. (2007). *The spiritual brain: A neuroscientist's case for the existence of the soul*. New York: HarperCollins Publishers.

Beauregard, M., & Paquette, V. (2006). Neural correlates of a mystical experience in Carmelite nuns. *Neuroscience Letters, 405*, 186–190; doi:10.1016/j.neulet.2006.06.060.

Brunette, J. (2004, November 16). *University of Wisconsin-Madison News*. Retrieved from www.news.wisc.edu/10420

Brunette, J. (2004, November 16). *University of Wisconsin-Madison News*. Retrieved from www.news.wisc.edu/10420. http://www.newscientist.com/article/dn8317. Ibid.

Cajete, G. (1994). *Look to the mountain: An ecology of indigenous education*. Durango: Kivaki Press.

Four Arrows. (2006). *Unlearning the language of conquest: Scholars expose anti-indianism in america*. Austin, TX: University of Texas Press.

Irwin, L. (2000). *Native american spirituality: A critical reader*. Lincoln, NE: University of Nebraska Press.

Johnson, G. (2007). God is in the d endrites. Can "neurotheology" bridge the gap between religion and science? *Slate*. Retrieved June 1, 2009, from http://www.slate.com/id/2165026/

Johnstone, B., & Glass, B. A. (2008). Support for a neuropsychological model of spirituality in persons with traumatic brain injury. *Neuroscience, 43*(4), 861–874; ISSN 0591-2385.

Lazar, S., Kerr, C. E., Wasserman, R., Gray, J. R., Greve, D. N., Treadway, M., et al. (2005, November 28). *Neuroscience, 16*(17), 1893–1897.

Lazar, S. W., Kerr, C. E., Wasserman, R. H., Ray, J., Greve, D., Treadway, M., et al. (2005, November 28). *Neuroreport, 17*, 1893–1897.

Lawlor, R. (1991). *Voices of the first day*. Rochester, NY: Inner Traditions International.

Lutz, A., Greishlar, L., Rawlings, N. B., Ricard, M., & Davidson, R. (2004, November 16). *Proceedings from the National Academy of Sciences of the USA, 101*(46), 16369–16373; doi:10.1073/pnas.0407401101.

Motluk, A. (2005, November 15). Meditation builds up the brain. *New Scientist*. Retrieved June 3, 2009, from http://www.newscientist.com/article/dn83111